THE
# Collins
BOOK OF
# Australian
# Poetry

THE

# Collins

BOOK OF

# Australian Poetry

occupied by genocide get out now!

*chosen by*

RODNEY HALL

COLLINS
*Sydney · London*

## By the Same Author

*Poetry*
Penniless till Doomsday
Statues & Lovers (in Four Poets)
Forty Beads on a Hangman's Rope
Eyewitness
The Autobiography of a Gorgon
The Law of Karma
Heaven, in a way
A Soapbox Omnibus
Selected Poems
Black Bagatelles

*Novels*
The Ship on the Coin
A Place Among People

*Biography*
Focus on Andrew Sibley
J. S. Manifold

*Anthologies*
New Impulses in Australian Poetry (with Thomas Shapcott)
Australian Poetry 1970
Poems from Prison
Stories from Australia (bi-lingual English/Bahasa Malaysia edition)
Australians Aware

This selection of poems © RODNEY HALL 1981

First published 1981 by William Collins Pty Ltd, Sydney
Reprinted August 1981
Typeset by Asco Trade Typesetting Ltd, Hong Kong
Printed in Hong Kong by South China Printing Co.
Designed by Jill Raphaeline

National Library of Australia
Cataloguing-in-Publication data:

The Collins book of Australian poetry.

Includes index
ISBN 0 00 216445 0

I. Australian poetry.    II. Hall, Rodney, 1935–.

A821'.008

## —— AUTHOR'S NOTE ——

I am grateful to the Literature Board of the Australia Council for a senior fellowship during the currency of which this book was compiled. I also wish to acknowledge the help offered me by Catherine Santamaria of the National Library, Canberra, and Marianne Ehrhardt of the Fryer Library, University of Queensland. For advice and assistance with the Aboriginal material, I must thank the staff of the Australian Institute of Aboriginal Studies, in particular Frank Wordick, Penny Taylor and Alice Moyle; also Professor R. M. W. Dixon of the Department of Linguistics at the Australian National University, and especially Tamsin Donaldson. An invaluable resource, while writing biographical notes on the contributors, was the National Library's archive of recorded interviews with authors, made by the indefatigable Hazel de Berg. Most of all, my gratitude goes to the poets for providing such superb work to choose from.

## —— PUBLISHER'S NOTE ——

The publisher would like to thank the Literature Board of the Australia Council for their generous assistance in the publication of this book.

# CONTENTS

# CONTENTS

# —— CONTENTS ——

# ——— CONTENTS ———

# CONTENTS

# CONTENTS

# CONTENTS

# CONTENTS

# CONTENTS

# CONTENTS

# CONTENTS

# CONTENTS

# CONTENTS

# CONTENTS

# —— INTRODUCTION ——

Australian poetry is not two hundred years old, as it is generally presented to us, but in all probability 40,000 years old. Traditional ceremonial songs such as 'The Moon-bone Song' of the Wonguri-Mandjigai people may well be as venerable as Moses. Neither we nor the Aborigines have any means of telling. Vast numbers of songs have been collected this century, recorded and transcribed. Many have been translated into English.

The problem with translation is, first, that these songs are not simply songs: they are dance, body-painting, music and social ceremony as well. But even accepting that the words by themselves cannot be much more than haunting stage directions, a second problem arises from the limitations of the translators. However dedicated and expert they may be in matters of anthropology or linguistics (and occasionally music), they have all been amateurs of poetry. So their attempted versified versions are mainly based on a nineteenth-century schooltext knowledge of verse forms and no dedication to poetic insight. So, while acknowledging their work with respect and gratitude, my view is that the Aboriginal songs in translation as we have them are shadows of great presences. But better the shadows than nothing. They at least supply a sense of scale and direction. Poetry in the white community has been seeking something of the kind for the past sixty years. We have suffered from the absence of a pre-literate mystical relationship with a homeland—the quality of relationship inseparable from the forms and rhythms of the language as well as its actual words. The fact that not one of the hundreds of Aboriginal dialects has an 's' sound in its vocabulary declares a more profound vernacular than the entire library of our books.

Given the absence of spiritual contact, is it surprising that our poetry has been so often obsessed with Nothingness and with Time as a measure of futility? And if we turn to Aboriginal chants we can perhaps console ourselves that the Psalms, so fruitful a source of poetry in all European languages, might not be any more accurately represented in the form we know than these are.

Certainly it seems incredible to me that only four entries recorded in Marianne Ehrhardt's exhaustive index of Australian anthologies from 1851 to 1980 include an Aboriginal song, three of them being the same one reprinted. For this reason I include some information which might be helpful in approaching these song-words as translated into English—information which ought to be commonplace knowledge in our heritage, had we not suffered an education by accountants and indoctrination into the Club of the Elite.

The ceremonial songs are traditional and often secret. They are, as Professor R. M. W. Dixon says in *The Languages of Australia*, 'simultaneously history, law and social ritual ... It is important to emphasize that Australian songs and song cycles do not have narrative structure; there is nothing similar to the European folk ballad. Each song will essentially throw up a single image ... In association with its accompanying legend a cycle of songs will be INTERPRETED as a narrative although the songs themselves each describe individual scenes with no overt linkage between them.' Several ceremonial songs are included in this anthology, chosen because they most clearly imply sacred meanings. I say 'imply' because the enigma of the sacred is that if you don't already experience it, you can't be told what it is.

The second category of Aboriginal song is the *tjapi* or *tyawi*. These are made up by individual singers for entertainment and are not respected as having any serious importance. Often enough we ourselves provide the subjects; sometimes humorous, sometimes bitter, sometimes baffled. They are still being composed and sung around the country. Those which I have included are arranged on the same basis as everything else; approximately in chronological order, taking into account the date they were collected and the age of the singer.

In 1788 came the invasion. And an eighteenth-century culture was grafted on the land. Convicts and military, tradespeople after the lucrative spice routes to the Indies, plus free settlers escaping the nastiness of the Industrial Revolution, took several bloody generations to create sufficient sense of community to begin writing poems as distinct from doggerel satires and adapted street songs. The process being gradual, it is not surprising that the poetic achievements of last century look a bit thin. Reading through creaking piles of these volumes, breathing their dried lucerne dust, turning brittle pages, peering among gardens of lichen for the precious word, I found the strongest thread was not Romantic literariness of the James Thomson to John Keats model (exemplified by Henry Kendall) but Augustan satire, and later the ballad.

With the coming of the ballad, Australian poetry found its voice. So we got under way—a frail boatload of garrulous yarnsters and rhyme-spinners on a vast Pacific of disorientation. But we were making head-way at least. The oars dipped and flashed to a monotonously predict-able metre, but that in itself was some kind of security.

Ballads were popular throughout the English-speaking world, but nowhere, I think, did they achieve a social environment so receptive as the itinerant bushworkers of Australia and the urban Australians who looked to these bush people as an image for their own virtues. Not so unexpected then, to find a Paterson achieving effortless virtuosity within the narrow range of weaving varied rhythms over the one metre; or Lawson with his command of narrative, his exact choice of detail to keep it moving and alive. Finally, though, it has to be admitted that the popular image of the sunburnt bushman is yet another aspect of the invasion, another attempt to master and possess the land, rather than learn to be possessed by it. Such images are the models we live by, just as the gods were in classical antiquity. This tradition is as touching and ridiculous as the Roman emperors claiming divinity for their fathers. Yet it looks enviably vigorous to an age where the hard, self-sacrificing greed of the pioneer has degenerated to the soft, suffocating greed of the speculator.

An overwhelming proportion of white Australian poetry has been, and still is, preoccupied with statements about the land, attempting just such a spiritual control as the Aborigines have, by adapting the English language to do duty in a landscape totally foreign to its vocabulary of meanings. The contrast with Aboriginal songs recreating the ritual act of naming places which is at the heart of survival itself could hardly be overstated.

At the turn of the century the flow of ballads had begun weakening to derivative posturings and jingoism. So instead of that frail rowing-boat progressing smoothly, the oarsmen lost their stroke, forgot where they were going, caught a few humiliating crabs, and then opted for the precaution of keeping the oars clear of the water altogether. They rowed the air with beautiful co-ordination. The form of the ballad had outlived its function when a ponderous newcomer, product of ambition in the young vigorous dissatisfied universities, climbed aboard. And the stern sank to the gunwale. Christopher Brennan and the serious commitment to profundity had arrived. But who would have had it any other way? Australian poetry changed course to face new challenges and a new perspective.

Far less welcome, as it turned out, was a chorus of the lost Celtique persuasion who set up a worship of whimsy. They produced, for tenacious decades, fairy verses mouldering into a plague of centaurs, hybrids with pastoralists' heads grafted on the woolly bestialities of hedonism. The climax of their influence came with Norman Lindsay. Hugh McCrae was the last (and most talented) poet of this tradition, though the best of his poems are of a less fanciful, more moving kind.

In the aftermath of the Great Depression 'Furnley Maurice' made a convincing effort to relocate the energy of poetry in the cities. Even so, the actual rescue came about because he and his generation were modest enough to accept the associations of words themselves as the basic material. Stimulated by the overseas example of Yeats, Owen and Frost, they learned to call 'Help!' instead of 'Art!'. Kenneth Slessor and Robert D. FitzGerald introduced a fresh flexibility of imagery. Meanwhile a different solution was being sought by the Jindyworobak Club in Adelaide. Reacting against British Imperialism, partly as a result of sufferings in the Depression, Rex Ingamells and his friends set out to establish environmental values. This they did in their poems by rejecting English words too weighty with overtones foreign to Australia and replacing them by images that attempted some native strength.

Both movements were admirably reasonable. The lack of spiritual identification with the land was indeed a challenge, and a revitalized use of English the only possible tool to meet it. The challenge is still being tackled by poets today.

This brings us to the end of the Second World War and a twenty-year period of poetry almost wholly governed by one man. Douglas Stewart was editor of the Red Page in The *Bulletin*, by far the most influential journal for the publication of poetry. He was also a member of the Commonwealth Literary Fund Committee which gave government subsidies to publishers issuing books of poetry. On top of which he became poetry editor of the country's principal poetry publishing house Angus & Robertson. Editors are a poet's most formative audience. By the very act of accepting or rejecting a poem, they markedly shape the author's next submissions, not to mention what advice they might offer on revising the manuscripts. In Stewart's case, he was the kind of editor ever anxious to be a helpful mentor. Hard-working and often generous to his friends, the end effect was a period in which everybody's poetry came more and more to resemble his own. There were outsiders, naturally, such as John Manifold, but they were excluded from the literary hierarchy. They had to make do with publication in small poetry magazines and quarterlies such as *Overland* and *Meanjin* or else establish themselves in America and England.

The break came when Vincent Buckley took over at The *Bulletin* in 1961 and in a brief couple of years transformed Australian poetry, introducing many new voices not previously heard. The somewhat cosy pastime of marvelling at bush eccentrics and looking to close-ups of insects and wildflowers for enlightenment on the larger issues in life vanished virtually overnight.

The poets writing today have no such battle to contend with. Although The *Bulletin* is making a strong bid to recover a position of literary influence under Geoffrey Dutton, the narrow uniformity has gone. I don't think the range has ever been more diverse or more contradictory at its extremes than now. For the first time, perhaps, we cannot say there is a dominant mainstream among the rising poets. This reflects what happened in the world at large during the '40s and '50s with the old certainties of politics and society suffering the angst of fatal rebuffs, followed by the widespread disaffection with authority in the '60s and '70s. Also radio and television have brought into the livingroom the savagery of the world where racial and ideological conflicts are fought between more equal adversaries than here.

One characteristic of living poets, whatever their age, distinguishes them from their predecessors: the ability to change style and experiment with new techniques. Lawson, or Gordon, or Brennan for that matter, began and ended working in one mode. Either they never got it right, or else endlessly rewrote the same few pieces. Then came Slessor whose one hundred poems gradually clarified, as he developed, into his tiny output of true poems, perhaps no more than thirty-five pages (a generous proportion of which are reproduced here). On these his reputation rests. And once he achieved them he didn't repeat himself. He stopped writing poetry altogether.

Now, we find poets learning to discover new possibilities, maybe new aspects of their personalities, and responding to developments in literary forms. Examples can be found by comparing the early and later poems of John Blight, Gwen Harwood, or Geoffrey Lehmann, for instance. Even in the small representations possible here, the changes are dramatic. The same applies to many others. Among the younger poets there is a drift away from the concept of the poet recreating a situation for the reader, externalizing it through imagery, towards oblique fragments suggesting what experience feels like from within. Both Jennifer Maiden and Martin Johnston write eloquently in this mode.

One of the basic decisions faced by any anthologist is in what order to present the poems. For this selection, since it attempts a comprehensive view so far as that is possible, I have opted for a general chronology. To do this I arrived at an average between the age of the poet and the span of years over which his or her best poetry has been written. Naturally, the result can only be approximate. Some poets have written memorably early in life, others of the same age have not begun till many years after. So it is, for example, that Slessor and Hope, born only six years apart are quite widely separated. Slessor had published all but a couple of his poems by 1939. Hope published his first collection in 1952 and is still writing into the 1980s.

In most cases I have also applied the method of date order to each poet's section, but occasionally readjustments have been desirable to bring out connections with other poets' work, a collective awareness that with the collapse of colonial powers in the Pacific we live among Melanesian, Polynesian and Asian peoples. Also there are the literary influences from Britain, America, east and west Europe which many share. I doubt that there has ever been any conflict between a sense of community among Australian poets and the ever-renewed influences from abroad. Thus it is equally mistaken to think of our poetry as an isolated self-sufficient flow, or as a chaotic scramble of rival individuals sycophantically aping Big Brother. And concerning the positions allotted to the Aboriginal song-words: if it is objected that they should all come at the beginning, that they represent a timeless tradition, my answer is that so do our Australian-English poems once we accept that our tradition is like other traditions and not the centre of the universe.

I should also be clear about my editorial intentions. I have set out to collect a book of what I judge to be the most alive of Australian poems—whatever their kind. I have not been interested in juggling reputations, the bugbear of so many anthologies. There are many writers with a batch of books to their name whose work I enjoy and respect but who never quite achieve the memorable quality required for a selection of this nature. In terms of reputation many of them would undoubtedly warrant inclusion, but I have not felt obliged to include them.

Far less have I attempted to set up a hierarchy of 'great' poets round whom the 'minor' poets are grouped. There is no such thing. Either the words they write are poetry, or not poetry. Poetry is an experience of a particular kind, and while it may vary in intensity, is without grade. Poets are men and women who tap the living energy of the language as they find it in their own time and place. This is the language they know deeply, because they have made it and been made by it. In that respect the poems in this book are in the Australian language. And it is a symptom of insecurity to load verses down with dinkum slang to declare their nationality, such slang being a capitulation. This Australian-English, created by us all, is the repository of our collective wisdom. The true poets are those who, far from ambitious to be 'great', dedicate themselves to the service of the language and as a result touch its richness.

This is the function of poetry: to be a living organ of language. Languages die, as we know, and often with startling rapidity. To stay alive, a language must exercise certain functions, one of which is poetry. There are examples in Australia of languages which have died in all other respects, but of which a few songs still remain; inscrutable repositories of knowledge by which the human spirit once survived. All living languages have their poetry. It is for the poet to take the responsibility of affirming this function in his own generation.

So it follows that a fixed pantheon of major poets is a ridiculous notion, while readers change and while the language—its forms and meanings—changes unceasingly. So a poem has to be re-read and re-created in terms of the new life of the language; it may be true for the reader or no longer true. There is no permanent place for anyone. Certain poets do touch the least-changing meanings of language and their poems may still be read as poems a thousand years later. Others, no less dedicated, cease to speak to us after a single generation.

My yardstick has been that this book has to be poetry in today's terms. I have carefully weighed the contribution to the whole made by each inclusion. For this reason, some well-known poems are not to be found here, where other poets have explored the material better. I have tried to be as willing to let the literature speak for itself as any one editor can. Therefore no attempt has been made to demonstrate a line— of pastoral verse, social satire or modernist verse—but to be open to whatever still works and speaks as poetry.

The selection is laid out so that each poet's contribution is seen to be part of the whole, rather than an isolated voice in a soundproof compartment; the poems interact and grow from one another. In this way I have done what I can to avoid building the anthology round competitive reputations. It is designed principally for pleasure, to be read through from beginning to end, brilliant and varied in its perceptions and development. If the poems have a secondary life, I would suggest it is not so much that of authorial ambition and achievement, as a special history of Australia.

For the convenience of students and teachers, however, each poet's poems are grouped together, making it easy to direct attention to the work of a particular writer. The copious biographical notes aim to be a lively introduction to each of the contributors and to give useful background information to the poems.

My method during the two years I took to compile this book was to go back to original sources and find what really lived best. This entailed reading some 700 books. Interestingly, I found that, by and large, the most gifted poets are indeed the ones who have become best-known. This was a disappointment, I'll admit, because I suppose I had been hoping to turn the whole assumption about what matters on its head. However, by way of compensation I discovered it is not always the best poems by which the poets survive. As a result this anthology offers fewer surprises in terms of poets included than I would have liked. On the other hand, there are many neglected poems I've had the pleasure of rescuing from obscurity.

One note, only, remains. Readers familiar with my editorial practice from various books and my eleven years as poetry editor of The

*Australian* will be surprised to find me including poems of my own (in the previous case of *New Impulses in Australian Poetry* I had an admirable co-editor, Tom Shapcott, so we were able to make selections for each other). Because I wouldn't know what to pick and because it goes against the grain to publish myself, I invited that most independent and perceptive of my fellow poets, Gwen Harwood, to make the decision for me. She is entirely responsible for choosing which and how many of my poems to include here. I am grateful to her for agreeing to make the selection. And if other readers find what I have chosen for the rest of the anthology as unexpected as I find Gwen Harwood's choice of mine, the book should provide fresh perspectives and a stimulating reappraisal all round.

*R.H.*
*Barragga Bay*
*October 1980*

# —— THE POEMS ——

# WONGURI-MANDJIGAI SONG

## *The Moon-bone Song*[1]

The people are making a camp of branches in that country at Arnhem
    Bay:
With the forked stick, the rail for the whole camp, the *Mandjigai* people
    are making it.
Branches and leaves are about the mouth of the hut: the middle is clear
    within.
They are thinking of rain, and of storing their clubs in case of a
    quarrel,
In the country of the Dugong, towards the wide clay pans made by
    the Moonlight.
Thinking of rain, and of storing the fighting sticks.
They put up the rafters of arm-band-tree wood, put the branches on to
    the camp, at Arnhem Bay, in that place of the Dugong...
And they block up the back of the hut with branches.
Carefully place the branches, for this is the camp of the Morning-
    Pigeon man,
And of the Middle-of-the-Camp man; of the Mangrove-Fish man; of
    two other head-men,
And of the Clay pan man; of the *Baiini*-Anchor man, and of the
    Arnhem Bay country man;
Of the Whale man and of another head-man; of the Arnhem Bay Creek
    man;
Of the Scales-of-the-Rock-Cod man; of the Rock Cod man, and of the
    Place-of-the-Water man.

             *       *       *

They are sitting about in the camp, among the branches, along the
    back of the camp:
Sitting along in lines in the camp, there in the shade of the paperbark
    trees:
Sitting along in a line, like the new white spreading clouds:
In the shade of the paperbarks, they are sitting resting like clouds.

[1] Translated from the Wonguri by Ronald M. Berndt

People of the clouds, living there like the mist; like the mist sitting
    resting with arms on knees,
In here towards the shade, in this Place, in the shadow of paperbarks.
Sitting there in rows, those *Wonguri-Mandjigai* people, paperbarks
    along like a cloud.
Living on cycad-nut bread; sitting there with white-stained fingers,
Sitting in there resting, those people of the Sandfly clan . . .
Sitting there like mist, at that place of the Dugong . . . and of the
    Dugong's Entrails . . .
Sitting resting there in the place of the Dugong . . .
In that place of the Moonlight Clay Pans, and at the place of the
    Dugong . . .
There at that Dugong place they are sitting all along.

\*    \*    \*

Wake up from sleeping! Come, we go to see the clay pan, at the place of
    the Dugong . . .
Walking along, stepping along, straightening up after resting:
Walking along, looking as we go down on to the clay pan.
Looking for lily plants as we go . . . and looking for lily foliage . . .
Circling around, searching towards the middle of the lily leaves to
    reach the rounded roots.
At that place of the Dugong . . .
At that place of the Dugong's Tail . . .
At that place of the Dugong; looking for food with stalks,
For lily foliage, and for the round-nut roots of the lily plant.

\*    \*    \*

The birds saw the people walking along.
Crying, the white cockatoos flew over the clay pan of the Moonlight;
From the place of the Dugong they flew, looking for lily-root food;
    pushing the foliage down and eating the soft roots.
Crying, the birds flew down and along the clay pan, at that place of the
    Dugong . . .
Crying, flying down there along the clay pan . . .
At the place of the Dugong, of the Tree-Limbs-Rubbing-Together, and
    of the Evening Star.
Where the lily-root clay pan is . . .
Where the cockatoos play, at that place of the Dugong . . .
Flapping their wings they flew down, crying, 'We saw the people!'
There they are always living, those clans of the white cockatoo . . .

And there is the Shag woman, and there her clan:
Birds, trampling the lily foliage, eating the soft round roots!

*　　*　　*

An animal track is running along: it is the track of the rat . . .
Of the male rat, and the female rat, and the young that hang to her
    teats as she runs,
The male rat hopping along, and female rat, leaving paw-marks as a
    sign´. . .
On the clay pans of the Dugong, and in the shade of the trees,
At the Dugong's place, and at the place of her Tail . . .
Thus, they spread paw-mark messages all along their tracks,
In that place of the Evening Star, in the place of the Dugong . . .
Among the lily plants and into the mist, into the Dugong place, and
    into the place of her Entrails.
Backwards and forwards the rats run, always hopping along . . .
Carrying swamp-grass for nesting, over the little tracks, leaving their
    signs.
Backwards and forwards they run on the clay pan, around the place of
    the Dugong.
Men saw their tracks at the Dugong's place, in the shade of the trees,
    on the white clay;
Roads of the rats, paw-marks everywhere, running into the mist.
All around are their signs; and there men saw them down on the clay
    pan, at the place of the Dugong.

*　　*　　*

A duck comes swooping down to the Moonlight clay pan, there at the
    place of the Dugong . . .
From far away. 'I saw her flying over, in here at the clay pan . . .'
Floating along, pushing the pool into ripples and preening her feathers.
(the duck speaks)
'I carried these eggs from a long way off, from inland to Arnhem
    Bay . . .'
Eggs, eggs, eggs; eggs she is carrying, swimming along.
She preens her feathers, and pulls at the lily foliage,
Drags at the lily leaves with her claws for food.
Swimming along, rippling the water among the lotus plants . . .
Backwards and forwards: she pulls at the foliage, swimming along,
    floating and eating.
This bird is taking her food, the lotus food in the clay-pan,

At the place of the Dugong there, at the place of the Dugong's Tail . . .
Swimming along for food, floating, and rippling the water, there at the
    place of the Lilies.
Taking the lotus, the rounded roots and stalks of the lily; searching and
    eating there as she ripples the water.
'Because I have eggs, I give to my young the sound of the water.'
Splashing and preening herself, she ripples the water, among the
    lotus . . .
Backwards and forwards, swimming along, rippling the water,
Floating along on the clay pan, at the place of the Dugong.

*    *    *

People were diving here at the place of the Dugong . . .
Here they were digging all around, following up the lily stalks,
Digging into the mud for the rounded roots of the lily,
Digging them out at that place of the Dugong, and of the Evening Star,
Pushing aside the water while digging, and smearing themselves with
    mud . . .
Piling up the mud as they dug, and washing the roots clean.
They saw arm after arm there digging: people thick like the mist . . .
The Shag woman too was there, following up the lily stalks.
There they saw arm after arm of the *Mandjigai* Sandfly clan,
Following the stalks along, searching and digging for food:
Always there together, those *Mandjigai* Sandfly people.
They follow the stalks of the lotus and lily, looking for food.
The lilies that always grow there at the place of the Dugong . . .
At that clay-pan, at the place of the Dugong, at the place of the lilies.

*    *    *

Now the leech is swimming along . . . It always lives there in the
    water . . .
It takes hold of the leaves of the lily and pods of the lotus, and climbs
    up on to their stalks.
Swimming along and grasping hold of the leaves with its head . . .
It always lives there in the water, and climbs up on to the people.
Always there, that leech, together with all its clan . . .
Swimming along towards the trees, it climbs up and waits for people.
Hear it swimming along through the water, its head out ready to grasp
    us . . .
Always living here and swimming along.

Because that leech is always there, for us, however it came there:
The leech that catches hold of those *Mandjigai* Sandfly people . . .

\*     \*     \*

The prawn is there, at the place of the Dugong, digging out mud with
     its claws . . .
The hard-shelled prawn living there in the water, making soft little
     noises.
It burrows into the mud and casts it aside, among the lilies . . .
Throwing aside the mud, with soft little noises . . .
Digging out mud with its claws at the place of the Dugong, the place of
     the Dugong's Tail . . .
Calling the bone invocation, the catfish invocation, the frog invocation,
     the sacred tree invocation . . .
The prawn is burrowing, coming up, throwing aside the mud, and
     digging . . .
Climbing up on to the lotus plants and on to their pods . . .

\*     \*     \*

Swimming along under the water, as bubbles rise to the surface, the
     tortoise moves in the swamp grass.
Swimming among the lily leaves and the grasses, catching them as she
     moves . . .
Pushing them with her short arms. Her shell is marked with designs,
This tortoise carrying her young, in the clay pan, at the place of the
     Dugong . . .
The short-armed *Madarba* tortoise, with special arm-bands, here at the
     place of the Dugong . . .
Backwards and forwards she swims, the short-armed one of the
     *Madarba*, and the *Dalwongu*.
Carrying eggs about, in the clay pan, at the place of the Dugong . . .
Her entrails twisting with eggs . . .
Swimming along through the grass, and moving her patterned shell.
The tortoise with her young, and her special arm-bands,
Swimming along, moving her shell, with bubbles rising;
Throwing out her arms towards the place of the Dugong . . .
This creature with the short arms, swimming and moving her shell;
This tortoise, swimming along with the drift of the water . . .
Swimming with her short arms, at the place of the Dugong . . .

\*     \*     \*

Wild-grape vines are floating there in the billabong:
Their branches, joint by joint, spreading over the water.
Their branches move as they lie, backwards and forwards,
In the wind and the waves, at the Moonlight clay pan, at the place of
    the Dugong . . .
Men see them lying there on the clay pan pool, in the shade of the
    paperbarks:
Their spreading limbs shift with the wind and the water:
Grape vines with their berries . . .
Blown backwards and forwards as they lie, there at the place of the
    Dugong.
Always there, with their hanging grapes, in the clay pan of the
    Moonlight . . .
Vine plants and roots and jointed limbs, with berry food, spreading
    over the water.

\*　　\*　　\*

Now the New Moon is hanging, having cast away his bone:
Gradually he grows larger, taking on new bone and flesh.
Over there, far away, he has shed his bone: he shines on the place of
    the Lotus Root, and the place of the Dugong,
On the place of the Evening Star, of the Dugong's Tail, of the
    Moonlight clay pan . . .
His old bone gone, now the New Moon grows larger;
Gradually growing, his new bone growing as well.
Over there, the horns of the old receding Moon bent down, sank into
    the place of the Dugong:
His horns were pointing towards the place of the Dugong.
Now the New Moon swells to fullness, his bone grown larger.
He looks on the water, hanging above it, at the place of the Lotus.
There he comes into sight, hanging above the sea, growing larger and
    older . . .
There far away he has come back, hanging over the clans near
    Milingimbi . . .
Hanging there in the sky, above those clans . . .
'Now I'm becoming a big moon, slowly regaining my roundness . . .'
In the far distance the horns of the Moon bend down, above
    Milingimbi,
Hanging a long way off, above Milingimbi Creek . . .
Slowly the Moon Bone is growing, hanging there far away.
The bone is shining, the horns of the Moon bend down.

First the sickle Moon on the old Moon's shadow; slowly he grows,
And shining he hangs there at the place of the Evening Star ...
Then far away he goes sinking down, to lose his bone in the sea;
Diving towards the water, he sinks down out of sight.
The old Moon dies to grow new again, to rise up out of the sea.

*     *     *

Up and up soars the evening Star, hanging there in the sky.
Men watch it, at the place of the Dugong and of the Clouds, and of the
    Evening Star,
A long way off, at the place of Mist, of Lilies and of the Dugong.
The Lotus, the Evening Star, hangs there on its long stalk, held by the
    Spirits.
It shines on that place of the Shade, on the Dugong place, and on to the
    Moonlight clay pan ...
The Evening Star is shining, back towards Milingimbi, and over the
    *Malag* people ...
Hanging there in the distance, towards the place of the Dugong,
The place of the Eggs, of the Tree-Limbs-Rubbing-Together, and of the
    Moonlight clay pan ...
Shining on its short stalk, the Evening Star, always there at the clay
    pan, at the place of the Dugong ...
There, far away, the long string hangs at the place of the Evening Star,
    the place of Lilies.
Away there at Milingimbi ... at the place of the Full Moon,
Hanging above the head of that *Wonguri* tribesman:
The Evening Star goes down across the camp, among the white gum
    trees ...
Far away, in those places near Milingimbi ...
Goes down among the *'Ngurulwulu* people, towards the camp and the
    gum trees,
At the place of the Crocodiles, and of the Evening Star, away towards
    Milingimbi ...
The Evening Star is going down, the Lotus Flower on its stalk ...
Going down among all those western clans ...
It brushes the heads of the uncircumcised people ...
Sinking down in the sky, that Evening Star, the Lotus ...
Shining on to the foreheads of all those headmen ...
On to the heads of all those Sandfly people ...
It sinks there into the place of the white gum trees, at Milingimbi.

# ANONYMOUS

## *Jim Jones*

O listen for a moment, lads, and hear me tell my tale,
How o'er the sea from England I was compelled to sail.
The jury says 'He's guilty,' and says the judge, says he,
'For life, Jim Jones, I'm sending you across the stormy sea.

'And take my tip before you ship to join the iron gang;
Don't get too gay at Botany Bay, or else you'll surely hang—
Or else you'll hang,' he says, says he, 'and after that, Jim Jones,
High up upon the gallows tree the crows will pick your bones.

'You'll have no time for mischief then, remember what I say;
They'll flog the poaching out of you, out there at Botany Bay.'
The waves were high upon the sea, the winds blew up in gales—
I would rather drown in misery than go to New South Wales.

The winds blew high upon the sea, and the pirates came along,
But the soldiers on our convict ship were full five hundred strong.
They opened fire and somehow drove that pirate ship away,
I'd rather have joined that pirate ship than come to Botany Bay.

For day and night the irons clang, and like poor galley-slaves
We toil and toil, and when we die must fill dishonoured graves.
But by and by I'll break my chain; into the bush I'll go,
And join the brave bushrangers there, Jack Donahue & Co.

And some dark night when everything is silent in the town
I'll kill the tyrants one and all, I'll shoot the floggers down;
I'll give the Law a little shock, remember what I say:
They'll yet regret they sent Jim Jones in chains to Botany Bay.

### Moreton Bay

One Sunday morning as I went walking, by Brisbane waters I chanced
    to stray;
I heard a prisoner his fate bewailing, as on the sunny river bank he
    lay:
'I am a native of Erin's island and banished now from my native shore;
They tore me from my aged parents and from the maiden whom I do
    adore.

'I've been a prisoner at Port Macquarie, at Norfolk Island and Emu
    Plains,
At Castle Hill and at cursed Toongabbie, at all those settlements I've
    worked in chains;
But of all places of condemnation and penal stations of New South
    Wales,
To Moreton Bay I have found no equal; excessive tyranny each day
    prevails.

'For three long years I was beastly treated, and heavy irons on my legs
    I wore;
My back with flogging is lacerated and often painted with my crimson
    gore.
And many a man from downright starvation lies mouldering now
    underneath the clay;
And Captain Logan he had us mangled at the triangles of Moreton Bay.

'Like the Egyptians and ancient Hebrews we were oppressed under
    Logan's yoke,
Till a native black lying there in ambush did give our tyrant his mortal
    stroke,
My fellow prisoners, be exhilarated that all such monsters such a death
    may find!
And when from bondage we are liberated our former sufferings shall
    fade from mind.'

# WILLIAM FORSTER

from *The Devil and the Governor*

DEVIL. In New South Wales, as I plainly see,
You're carving out plentiful jobs for me.
But forgive me for hinting your zeal is such
That I'm only afraid you'll do too much.
I know this well—To subject mankind
You must tickle before you attempt to bind!
Nor lay on his shoulder the yoke until
Through his habits you've first enslaved his will.
You're too violent far—you rush too madly
At your favourite ends and spoil them sadly.
Already, I warn you, your system totters,
They're a nest of hornets these rascally Squatters,
Especially when you would grasp their cash—
Excuse me, George, but I think you're rash.

GOVERNOR. Rash! d——n it, rash!

DEVIL. . . . Don't fly in a passion,
In the higher circles 'tis not the fashion;
And swearing, besides, you must allow,
Is neither polite nor useful now.

GOVERNOR. Would you have me forego the rights of the Crown,
To be laughed at all over this factious town?
I'll teach these Squatters to pay their rent,
And don't care one rush for their discontent;
They've abused me in print, they've made orations,
They've their papers and pastoral associations;
To England they've sent their vile petitions—
They've their Agents in swarms like heathen missions;
They've gone to the length of caricaturing—
But I'll show them the evil's past their curing.

DEVIL. Come, come, be cool or your aim you'll miss,
Your temper's too hot for work like this;

This people I say will submit the more readily
If you've only the wit to grind them steadily.
You've a snug little tyranny under your thumb—
But manage it well, or down 'twill come.
'Twere a pity to peril this rich possession
By a foolish rashness or indiscretion;
Wentworth and Windeyer are troublesome chaps,
And the Council's a thorn in your side, perhaps;
But let them grumble and growl their fill,
You know very well their power is nil. . . .
Then calmly proceed, and with prudence act;
'In the middle lies safety'—that's a fact—
Subdue by degrees, and slowly oppress,
Or, I tell you, you'll get yourself into a mess.
While people petition, they'll find it 'a sell'
But don't push them too hard, they might rebel.

GOVERNOR. Rebel! ha! ha! you're surely in joke;
Rebellion here—a mere puff of smoke.
What would the people of England say
A rebellion! how queer! in Botany Bay!
Pick-pockets, swindlers, thieves, and jobbers,
Cut-throats, and burglars, and highway robbers—
A mob that escaped the gallows at home
'Tis worse than 'the servile wars at Rome'!
A handful of troops would put them down,
And the higher classes would join the Crown.

DEVIL. It might be so, but just mark, my friend—
Who come to be losers in the end?
No doubt there'd be fun well worth enjoying—
Burning, and plundering, and destroying;
Fighting for towns not worth disputing—
Skirmishing, robbing, and rifle-shooting
From bushes and trees, and rocks for barriers—
Murdering of post boys and plundering of carriers,
Storming of camp by midnight entries
Driving off horses, and popping off sentries—
Seizing of stock for purposes royal,

Pressing of men to make them loyal;
Some heroes might fall in that petty strife,
Whom bondage had taught a contempt of life,
Some patriots leading in civil storms,
Might dangle on gibbets their martyr forms
Or exiled afar, to return no more,
Might bury their bones on a foreign shore,
Proscribed by the tyrants they dared to brave
And mocked by the people they fought to save;
But not in vain would they bear or bleed,
This land would have gained what most they need.
John Bull from his drowsy indifference waking,
Would give some of you despots a terrible shaking;
You'd be robbed of your berth and your reputation,
For causing your masters so much vexation—
And the people your chains so closely bind,
A tardy justice would seek and find.
Take my advice, I offer it cheap—
Why, as I live, the man's asleep!
George, George, your manners much want reforming,
But I'll give your nose a bit of a warming.
    [*Tweaks his nose and vanishes.*]


### Sonnet on the Crimean War

*Published in the* SYDNEY EMPIRE, *about the time of the peace.*

'Twixt East and West a giant shape she grew
To both akin, and making both afraid—
Casting a lurid shadow on the new
And ancient world, her greedy eyes betrayed
The tiger's heart, and ominously surveyed
The peoples destined for her future prey.
From polar steppes, and ice-encumbered seas,
To where the warm and blue Symplegades
Perplex the splendour of a Grecian day,
She stretched her long grasp, conquering by degrees,
And when at length the banded nations rose

In armed resistance, their combined array
   With equal arms she shrank not to oppose,
   But bravely stood where still she stands at bay.


### Love has Eyes

Dear friend! Believe me, Love's not always blind,
   But as an idiot's spiritual night,
   By sudden inspiration set alight,
May teach mysterious wisdom to mankind,
So amorous insight flashes on the mind,
   And shows your naked soul—even as you are
   With all your womanly faults, yet lovelier far
Than any perfect creature I can find
In this imperfect world by God designed—
   Faults, that like spots upon the peerless sun,
   Into unexpected light and beauty run—
Gazing whereon methinks I leave behind
Earth's vapid shows, and my delighted eyes
Throb as with beams intense, and splendour of the skies.


### The Poor of London

Lift up, ye poor! your everlasting prayer!
   We have you with us always, as foretold
   By the great Teacher, in the times of old—
We have you with us always—everywhere.
Your spectral faces haunt us through the glare
   Of this great city—from its storied stones
   In chorus rise your immemorial groans—
Your rags and misery taint the turbid air—
Lift up your million voices, and prepare
   The prosperous thousands for that ominous day,
   When your grim choirs, grown ghastlier by delay,
And sick with hope deferred, from every lair
   Issuing, shall seize the citadels of power,
And brandish vested rights to pillage and devour.

# ANONYMOUS

## *The Streets of Forbes*

Come all you Lachlan men, and a sorrowful tale I'll tell
Concerning of a hero bold who through misfortune fell.
His name it was Ben Hall, a man of good renown
Who was hunted from his station, and like a dog shot down.

Three years he roamed the roads, and he showed the traps some fun;
A thousand pound was on his head, with Gilbert and John Dunn.
Ben parted from his comrades, the outlaws did agree
To give away bushranging and to cross the briny sea.

Ben went to Goobang Creek, and that was his downfall;
For riddled like a sieve was valiant Ben Hall.
'Twas early in the morning upon the fifth of May
When the seven police surrounded him as fast asleep he lay.

Bill Dargin he was chosen to shoot the outlaw dead;
The troopers then fired madly, and filled him full of lead.
They rolled him in a blanket, and strapped him to his prad,
And led him through the streets of Forbes to show the prize they had.

# CHARLES HARPUR

## *Bush Justice*

A Dealer, bewitched by gain-promising dreams
Settled down near my Station, to trade with my Teams,
And to sell to my men too! from whom, through the nose,
Until then, I had screw'd just what prices I chose;
And for this, to be sure, I so hated the man,
That I swore ne'er to rest till I'd settled some plan
Whereby in the Lockup to cleverly cram him!
And so to my Super the matter I put,

Who thereupon 'found' a sheep's head near his hut,
And the 'how came it there?' was sufficient to damn him,
The Beak before who I then lugg'd him, as you
May suppose, being neck-deep in Squattery too.

'Twas a beautiful Hearing, as noted at large
By the Clerk (who was bonuss'd)—sheep-stealing the charge;
'Twould make your hearts laugh in the Records to see
How we bullied him out of his wits!—I say *we*,
Because while on this side against him I banged,
On the other the Beak said he ought to be hanged,
For a gallows-grained, scandalous son of transgression!
And committing him then—the case being so plain,
We sent him three hundred miles 'down on the chain'
To his Trial—and eke to his 'acquittal', at Session!
For what care we Squatters for Law on a push?
And for Justice! what has she to do with the Bush?


### Marvellous Martin

Who sees him walk the street, can scarce forbear
To question thus his friend, What prig goes there?
So much hath Nature, as 'tis oft her plan,
Stamped inward trickery on the outward man!
And yet, with her great interdiction deep
Impressed thus on his being, see him creep
Into our Parliament, and dare to prate
About the god-like principles of State;
With this sole claim address him to the work,
That he has read that prince of sophists, Burke!
And though a dreary Plunkett's glad to praise
His talent, seeing that their feeble rays
Have just that kindred with his own pinched mind
Which (says the proverb) makes us wond'rous kind.
No more could such a creature feel or think
Beyond Expediency's most beaten brink,
Or sum the onward pressure of our race,
Than I could heave a mountain from its base!

Nay, even the dogmas of his vaunted Burke
Work in him to no end, or backward work,
Or dwindle in his view, like heaven's wide cope
Seen through the wrong end of a telescope.

How then might such a 'thing', with all the gang
That yet like vermin about Wentworth hang,
Rear-ranked with hirelings,—how might he and these,
(Any-thing snobs and no-thing Nominees!)
Devise a Government intoned and twined
With all that's true and fetterless in mind
And free in body—one, in short, designed
Not for the pigmies of the passing hour,
But for Australia's future sons of Power?
No! they can spin but feudal cobwebs, soon
By Freedom to be blown into the moon,
Or back to Norfolk Island, whence, 'tis plain,
Their slimy embryos came in youthful Lottery's brain.

### from *A Coast View*

Dead city walls may pen us in, but still
Her[1] influence seeks, to find us,—even there,
Through many a simple means. A vagrant mass
Of sunshine, falling into some void place,
Shall warm us to the heart, and trade awhile,
Though through some sorrowful reminiscence,
With instincts which, regenerated thus,
Make us child-happy. A stray gust of wind
Pent in and wasting up the narrow lanes,
Shall breathe insinuations to our age
Of youth's fresh promise. Even a bird, though caged,
Shall represent past freedom, and its notes
Be spirited with memories that call
Around us the fresh fumes of bubbling brooks

[1] Nature.

And far wild woods. Nay, even a scanty vine,
Trailing along some backyard wall, shall speak
Love's first green language; and (so cheap is truth)
A bucket of clear water from the well
Be in its homely brightness beautiful.


## from *The Creek of the Four Graves*

I verse a Settler's tale of olden times—
One told me by our sage friend, Egremont;
Who then went forth, meetly equipt, with four
Of his most trusty and adventurous men
Into the wilderness,—went forth to seek
New streams and wider pastures for his fast
Augmenting flocks and herds. On foot were all,
For horses then were beasts of too great price
To be much ventured upon mountain routes,
And over wild wolds clouded up with brush,
And cut with marshes, perilously pathless.

So went they forth at dawn: and now the sun
That rose behind them as they journeyed out,
Was firing with his nether rim a range
Of unknown mountains that, like rampires, towered
Full in their front, and his last glances fell
Into the gloomy forest's eastern glades
In golden masses, transiently, or flashed
Down on the windings of a nameless Creek,
That noiseless ran betwixt the pioneers
And those new Apennines;—ran, shaded up
With boughs of the wild willow, hanging mixed
From either bank, or duskily befringed
With upward tapering, feathery swamp-oaks—
The sylvan eyelash always of remote
Australian waters, whether gleaming still
In lake or pool, or bickering along
Between the marges of some eager stream.

Before them, thus extended, wilder grew
The scene each moment—beautifully wilder!
For when the sun was all but sunk below
Those barrier mountains,—in the breeze that o'er
Their rough enormous backs deep fleeced with wood
Came whispering down, the wide upslanting sea
Of fanning leaves in the descending rays
Danced interdazzlingly, as if the trees
That bore them, were all thrilling,—tingling all
Even to the roots for very happiness.


# ADAM LINDSAY GORDON


### A Dedication
To the author of *Holmby House*

They are rhymes rudely strung with intent less
   Of sound than of words,
In lands where bright blossoms are scentless,
   And songless bright birds;
Where, with fire and fierce drought on her tresses,
Insatiable Summer oppresses
Sere woodlands and sad wildernesses,
   And faint flocks and herds.

Where in dreariest days, when all dews end,
   And all winds are warm,
Wild Winter's large flood-gates are loosen'd,
   And floods, freed by storm,
From broken up fountain heads, dash on
Dry deserts with long pent up passion—
Here rhyme was first framed without fashion,
   Song shaped without form.

Whence gather'd?—The locust's glad chirrup
   May furnish a stave;

The ring of a rowel and stirrup,
  The wash of a wave.
The chaunt of the marsh frog in rushes,
  That chimes through the pauses and hushes
  Of nightfall, the torrent that gushes,
    The tempests that rave.


from *Hippodromania; or Whiffs From the Pipe*

Rest, and be thankful! On the verge
  Of the tall cliff rugged and grey,
But whose granite base the breakers surge,
  And shiver their frothy spray,
Outstretched, I gaze on the eddying wreath
  That gathers and flits away,
With the surf beneath, and between my teeth
  The stem of the 'ancient clay'.

With the anodyne cloud on my listless eyes,
  With its spell on my dreamy brain,
As I watch the circling vapours rise
From the brown bowl up to the sullen skies.
  My vision becomes more plain,
Till a dim kaleidoscope succeeds
  Through the smoke-rack drifting and veering,
Like ghostly riders on phantom steeds
  To a shadowy goal careering.

In their own generation the wise may sneer,
  They hold our sports in derision;
Perchance to sophist, or sage, or seer,
  Were allotted a graver vision.
Yet if man, of all the Creator plann'd,
  His noblest work is reckoned,
Of the works of His hand, by sea or by land,
  The horse may at least rank second.

Did they quail, those steeds of the squadrons light,
  Did they flinch from the battle's roar,

When they burst on the guns of the Muscovite,
  By the echoing Black Sea shore?
On! on! to the cannon's mouth they stride,
  With never a swerve nor a shy,
Oh! the minutes of yonder maddening ride,
  Long years of pleasure outvie!

No slave, but a comrade staunch, in this,
  Is the horse, for he takes his share,
Not in peril alone, but in feverish bliss,
  And in longing to do and dare.
Where bullets whistle, and round shot whiz,
  Hoofs trample, and blades flash bare,
God send me an ending as fair as his
  Who died in his stirrups there!

### *How We Beat the Favourite*
A LAY OF THE LOAMSHIRE HUNT CUP

'Aye, squire,' said Stevens, 'they back him at evens;
  The race is all over, bar shouting, they say;
The Clown ought to beat her; Dick Neville is sweeter
  Than ever—he swears he can win all the way.

'A gentleman rider—well, I'm an outsider,
  But if he's a gent who the mischief's a jock?
You swells mostly blunder, Dick rides for the plunder,
  He rides, too, like thunder—he sits like a rock.

'He calls "hunted fairly" a horse that has barely
  Been stripp'd for a trot within sight of the hounds,
A horse that at Warwick beat Birdlime and Yorick,
  And gave Abdelkader at Aintree nine pounds.

'They say we have no test to warrant a protest;
  Dick rides for a lord and stands in with a steward;
The light of their faces they show him—his case is
  Prejudged and his verdict already secured.

'But none can outlast her, and few travel faster,
    She strides in her work clean away from The Drag;
You hold her and sit her, she couldn't be fitter,
    Whenever you hit her she'll spring like a stag.

'And p'rhaps the green jacket, at odds though they back it,
    May fall, or there's no knowing what may turn up.
The mare is quite ready, sit still and ride steady,
    Keep cool; and I think you may just win the Cup.'

Dark-brown with tan muzzle, just stripped for the tussle,
    Stood Iseult, arching her neck to the curb,
A lean head and fiery, strong quarters and wiry,
    A loin rather light, but a shoulder superb.

Some parting injunction, bestowed with great unction,
    I tried to recall, but forgot like a dunce,
When Reginald Murray, full tilt on White Surrey,
    Came down in a hurry to start us at once.

'Keep back in the yellow! Come up on Othello!
    Hold hard on the chestnut! Turn round on The Drag!
Keep back there on Spartan! Back you, sir, in tartan!
    So, steady there, easy!' and down went the flag.

We started, and Kerr made strong running on Mermaid,
    Through furrows that led to the first stake-and-bound,
The crack, half extended, look'd bloodlike and splendid,
    Held wide on the right where the headland was sound.

I pulled hard to baffle her rush with the snaffle,
    Before her two-thirds of the field got away;
All through the wet pasture where floods of the last year
    Still loitered, they clotted my crimson with clay.

The fourth fence, a wattle, floor'd Monk and Bluebottle;
    The Drag came to grief at the blackthorn and ditch,
The rails toppled over Redoubt and Red Rover,
    The lane stopped Lycurgus and Leicestershire Witch.

She passed like an arrow Kildare and Cock Sparrow,
   And Mantrap and Mermaid refused the stone wall;
And Giles on The Greyling came down at the paling,
   And I was left sailing in front of them all.

I took them a burster, nor eased her nor nursed her
   Until the Black Bullfinch led into the plough,
And through the strong bramble we bored with a scramble—
   My cap was knock'd off by the hazel-tree bough.

Where furrows looked lighter I drew the rein tighter—
   Her dark chest all dappled with flakes of white foam,
Her flanks mud-bespattered, a weak rail she shattered—
   We landed on turf with our heads turn'd for home.

Then crash'd a low binder, and then close behind her
   The sward to the strokes of the favourite shook;
His rush roused her mettle, yet ever so little
   She shorten'd her stride as we raced at the brook.

She rose when I hit her. I saw the stream glitter,
   A wide scarlet nostril flashed close to my knee,
Between sky and water The Clown came and caught her,
   The space that he cleared was a caution to see.

And forcing the running, discarding all cunning,
   A length to the front went the rider in green;
A long strip of stubble, and then the big double,
   Two stiff flights of rails with a quickset between.

She raced at the rasper, I felt my knees grasp her,
   I found my hands give to her strain on the bit;
She rose when The Clown did—our silks as we bounded
   Brush'd lightly, our stirrups clash'd loud as we lit.

A rise steeply sloping, a fence with stone coping—
   The last—we diverged round the base of the hill;
His path was the nearer, his leap was the clearer,
   I flogg'd up the straight and he led sitting still.

She came to his quarter, and on still I brought her,
    And up to his girth, to his breastplate she drew,
A short prayer from Neville just reach'd me, 'The Devil!'
    He muttered—lock'd level the hurdles we flew.

A hum of hoarse cheering, a dense crowd careering,
    All sights seen obscurely, all shouts vaguely heard;
'The green wins!' 'The crimson!' The multitude swims on,
    And figures are blended and features are blurr'd.

'The horse is her master!' 'The green forges past her!'
    'The Clown will outlast her!' 'The Clown wins!' 'The Clown!'
The white railing races with all the white faces,
    The chestnut outpaces, outstretches the brown.

On still past the gateway she strains in the straightway,
    Still struggles, 'The Clown by a short neck at most,'
He swerves, the green scourges, the stand rocks and surges,
    And flashes, and verges, and flits the white post.

Aye! so ends the tussle,—I knew the tan muzzle
    Was first, though the ring-men were yelling 'Dead heat!'
A nose I could swear by, but Clarke said, 'The mare by
    A short head.' And that's how the favourite was beat.


### The Sick Stockrider

Hold hard, Ned! Lift me down once more, and lay me in the shade.
    Old man, you've had your work cut out to guide
Both horses, and to hold me in the saddle when I sway'd,
    All through the hot, slow, sleepy, silent ride.

The dawn at 'Moorabinda' was a mist rack dull and dense,
    The sunrise was a sullen, sluggish lamp;
I was dozing in the gateway at Arbuthnot's bound'ry fence,
    I was dreaming on the Limestone cattle camp.
We crossed the creek at Carricksford, and sharply through the haze,
    And suddenly the sun shot flaming forth;

To southward lay 'Katâwa', with the sandpeaks all ablaze,
   And the flush'd fields of Glen Lomond lay to north.


Now westward winds the bridle path that leads to Lindisfarm,
   And yonder looms the double-headed Bluff;
From the far side of the first hill, when the skies are clear and calm,
   You can see Sylvester's woolshed fair enough.
Five miles we used to call it from our homestead to the place
   Where the big tree spans the roadway like an arch;
'Twas here we ran the dingo down that gave us such a chase
   Eight years ago—or was it nine?—last March.


'Twas merry in the glowing morn, among the gleaming grass,
   To wander as we've wandered many a mile,
And blow the cool tobacco cloud, and watch the white wreaths pass,
   Sitting loosely in the saddle all the while.
'Twas merry 'mid the blackwoods, when we spied the station roofs,
   To wheel the wild scrub cattle at the yard,
With a running fire of stockwhips and a fiery run of hoofs;
   Oh! the hardest day was never then too hard!


Aye! we had a glorious gallop after 'Starlight' and his gang,
   When they bolted from Sylvester's on the flat;
How the sun-dried reed-beds crackled, how the flintstrewn ranges rang
   To the strokes of 'Mountaineer' and 'Acrobat'.
Hard behind them in the timber, harder still across the heath,
   Close beside them through the tea-tree scrub we dash'd;
And the golden-tinted fern leaves, how they rustled underneath!
   And the honeysuckle osiers, how they crash'd!


We led the hunt throughout, Ned, on the chestnut and the grey,
   And the troopers were three hundred yards behind,
While we emptied our six-shooters on the bushrangers at bay,
   In the creek with stunted box-tree for a blind!
There you grappled with the leader, man to man and horse to horse,
   And you roll'd together when the chestnut rear'd;
He blazed away and missed you in that shallow watercourse—
   A narrow shave—his powder singed your beard!

In these hours when life is ebbing, how those days when life was
    young
  Come back to us; how clearly I recall
Even the yarns Jack Hall invented, and the songs Jem Roper sung;
  And where are now Jem Roper and Jack Hall?

Aye! nearly all our comrades of the old colonial school,
  Our ancient boon companions, Ned, are gone;
Hard livers for the most part, somewhat reckless as a rule,
  It seems that you and I are left alone.

There was Hughes, who got in trouble through that business with the
    cards,
  It matters little what became of him;
But a steer ripp'd up MacPherson in the Cooraminta yards,
  And Sullivan was drown'd at Sink-or-swim.

And Mostyn—poor Frank Mostyn—died at last a fearful wreck,
  In 'the horrors', at the Upper Wandinong;
And Carisbrooke, the rider, at the Horsefall broke his neck,
  Faith! the wonder was he saved his neck so long!
Ah! those days and nights we squandered at the Logans' in the glen—
  The Logans, man and wife, have long been dead.
Elsie's tallest girl seems taller than your little Elsie then;
  And Ethel is a woman grown and wed.

I've had my share of pastime, and I've done my share of toil,
  And life is short—the longest life a span;
I care not now to tarry for the corn or for the oil,
  Or for the wine that maketh glad the heart of man.
For good undone and gifts misspent and resolutions vain,
  'Tis somewhat late to trouble. This I know—
I should live the same life over, if I had to live again;
  And the chances are I go where most men go.

The deep blue skies wax dusky, and the tall green trees grow dim,
  The sward beneath me seems to heave and fall;
And sickly, smoky shadows through the sleepy sunlight swim,
  And on the very sun's face weave their pall.

Let me slumber in the hollow where the wattle blossoms wave,
　　With never stone or rail to fence my bed;
Should the sturdy station children pull the bush flowers on my grave,
　　I may chance to hear them romping overhead.


# ARANDA SONG

### *Ankotarinya*[1]


*Ankotarinya in his burrow is decorated with red down.*
　　Red is the down which is covering me
　　Red I am as though I was burning in a fire.

　　Red I am as though I was burning in a fire
　　Bright red gleams the ochre with which I have rubbed my body.

　　Red I am as though I was burning in a fire
　　Red, too, is the hollow in which I am lying.

　　Red I am like the heart of a flame of fire
　　Red, too, is the hollow in which I am lying.

　　The red tjurunga is resting upon my head
　　Red, too, is the hollow in which I am lying.

*The great tnatantja stands on his head and shoots up to the sky.*
　　Like a whirlwind it is towering to the sky
　　Like a pillar of red sand it is towering to the sky.

　　The tnatantja is towering to the sky
　　Like a pillar of red sand it is towering to the sky.


[1] Translated from the Aranda by T. G. H. Strehlow

*He describes the country in the vicinity of Ankota.*
  A mass of red pebbles covers the plains
  Little white sand-rills cover the plains.

  Lines of red pebbles streak the plains
  Lines of white sand-rills streak the plains.

*After he has caught the scent of people an underground pathway opens up.*
  An underground pathway lies open before me
  Leading straight west, it lies open before me.

  A cavernous pathway lies open before me
  Leading straight west, it lies open before me.

*He follows up the scent.*
  He is sucking his beard into his mouth in anger
  Like a dog he follows the trail by scent.

  He hurries on swiftly, like a keen dog
  Like a dog he follows the trail by scent.

  Irresistible and foaming with rage—
  Like a whirlwind he rakes them together.

*He devours the tjilpa men. And after being struck down, returns to
    Ankota.*
  Out yonder, not far from me, lies Ankota
  The underground hollow is gaping open before me.

  A straight track is gaping open before me
  An underground hollow is gaping open before me.

  A cavernous pathway is gaping open before me
  An underground pathway is gaping open before me.

*Once more he is back in his old home.*
  Red I am, like the heart of a flame of fire
  Red, too, is the hollow in which I am resting.

### Aranda Song[1]

The sun is going down. His spearthrower lies on the ground, and his staff is lying on top of his spearthrower. Now all is darkness. He stretches himself out, weary from carrying the heavy animal. He lies on the ground.

He is lying where he had flung himself down at twilight. He is lying motionless. Never to stir again he is lying there, unable to turn over, stretched out on his back. Deep midnight gathers about him: he is lying motionless. Without a thought he lies there; never will he move again.

The earth is growing light. The darkness is lifting; the eastern sky grows bright: he is still lying as he had flung himself down in the twilight, nor does he wake up. The sun looks over the horizon. The sun spies him, still without a move. Never to rise again he lies there. Without a thought he lies there. And the sun is rising in the sky.

## HENRY KENDALL

### The Last of His Tribe

He crouches, and buries his face on his knees,
   And hides in the dark of his hair;
For he cannot look up to the storm-smitten trees,
   Or think of the loneliness there—
   Of the loss and the loneliness there.

[1] Translated from the Aranda by T. G. H. Strehlow

The wallaroos grope through the tufts of the grass,
    And turn to their covers for fear;
But he sits in the ashes and lets them pass
    Where the boomerangs sleep with the spear—
    With the nullah, the sling, and the spear.

Uloola, behold him! The thunder that breaks
    On the tops of the rocks with the rain,
And the wind which drives up with the salt of the lakes,
    Have made him a hunter again—
    A hunter and fisher again.

For his eyes have been full with a smouldering thought;
    But he dreams of the hunts of yore,
And of foes that he sought, and of fights that he fought
    With those who will battle no more—
    Who will go to the battle no more.

It is well that the water which tumbles and fills,
    Goes moaning and moaning along;
For an echo rolls out from the sides of the hills,
    And he starts at a wonderful song—
    At the sounds of a wonderful song.

And he sees through the rents of the scattering fogs,
    The corroboree warlike and grim,
And the lubra who sat by the fire on the logs,
    To watch, like a mourner, for him—
    Like a mother and mourner for him.

Will he go in his sleep from these desolate lands,
    Like a chief, to the rest of his race,
With the honey-voiced woman who beckons and stands,
    And gleams like a dream in his face—
    Like a marvellous dream in his face?

## Orara[1]

The strong sob of the chafing stream
   That seaward fights its way
Down crags of glitter, dells of gleam,
   Is in the hills to-day.

But far and faint, a grey-winged form
   Hangs where the wild lights wane—
The phantom of a bygone storm,
   A ghost of wind and rain.

The soft white feet of afternoon
   Are on the shining meads,
The breeze is as a pleasant tune
   Amongst the happy reeds.

The fierce, disastrous, flying fire,
   That made the great caves ring,
And scarred the slope, and broke the spire,
   Is a forgotten thing.

The air is full of mellow sounds,
   The wet hill-heads are bright,
And, down the fall of fragrant grounds,
   The deep ways flame with light.

A rose-red space of stream I see,
   Past banks of tender fern;
A radiant brook, unknown to me
   Beyond its upper turn.

The singing silver life I hear,
   Whose home is in the green,
Far-folded woods of fountains clear,
   Where I have never been.

[1] A tributary of the Clarence River

Ah, brook above the upper bend,
　I often long to stand
Where you in soft, cool shades descend
　From the untrodden land!

Ah, folded woods, that hide the grace
　Of moss and torrents strong,
I often wish to know the face
　Of that which sings your song!

But I may linger, long, and look
　Till night is over all:
My eyes will never see the brook,
　Or sweet, strange waterfall.

The world is round me with its heat,
　And toil, and cares that tire;
I cannot with my feeble feet
　Climb after my desire.

But, on the lap of lands unseen,
　Within a secret zone,
There shine diviner gold and green
　Than man has ever known.

And where the silver waters sing
　Down hushed and holy dells,
The flower of a celestial Spring—
　A tenfold splendour, dwells.

Yea, in my dream of fall and brook
　By far sweet forests furled,
I see that light for which I look
　In vain through all the world—

The glory of a larger sky
　On slopes of hills sublime,
That speak with God and morning, high
　Above the ways of Time!

Ah! haply, in this sphere of change
  Where shadows spoil the beam,
It would not do to climb that range
  And test my radiant Dream.

The slightest glimpse of yonder place,
  Untrodden and alone,
Might wholly kill that nameless grace
  The charm of the unknown:

And therefore, though I look and long,
  Perhaps the lot is bright
Which keeps the river of the song
  A beauty out of sight.


### Christmas Creek

Phantom streams were in the distance—mocking lights of lake and
    pool—
Ghosts of trees of soft green lustre—groves of shadows deep and cool!
Yea, some devil ran before them changing skies of brass to blue,
Setting bloom where curse is planted, where a grassblade never grew.
Six there were, and high above them glared a wild and wizened sun,
Ninety leagues from where the waters of the singing valleys run.
There before them, there behind them, was the great, stark, stubborn
    plain,
Where the dry winds hiss for ever, and the blind earth moans for rain!
Ringed about by tracks of furnace, ninety leagues from stream and
    tree,
Six there were, with wasted faces, working northwards to the sea!

          *    *    *

Ah, the bitter, hopeless desert! Here these broken human wrecks
Trod the wilds where sand of fire is with the spiteful spinifex,
Toiled through spheres that no bird knows of, where with fiery
    emphasis
Hell hath stamped its awful mint-mark deep on every thing that is!
Toiled and thirsted, strove and suffered! *This* was where December's
    breath

As a wind of smiting flame is on weird, haggard wastes of death!
*This* was where a withered moan is, and the gleam of weak, wan star,
And a thunder full of menace sends its mighty voices far!
*This* was where black execrations, from some dark tribunal hurled,
Set the brand of curse on all things in the morning of the world!

      *  *  *

One man yielded—then another—then a lad of nineteen years
Reeled and fell, with English rivers singing softly in his ears,
English grasses started round him—then the grace of Sussex lea
Came and touched him with the beauty of a green land by the sea!

Old-world faces thronged about him—old-world voices spoke to him;
But his speech was like a whisper, and his eyes were very dim.
In a dream of golden evening, beaming on a quiet strand,
Lay the stranger till a bright One came and took him by the hand.
England vanished, died the voices! but he heard a holier tone,
And an angel that we know not led him to the lands unknown!

      *  *  *

Six there were, but three were taken! Three were left to struggle still;
But against the red horizon flamed a horn of brindled hill!
But beyond the northern skyline, past a wall of steep austere,
Lay the land of light and coolness in an April-coloured year!
'Courage, brothers!' cried the leader. 'On the slope of yonder peak
There are tracts of herb and shadow, and the channels of the creek!'
So they made one last great effort—haled their beasts through brake
  and briar—
Set their feet on spurs of furnace—grappled spikes and crags of fire—
Fought the stubborn mountain forces, smote down naked, natural
  powers,
Till they gazed from thrones of Morning on a sphere of streams and
  flowers.

Out behind them was the desert, glaring like a sea of brass!
Here before them were the valleys, fair with moon-light-coloured grass!
At their backs were haggard waste-lands, bickering in a wicked blaze!
In their faces beamed the waters, marching down melodious ways!
Touching was the cool, soft lustre over laps of lawn and lea;
And majestic was the great road Morning made across the sea.
On the sacred day of Christmas, after seven months of grief,

Rested three of six who started, on a bank of moss and leaf—
Rested by a running river, in a hushed, a holy week;
And they named the stream that saved them—named it fitly—
    'Christmas Creek'.


# BARCROFT BOAKE

### An Allegory

The fight was over, and the battle won.
A soldier, who beneath his chieftain's eye
Had done a mighty deed and done it well,
And done it as the world will have it done—
A stab, a curse, some quick play of the butt,
Two skulls cracked crosswise, *but the colours saved*—
Proud of his wounds, proud of the promised cross,
Turned to his rear-rank man, who on his gun
Leant heavily apart. 'Ho, friend!' he called,
'You did not fight then: were you left behind?
I saw you not.' The other turned and showed
A gaping, red-lipped wound upon his breast.
'Ah,' said he sadly, 'I was in the smoke!'
Threw up his arms, shivered, and fell and died.


### At Devlin's Siding

What made the porter stare so hard? what made the porter stare
And eye the tall young woman and the bundle that she bare?

What made the tall young woman flush, and strive to hide her face,
As the train slid past the platform and the guard swung in his place?

What made her look so stealthily both up and down the line,
And quickly give the infant suck to still its puny whine?

Why was the sawmill not at work? why were the men away?
They might have turned a woman from a woeful deed that day.

Why did the pine-scrub stand so thick? why was the place so lone
That nothing but the soldier-birds might hear a baby moan?

Why doth the woman tear the child? why doth the mother take
The infant from her breast, and weep as if her heart would break?

Why doth she moan, and grind her teeth, and weave an awful curse
To fall on him who made of her a harlot—ay, and worse?

Why should she fall upon her knees and, with a trembling hand,
Clear off the underbrush and scrape a cradle in the sand?

Why doth she shudder as she hears the buzz of eager flies,
And bind a handkerchief across the sleeping infant's eyes?

Why doth she turn, but come again and feverishly twine,
To shield it from the burning sun, the fragrant fronds of pine?

Why, as she strides the platform, does she try hard not to think
That somewhere in the scrub a babe is calling her for drink?

Why, through the alleys of the pine, do languid breezes sigh
A low refrain that seems to mock her with a baby's cry?

Seek not to know! but pray for her, and pity, as the train
Carries a white-faced woman back to face the world again.


### Where the Dead Men Lie

Out on the wastes of the Never Never—
    That's where the dead men lie!
There where the heat-waves dance for ever—
    That's where the dead men lie!
That's where the Earth's loved sons are keeping

Endless tryst: not the west wind sweeping
Feverish pinions can wake their sleeping—
   Out where the dead men lie!

Where brown Summer and Death have mated—
   That's where the dead men lie!
Loving with fiery lust unsated—
   That's where the dead men lie!
Out where the grinning skulls bleach whitely
Under the saltbush sparkling brightly;
Out where the wild dogs chorus nightly—
   That's where the dead men lie!

Deep in the yellow, flowing river—
   That's where the dead men lie!
Under the banks where the shadows quiver—
   That's where the dead men lie!
Where the platypus twists and doubles,
Leaving a train of tiny bubbles;
Rid at last of their earthly troubles—
   That's where the dead men lie!

East and backward pale faces turning—
   That's how the dead men lie!
Gaunt arms stretched with a voiceless yearning—
   That's how the dead men lie!
Oft in the fragrant hush of nooning
Hearing again their mothers' crooning,
Wrapt for aye in a dreamful swooning—
   That's how the dead men lie!

Only the hand of Night can free them—
   That's when the dead men fly!
Only the frightened cattle see them—
   See the dead men go by!
Cloven hoofs beating out one measure,
Bidding the stockman know no leisure—
That's when the dead men take their pleasure!
   That's when the dead men fly!

Ask, too, the never-sleeping drover:
    He sees the dead pass by;
Hearing them call to their friends—the plover,
    Hearing the dead men cry;
Seeing their faces stealing, stealing,
Hearing their laughter pealing, pealing,
Watching their grey forms wheeling, wheeling
    Round where the cattle lie!

Strangled by thirst and fierce privation—
    That's how the dead men die!
Out on Moneygrub's farthest station—
    That's how the dead men die!
Hardfaced greybeards, youngsters callow;
Some mounds cared for, some left fallow;
Some deep down, yet others shallow;
    Some having but the sky.

Moneygrub, as he sips his claret,
    Looks with complacent eye
Down at his watch-chain, eighteen-carat—
    There, in his club, hard by:
Recks not that every link is stamped with
Names of the men whose limbs are cramped with
Too long lying in grave mould, camped with
    Death where the dead men lie.


# WENBERI

## Wenberi's Song[1]

We all go to the bones
    all of them shining white in this Dulur country.

The noise of our father Bunjil
    rushing down singing inside this breast of mine.

---

[1] Translated from the Woiworung by A. W. Howitt

HENRY LAWSON : A real poet.

*Faces in the Street*

They lie, the men who tell us for reasons of their own
That want is here a stranger, and that misery's unknown;
For where the nearest suburb and the city proper meet
My window-sill is level with the faces in the street—
     Drifting past, drifting past,
     To the beat of weary feet—
While I sorrow for the owners of those faces in the street.

And cause I have to sorrow, in a land so young and fair,
To see upon those faces stamped the marks of Want and Care;
I look in vain for traces of the fresh and fair and sweet
In sallow, sunken faces that are drifting through the street—
     Drifting on, drifting on,
     To the scrape of restless feet;
I can sorrow for the owners of the faces in the street.

In hours before the dawning dims the starlight in the sky
The wan and weary faces first begin to trickle by,
Increasing as the moments hurry on with morning feet,
Till like a pallid river flow the faces in the street—
     Flowing in, flowing in,
     To the beat of hurried feet—
Ah! I sorrow for the owners of those faces in the street.

The human river dwindles when 'tis past the hour of eight,
Its waves go flowing faster in the fear of being late;
But slowly drag the moments, whilst beneath the dust and heat
The city grinds the owners of the faces in the street—
     Grinding body, grinding soul,
     Yielding scarce enough to eat—
O I sorrow for the owners of the faces in the street.

And then the only faces till the sun is sinking down
Are those of outside toilers and the idlers of the town,

Save here and there a face that seems a stranger in the street
Tells of the city's unemployed upon his weary beat—
    Drifting round, drifting round,
    To the tread of listless feet—
Ah! My heart aches for the owner of that sad face in the street.

And when the hours on lagging feet have slowly dragged away,
And sickly yellow gaslights rise to mock the going day,
Then flowing past my window like a tide in its retreat,
Again I see the pallid stream of faces in the street—
    Ebbing out, ebbing out,
    To the drag of tired feet,
While my heart is aching dumbly for the faces in the street.

And now all blurred and smirched with vice the day's sad pages end,
For while the short 'large hours' towards the longer 'small hours' trend,
With smiles that mock the wearer, and with words that half entreat,
Delilah pleads for custom at the corner of the street—
    Sinking down, sinking down,
    Battered wreck by tempests beat—
A dreadful, thankless trade is hers, that Woman of the Street.

But, ah! to dreader things than these our fair young city comes,
For in its heart are growing thick the filthy dens and slums,
Where human forms shall rot away in sties for swine unmeet,
And ghostly faces shall be seen unfit for any street—
    Rotting out, rotting out,
    For the lack of air and meat—
In dens of vice and horror that are hidden from the street.

I wonder would the apathy of wealthy men endure
Were all their windows level with the faces of the Poor?
Ah! Mammon's slaves, your knees shall knock, your hearts in terror
    beat,
When God demands a reason for the sorrows of the street,
    The wrong things and the bad things
    And the sad things that we meet
In the filthy lane and alley, and the cruel, heartless street.

I left the dreadful corner where the steps are never still,
And sought another window overlooking gorge and hill;
But when the night came dreary with the driving rain and sleet,
They haunted me—the shadows of those faces in the street,
>> Flitting by, flitting by,
>> Flitting by with noiseless feet,
And with cheeks but little paler than the real ones in the street.

Once I cried: 'O God Almighty! if Thy might doth still endure,
Now show me in a vision for the wrongs of Earth a cure.'
And, lo! with shops all shuttered I beheld a city's street,
And in the warning distance heard the tramp of many feet,
>> Coming near, coming near,
>> To a drum's dull distant beat,
And soon I saw the army that was marching down the street.

Then, like a swollen river that has broken bank and wall,
The human flood came pouring with the red flags over all,
And kindled eyes all blazing bright with revolution's heat,
And flashing swords reflecting rigid faces in the street—
>> Pouring on, pouring on,
>> To a drum's loud threatening beat,
And the war-hymns and the cheering of the people in the street.

And so it must be while the world goes rolling round its course,
The warning pen shall write in vain, the warning voice grow hoarse,
But not until a city feels Red Revolution's feet
Shall its sad people miss awhile the terrors of the street—
>> The dreadful everlasting strife
>> For scarcely clothes and meat
In that pent track of living death—the city's cruel street.


### The Teams

>> A cloud of dust on the long white road,
>> And the teams go creeping on
>> Inch by inch with the weary load;

And by the power of the green-hide goad
    The distant goal is won.

With eyes half-shut to the blinding dust,
    And necks to the yokes bent low,
The beasts are pulling as bullocks must;
And the shining tires might almost rust
    While the spokes are turning slow.

With face half-hid 'neath a broad-brimmed hat
    That shades from the heat's white waves,
And shouldered whip with its green-hide plait,
The driver plods with a gait like that
    Of his weary, patient slaves.

He wipes his brow, for the day is hot,
    And spits to the left with spite;
He shouts at Bally, and flicks at Scot,
And raises dust from the back of Spot,
    And spits to the dusty right.

He'll sometimes pause as a thing of form
    In front of a settler's door,
And ask for a drink, and remark, 'It's warm,'
Or say, 'There's signs of a thunderstorm;'
    But he seldom utters more.

The rains are heavy on roads like these;
    And, fronting his lonely home,
For days together the settler sees
The waggons bogged to the axletrees,
    Or ploughing the sodden loam.

And then when the roads are at their worst,
    The bushman's children hear
The cruel blows of the whips reversed
While bullocks pull as their hearts would burst,
    And bellow with pain and fear.

And thus—with glimpses of home and rest—
  Are the long, long journeys done;
And thus—'tis a thankless life at the best—
Is distance fought in the mighty West,
  And the lonely battles won.


### The Horseman on the Skyline

Who's that mysterious rider,
  Full-sized, yet far away,
Seen by the Western-sider—
  A spectre of the day?
On ridge or seeming high line
  Where East the plain expands,
The horseman on the skyline
  Is known in many lands.

With summer insects drumming
  And summer skies aglow,
He's there—none saw him coming—
  He's gone—none saw him go.
Too plain for superstition,
  Too blurred for one we sought,
He rides across our vision
  To vanish like a thought.

He never halts nor hurries,
  But slowly, in broad day,
Along the skyline eastward
  He seems to pick his way.
He rides against the sunrise,
  He rides against the gloom,
Where suddenly, in summer,
  The lurid storm-clouds loom.

He never rides in starlight,
  Nor underneath the moon,
But often in the distant
  And dazzling haze of noon.

The sad Australian sunset
   (Too sad for pen or tongue)
Has often seen him riding
   Out where the night was young.

On rolling cattle ranches,
   In 'country' far away,
Where cowboys took their chances,
   They saw him every day.
And many try to find him
   Where riders never tire—
He leaves no trail behind him
   And never lights a fire.

On run and ranch and veldtland
   He leaves them all in doubt—
A cowboy, or a stockman,
   A horse thief, or a scout.
The glass brings him no nearer,
   Nor hints the way he came;
His features are no clearer,
   He vanishes the same.

Too blurred and dark his clothing
   To hint of his degree;
Inquiries lead to nothing,
   No hoof-marks do we see.
He leaves the watcher puzzled,
   Or leaves the watcher pained:
The horseman on the skyline
   Has never been explained.

Still, where by foot or saddle,
   Or train or motor car,
The people hurry westward—
   It matters not how far—
And, plainly seen by many,
   The greatest and the least—
The rider on the skyline
   Is scouting to the east.

## Up the Country

I am back from up the country—very sorry that I went—
Seeking for the Southern poets' land whereon to pitch my tent;
I have lost a lot of idols, which were broken on the track,
Burnt a lot of fancy verses, and I'm glad that I am back.
Further out may be the pleasant scenes of which our poets boast,
But I think the country's rather more inviting round the coast.
Anyway, I'll stay at present at a boarding-house in town,
Drinking beer and lemon-squashes, taking baths and cooling down.

'Sunny plains!' Great Scott!—those burning wastes of barren soil and
    sand
With their everlasting fences stretching out across the land!
Desolation where the crow is! Desert where the eagle flies,
Paddocks where the luny bullock starts and stares with reddened eyes;
Where, in clouds of dust enveloped, roasted bullock-drivers creep
Slowly past the sun-dried shepherd dragged behind his crawling sheep.
Stunted peak of granite gleaming, glaring like a molten mass
Turned from some infernal furnace on a plain devoid of grass.

Miles and miles of thirsty gutters—strings of muddy water-holes
In the place of 'shining rivers'—'walled by cliffs and forest boles'.
Barren ridges, gullies, ridges! where the everlasting flies—
Fiercer than the plagues of Egypt—swarm about your blighted eyes!
Bush! where there is no horizon! where the buried bushman sees
Nothing—Nothing! but the sameness of the ragged, stunted trees!
Lonely hut where drought's eternal—suffocating atmosphere—
Where the God-forgotten hatter dreams of city life and beer.

Treacherous tracks that trap the stranger, endless roads that gleam and
    glare,
Dark and evil-looking gullies, hiding secrets here and there!
Dull dumb flats and stony rises, where the toiling bullocks bake,
And the sinister 'gohanna', and the lizard, and the snake.
Land of day and night—no morning freshness, and no afternoon,
When the great white sun in rising brings the summer heat in June.
Dismal country for the exile, when the shades begin to fall
From the sad heart-breaking sunset, to the newchum worst of all.

Dreary land in rainy weather, with the endless clouds that drift
O'er the bushman like a blanket that the Lord will never lift—
Dismal land when it is raining—growl of floods, and, O the woosh
Of the rain and wind together on the dark bed of the bush—
Ghastly fires in lonely humpies where the granite rocks are piled
In the rain-swept wildernesses that are wildest of the wild.

Land where gaunt and haggard women live alone and work like men,
Till their husbands, gone a-droving, will return to them again:
Homes of men! if homes had ever such a God-forgotten place,
Where the wild selector's children fly before a stranger's face.
Home of tragedy applauded by the dingoes' dismal yell,
Heaven of the shanty-keeper—fitting fiend for such a hell—
And the wallaroos and wombats, and, of course, the curlew's call—
And the lone sundowner tramping ever onward through it all!

I am back from up the country, up the country where I went
Seeking for the Southern poets' land whereon to pitch my tent;
I have shattered many idols out along the dusty track,
Burnt a lot of fancy verses—and I'm glad that I am back.
I believe the Southern poets' dream will not be realized
Till the plains are irrigated and the land is humanized.
I intend to stay at present, as I said before, in town
Drinking beer and lemon-squashes, taking baths and cooling down.


*Ned's Delicate Way*


Ned knew I was short of tobacco one day,
    And that I was too proud to ask for it;
He hated such pride, but his delicate way
    Forbade him to take me to task for it.


I loathed to be cadging tobacco from Ned,
    But, when I was just on the brink of it:
'I've got a new brand of tobacco,' he said—
    'Try a smoke, and let's know what you think of it.'

## Will Yer Write it Down for Me?

In the parlour of the shanty where the lives have all gone wrong,
When a singer or reciter gives a story or a song,
Where the poet's heart is speaking to their hearts in every line,
Till the hardest curse and blubber at the thoughts of Auld Lang Syne;
Then a boozer lurches forward with an oath for all disguise—
Prayers and curses in his soul, and tears and liquor in his eyes—
Grasps the singer or reciter with a death-grip by the hand:
'That's the truth, bloke! Sling it at 'em! O Gorbli'me, that was grand!
Don't mind me; I've got 'em. *You* know! What's yer name, bloke! Don't
    yer *see*?
Who's the bloke what wrote the po'try? *Will* yer write it down fer
    me?'

And the backblocks bard goes through it, ever seeking as he goes
For the line of least resistance to the hearts of men he knows;
And he tracks their hearts in mateship, and he tracks them out alone—
Seeking for the power to sway them, till he finds it in his own,
Feels what they feel, loves what they love, learns to hate what they
    condemn,
Takes his pen in tears and triumph, and he writes it down for them.

## Ripperty! Kye! Ahoo!

There was a young woman, as I've heard tell
    (Ripperty! Kye! Ahoo!),
Lived near the sea in a nice little hell
That she made for herself and her husband as well;
But that's how a good many married folk dwell—
    Ripperty! Kye! Ahoo!

She kept a big mongrel that murdered his fowls
    (Ripperty! Kye! Ahoo!)
And kept him awake with his barks and his growls.
    (Ripperty! Kye! Ahoo!)
She also had cats that assisted with yowls;
She gave him old dishcloths and nightgowns for tow'ls,

And called in the neighbours to witness his growls—
      Ripperty! Kye! A-hoo!

You'd think 'twas the limit, but *she* didn't—quite
      (Ripperty! Kye! Ahoo!);
He had to sleep out in the fowlhouse at night
      (Ripperty! Kye! Ahoo!)
And make his own breakfast before it was light;
Then go to his work, and then keep out of sight
When he came home to dinner—and that wasn't right—
      (*Singing*): Ripperty! Kye! A-hoo!

She'd find him and chase him with pot-stick and fist
      (Ripperty! Kye! Ahoo!);
He'd an arm like a navvy, and also a wrist—
      (Ripperty! Kye! Ahoo!)
Why *didn't* he give her a jolt or a twist?
Then, because she so crowed for the hiding she missed,
She'd shriek: 'You great coward! why don't you enlist?'
      Ripperty! Kye! A-hoo!

She'd invite all her relatives down for the day
      (Ripperty! Kye! A-hoo!)
And also invite *his* relations to stay.
      (Ripperty! Kye! Ahoo!)
He found his own worst, as is often the way;
(They told her his father was locked up one day);
His red beard went white, and his brown hair went grey.
      (*Sadly*): Rip-per-ty! Kye! A-hoo!

Her parents were German, as he was aware.
      (Ripperty! Kye! Ahoo!),
He said to himself: 'I had better be there!'
      (Ripperty! Kye! Ahoo!)
He went to the Depot and made himself bare,
And was straightway accepted, and passed then and there—
He clapped his great wings and he *crowed* (so they swear):
      Ripperty! Kye! A-hoo!

He came home for 'Final' and filled up with rum.
    (Ripperty! Kye! A-hic-hoo!)
She said, when she saw him: 'I thought you would come!
    (Ripperty! Kye! Ahoo!)
You'd best make yer will and make over the home
And arrange the allowance, and don't look so glum!'
He did as she told him, and went away, dumb—
    Ripperty! Kye! A-hoo!

He went to the Front, and he fought for the French.
    (Ripperty! Kye! Ahoo!)
He went for the Germans and cleared out a trench;
    (Ripperty! Kye! Ahoo!)
They tumbled like drunken men over a bench;
He finished them off with a jab and a wrench,
And loudly he yelled, in the mix-up and stench,
    'Ripperty! Kye! A-hoo!'

He came back at last with ideas that were new.
    (Ripperty! Kye! A-hoo!)
He went for the mongrel, and ran him right through;
    (Ripperty! Kye! Ahoo!)
He potted three cats on the ridge-capping, too;
North, southward and eastward the relatives flew;
Then he said: 'Now, old woman, I'm coming for you!
    RIPPERTY! KYE! A-HOO!'

Three times round the house and the fowlhouse she fled
    (Ripperty! Kye! A-hoo!)
Three inches in front of his bayonet red;
    (Ripperty! Kye! Ahoo!)
He yelled, and she shrieked fit to shriek off her head,
He fired at the house and the fowlhouse and shed,
Till she fell on the dungheap quite three-quarters dead.
    Ripperty! Kye! A-hoo!

Now, there's a young woman, as I've heard tell
    (*Sing gently*): Ripperty! Kye! A-hoo!
Lives near the sea in a nice little shell,
    (*Sing softly*): Ripperty! Kye! Ahoo!

That's built of brick, wood, and red tiles, at Rozelle;
She's fond of her husband, and he's doing well—
And—that's how a good many married folk dwell.
    (*Sing exultantly*): Ripperty! Kye! A-hoo!


# ANONYMOUS

## Much Distressed

'Her Majesty the Queen was much distressed at the terrible news of the wreck
of the steamer *Elbe*.'

The noisy urchins scampered round
    Amidst the careless crowd:
'An orful wreck! Three 'underd drown'd!'
    They cried the news aloud.
We bought a paper, paused, and read
    With melancholy zest,
Then winked our other eye, and said—
    'The Queen will be distressed.'

We felt it coming from the first;
    Court flunkeys took the hint,
And promptly got a royal burst
    Of sorrow into print.
The cable told the touching tale
    Exactly as we guessed—
We never knew her grief to fail,
    The Queen *was* much distressed.

In time of war, should British blood
    Be shed by niggers mean,
Or when an earthquake, or a flood,
    Appears upon the scene;
Or accidents in mines excite
    Some public interest,
Then, posing in a blaze of light,
    The Queen is much distressed.

# A. B. ('BANJO') PATERSON

*The Road to Hogan's Gap*

Now look, you see, it's this way like—
  You cross the broken bridge
And run the crick down, till you strike
  The second right-hand ridge.

The track is hard to see in parts,
  But still it's pretty clear;
There's been two Injun hawkers' carts
  Along that road this year.

Well, run that right-hand ridge along—
  It ain't, to say, too steep—
There's two fresh tracks might put you wrong
  Where blokes went out with sheep.

But keep the crick upon your right,
  And follow pretty straight
Along the spur, until you sight
  A wire and sapling gate.

Well, that's where Hogan's old grey mare
  Fell off and broke her back;
You'll see her carcass layin' there,
  Jist down below the track.

And then you drop two mile, or three,
  It's pretty steep and blind;
You want to go and fall a tree
  And tie it on behind.

And then you pass a broken cart
  Below a granite bluff;
And that is where you strike the part
  They reckon pretty rough.

But by the time you've got that far
   It's either cure or kill,
So turn your horses round the spur
   And face 'em up the hill.

For look, if you should miss the slope
   And get below the track,
You haven't got the slightest hope
   Of ever gettin' back.

An' half way up you'll see the hide
   Of Hogan's brindled bull;
Well, mind and keep the right-hand side.
   The left's too steep a pull.

And both the banks is full of cracks;
   An' just about at dark
You'll see the last year's bullock tracks
   Where Hogan drew the bark.

The marks is old and pretty faint—
   O'ergrown with scrub and such;
Of course the track to Hogan's ain't
   A road that's travelled much.

But turn and run the tracks along
   For half a mile or more,
And then, of course, you can't go wrong—
   You're right at Hogan's door.

When first you come to Hogan's gate
   He mightn't show perhaps;
He's pretty sure to plant, and wait
   To see it ain't the traps.

I wouldn't call it good enough
   To let your horses out;
There's some that's pretty extra rough
   Is livin' round about.

It's likely, if your horses did
    Get feedin' near the track,
It's going to cost at least a quid
    Or more to get them back.

So, if you find they're off the place,
    It's up to you to go
And flash a quid in Hogan's face—
    He'll know the blokes that know.

But listen—if you're feelin' dry,
    Just see there's no one near,
And go and wink the other eye
    And ask for ginger beer.

The blokes come in from near and far
    To sample Hogan's pop;
They reckon once they breast the bar
    They stay there till they drop.

On Sundays you can see them spread
    Like flies around the tap.
It's like that song 'The Livin' Dead'
    Up there at Hogan's Gap.

They like to make it pretty strong
    Whenever there's a chance;
So when a stranger comes along
    They always hold a dance.

There's recitations, songs, and fights—
    A willin' lot you'll meet.
There's one long bloke up there recites;
    I tell you he's a treat.

They're lively blokes all right up there,
    It's never dull a day.
I'd go meself if I could spare
    The time to get away.

*    *    *

The stranger turned his horses quick.
   He didn't cross the bridge;
He didn't go along the crick
   To strike the second ridge;

He didn't make the trip, because
   He wasn't feeling fit.
His business up at Hogan's was
   To serve him with a writ.

He reckoned, if he faced the pull
   And climbed the rocky stair,
The next to come might find his hide
A landmark on the mountain side,
Along with Hogan's brindled bull
   And Hogan's old grey mare!


### The Travelling Post Office

The roving breezes come and go, the reed-beds sweep and sway,
The sleepy river murmurs low, and loiters on its way,
It is the land of lots o' time along the Castlereagh.

      \*     \*     \*

The old man's son had left the farm, he found it dull and slow,
He drifted to the great North-west, where all the rovers go.
'He's gone so long,' the old man said, 'he's dropped right out of mind,
But if you'd write a line to him I'd take it very kind;
He's shearing here and fencing there, a kind of waif and stray—
He's droving now with Conroy's sheep along the Castlereagh.

'The sheep are travelling for the grass, and travelling very slow;
They may be at Mundooran now, or past the Overflow,
Or tramping down the black-soil flats across by Waddiwong
But all those little country towns would send the letter wrong.
The mailman, if he's extra tired, would pass them in his sleep;
It's safest to address the note to "Care of Conroy's sheep",
For five and twenty thousand head can scarcely go astray,
You write to "Care of Conroy's sheep along the Castlereagh".'

      \*     \*     \*

By rock and ridge and riverside the western mail has gone
Across the great Blue Mountain Range to take that letter on.
A moment on the topmost grade, while open fire-doors glare,
She pauses like a living thing to breathe the mountain air,
Then launches down the other side across the plains away
To bear that note to 'Conroy's sheep along the Castlereagh'.

And now by coach and mailman's bag it goes from town to town,
And Conroy's Gap and Conroy's Creek have marked it 'Further down'.
Beneath a sky of deepest blue, where never cloud abides,
A speck upon the waste of plain the lonely mailman rides.

Where fierce hot winds have set the pine and myall boughs asweep
He hails the shearers passing by for news of Conroy's sheep.
By big lagoons where wildfowl play and crested pigeons flock,
By camp-fires where the drovers ride around their restless stock,
And past the teamster toiling down to fetch the wool away
My letter chases Conroy's sheep along the Castlereagh.


## Waltzing Matilda

Once a jolly swagman camped by a billabong
Under the shade of a coolibah tree;
And he sang, as he watched and waited while his billy boiled:
'Who'll come a-waltzing Matilda with me?'

*Chorus*
Waltzing Matilda, Waltzing Matilda,
Who'll come a-waltzing Matilda with me?
And he sang as he watched and waited while his billy boiled:
'Who'll come a-waltzing Matilda with me?'

Down came a jumbuck to drink at that billabong,
Up jumped the swagman and grabbed him with glee;
And he sang as he shoved that jumbuck in his tucker-bag,
'You'll come a-waltzing Matilda with me!'

*Chorus*
Waltzing Matilda, Waltzing Matilda,
You'll come a-waltzing Matilda with me;
And he sang as he shoved that jumbuck in his tucker-bag:
'You'll come a-waltzing Matilda with me!'

Up came the squatter, mounted on his thoroughbred,
Up came the troopers—one—two—three!
'Whose that jolly jumbuck you've got in your tucker-bag?
You'll come a-waltzing Matilda with me!'

*Chorus*
Waltzing Matilda, Waltzing Matilda,
You'll come a-waltzing Matilda with me:
'Whose that jolly jumbuck you've got in your tucker-bag?
You'll come a-waltzing Matilda with me!'

Up jumped the swagman and sprang into the billabong,
'You'll never catch me alive!' said he,
And his ghost may be heard as you pass by that billabong,
'You'll come a-waltzing Matilda with me!'

*Chorus*
Waltzing Matilda, Waltzing Matilda,
You'll come a-waltzing Matilda with me!
And his ghost may be heard as you pass by that billabong,
'You'll come a-waltzing Matilda with me!'


## The Man from Snowy River

There was movement at the station, for the word had passed around
  That the colt from old Regret had got away,
And had joined the wild bush horses—he was worth a thousand
    pound,
  So all the cracks had gathered to the fray.
All the tried and noted riders from the stations near and far
  Had mustered at the homestead overnight,

For the bushmen love hard riding where the wild bush horses are,
    And the stock-horse snuffs the battle with delight.

There was Harrison, who made his pile when Pardon won the cup,
    The old man with his hair as white as snow;
But few could ride beside him when his blood was fairly up—
    He would go wherever horse and man could go,
And Clancy of the Overflow came down to lend a hand,
    No better horseman ever held the reins;
For never horse could throw him while the saddle-girths would
        stand—
    He learnt to ride while droving on the plains.

And one was there, a stripling on a small and weedy beast;
    He was something like a racehorse undersized,
With a touch of Timor pony—three parts thoroughbred at least—
    And such as are by mountain horsemen prized.
He was hard and tough and wiry—just the sort that won't say die—
    There was courage in his quick impatient tread;
And he bore the badge of gameness in his bright and fiery eye,
    And the proud and lofty carriage of his head.

But still so slight and weedy, one would doubt his power to stay,
    And the old man said, 'That horse will never do
For a long and tiring gallop—lad, you'd better stop away,
    Those hills are far too rough for such as you.'
So he waited, sad and wistful—only Clancy stood his friend—
    'I think we ought to let him come,' he said;
'I warrant he'll be with us when he's wanted at the end,
    For both his horse and he are mountain bred.

'He hails from Snowy River, up by Kosciusko's side,
    Where the hills are twice as steep and twice as rough;
Where a horse's hoofs strike firelight from the flint stones every stride,
    The man that holds his own is good enough.
And the Snowy River riders on the mountains make their home,
    Where the river runs those giant hills between;
I have seen full many horsemen since I first commenced to roam,
    But nowhere yet such horsemen have I seen.'

So he went; they found the horses by the big mimosa clump,
   They raced away towards the mountain's brow,
And the old man gave his orders, 'Boys, go at them from the jump,
   No use to try for fancy riding now.
And, Clancy, you must wheel them, try and wheel them to the right.
   Ride boldly, lad, and never fear the spills,
For never yet was rider that could keep the mob in sight,
   If once they gain the shelter of those hills.'

So Clancy rode to wheel them—he was racing on the wing
   Where the best and boldest riders take their place,
And he raced his stock-horse past them, and he made the ranges ring
   With the stockwhip, as he met them face to face.
Then they halted for a moment, while he swung the dreaded lash,
   But they saw their well-loved mountain full in view,
And they charged beneath the stockwhip with a sharp and sudden
     dash,
   And off into the mountain scrub they flew.

Then fast the horsemen followed, where the gorges deep and black
   Resounded to the thunder of their tread,
And the stockwhips woke the echoes, and they fiercely answered back
   From cliffs and crags that beetled overhead.
And upward, ever upward, the wild horses held their way,
   Where mountain ash and kurrajong grew wide;
And the old man muttered fiercely, 'We may bid the mob good day,
   *No* man can hold them down the other side.'

When they reached the mountain's summit, even Clancy took a pull—
   It well might make the boldest hold their breath;
The wild hop scrub grew thickly, and the hidden ground was full
   Of wombat holes, and any slip was death.
But the man from Snowy River let the pony have his head,
   And he swung his stockwhip round and gave a cheer,
And he raced him down the mountain like a torrent down its bed,
   While the others stood and watched in very fear.

He sent the flint-stones flying, but the pony kept his feet,
   He cleared the fallen timber in his stride,

And the man from Snowy River never shifted in his seat—
  It was grand to see that mountain horseman ride.
Through the stringy barks and saplings, on the rough and broken
    ground,
  Down the hillside at a racing pace he went;
And he never drew the bridle till he landed safe and sound
  At the bottom of that terrible descent.

He was right among the horses as they climbed the farther hill,
  And the watchers on the mountain, standing mute,
Saw him ply the stockwhip fiercely; he was right among them still,
  As he raced across the clearing in pursuit.
Then they lost him for a moment, where two mountain gullies met
  In the ranges—but a final glimpse reveals
On a dim and distant hillside the wild horses racing yet,
  With the man from Snowy River at their heels.

And he ran them single-handed till their sides were white with foam;
  He followed like a bloodhound on their track,
Till they halted, cowed and beaten; then he turned their heads for
    home,
  And alone and unassisted brought them back.
But his hardy mountain pony he could scarcely raise a trot,
  He was blood from hip to shoulder from the spur;
But his pluck was still undaunted, and his courage fiery hot,
  For never yet was mountain horse a cur.

And down by Kosciusko, where the pine-clad ridges raise
  Their torn and rugged battlements on high,
Where the air is clear as crystal, and the white stars fairly blaze
  At midnight in the cold and frosty sky,
And where around the Overflow the reed-beds sweep and sway
  To the breezes, and the rolling plains are wide,
The Man from Snowy River is a household word today,
  And the stockmen tell the story of his ride.

# ANONYMOUS

## The Boss's Wife

The warm winds crossed from the eastern coast,
Grew hot through the mountain passes
And picked up the breath of the burning plains
And touched on the station grasses.

And the grasses shrivelled, all dry and brown,
And shrunk to a dusty grey,
And the brown earth cracked, and the fiery drought
Came down on the land to stay.

The waters in on the homestead holes
Sank down to the blue-clay rim,
And the ibis came in their circling flocks
To feast on the bony bream.

'Twas shift all stock to the breeders' run,
With never the slightest doubt—
For the station boss 'twas a total loss
If the breeders' run gave out.

And the boss must wrestle and scheme and toil
And stick to the uphill job,
And battle it out with the fiery drought
For the sake of the starving mob.

And at night he'd go to the stockmen's hut,
For word of the day's work done,
And he'd stay for a smoke, or a yarn and a joke,
And talk of the outside run.

But it seemed somehow to the boss's wife,
A deep and rankling slight
That his plans were made with outside aid
When it came to an uphill fight.

And at night when he'd gone she'd wait and watch
In loneliest contemplation
Of the lot and life of a station wife
And the ways of an outback station.

And she'd gaze at the stockmen's huts below,
And across to the servant's light,
And she'd wait and brood in the doleful mood
That comes with the silent night.

And out of the darkness a notion grew,
A dim little gleaming dart,
It grew and flashed like a fiery sword,
And struck at the wifely heart.

'Twas a notion founded on logic's rites,
And womanly intuition,
By the housemaid's light when it sank at night,
And a shadowy apparition.

She gave no sign, but she watched each night,
Till there wasn't much room for doubt,
And she timed when the boss came in at night,
From the time that the lights went out.

And she hid the hurt with a woman's skill,
And she studied the housemaid's lighting;
To be betrayed for an artless maid—
'Twas time to be up and fighting.

When the boss was gone to stockmen's hut
She lost no time in the going,
With a friendly smile and a bit of guile,
Would the maid come and help with the sewing?

And the maid agreed with a ready nod,
She'd nothing much to do,
She went with a smile, and fell for a pile
Would last for an hour or two.

And the wife, when the work was well in swing,
Slipped off to the housemaid's room,
And safe in the camp she blew the lamp,
And waited there in the gloom.

Till the footsteps soft on the beaten track
Turned in at the darkened door,
With scarce a rap, or the slightest tap,
For he'd been there oft before.

She spoke no word, and the darkened room
No change in the form betrayed,
Nor the greeting kiss with the meeting miss,
'Twas much as the melting maid.

'Twas a woman's style and a wifely wile,
To play the maid of the quarters,
She played with the skill and the strength of will,
And the guile of Eve's own daughters.

She played, and sudden she flashed a torch,
One horrified glance she took;
She dropped the light and she fainted quite,
'Twas Chin-ti, the Chinese cook!

# EDWARD DYSON

## The Old Whim Horse

He's an old grey horse, with his head bowed sadly,
   And with dim old eyes and a queer roll aft,
With the off-fore sprung and the hind screwed badly
   And he bears all over the brands of graft;
And he lifts his head from the grass to wonder
   Why by night and day now the whim is still,
Why the silence is, and the stampers' thunder
   Sounds forth no more from the shattered mill.

In that whim he worked when the night winds bellowed
   On the riven summit of Giant's Hand,
And by day when prodigal Spring had yellowed
   All the wide, long sweep of enchanted land;
And he knew his shift, and the whistle's warning,
   And he knew the calls of the boys below;
Through the years, unbidden, at night or morning,
   He had taken his stand by the old whim bow.

But the whim stands still, and the wheeling swallow
   In the silent shaft hangs her home of clay,
And the lizards flirt and the swift snakes follow
   O'er the grass-grown brace in the summer day;
And the corn springs high in the cracks and corners
   Of the forge, and down where the timber lies;
And the crows are perched like a band of mourners
   On the broken hut on the Hermit's Rise.

All the hands have gone, for the rich reef paid out,
   And the company waits till the calls come in;
But the old grey horse, like the claim, is played out,
   And no market's near for his bones and skin.
So they let him live, and they left him grazing
   By the creek, and oft in the evening dim
I have seen him stand on the rises, gazing
   At the ruined brace and the rotting whim.

The floods rush high in the gully under,
   And the lightnings lash at the shrinking trees,
Or the cattle down from the ranges blunder
   As the fires drive by on the summer breeze.
Still the feeble horse at the right hour wanders
   To the lonely ring, though the whistle's dumb,
And with hanging head by the bow he ponders
   Where the whim boy's gone—why the shifts don't come.

But there comes a night when he sees lights glowing
   In the roofless huts and the ravaged mill,
When he hears again all the stampers going—
   Though the huts are dark and the stampers still:

When he sees the steam to the black roof clinging
   As its shadows roll on the silver sands,
And he knows the voice of his driver singing,
   And the knocker's clang where the braceman stands.

See the old horse take, like a creature dreaming,
   On the ring once more his accustomed place;
But the moonbeams full on the ruins streaming
   Show the scattered timbers and grass-grown brace.
Yet *he* hears the sled in the smithy falling,
   And the empty truck as it rattles back,
And the boy who stands by the anvil, calling;
   And he turns and backs, and he 'takes up slack.'

While the old drum creaks, and the shadows shiver
   As the wind sweeps by, and the hut doors close,
And the bats dip down in the shaft or quiver
   In the ghostly light, round the grey horse goes;
And he feels the strain on his untouched shoulder,
   Hears again the voice that was dear to him,
Sees the form he knew—and his heart grows bolder
   As he works his shift by the broken whim.

He hears in the sluices the water rushing
   As the buckets drain and the doors fall back:
When the early dawn in the east is blushing,
   He is limping still round the old, old track.
Now he pricks his ears, with a neigh replying
   To a call unspoken, with eyes aglow,
And he sways and sinks in the circle, dying,
   From the ring no more will the grey horse go.

In a gully green, where a dam lies gleaming,
   And the bush creeps back on a worked-out claim,
And the sleepy crows in the sun sit dreaming
   On the timbers grey and a charred hut frame,
Where the legs slant down, and the hare is squatting
   In the high rank grass by the dried-up course,
Nigh a shattered drum and a king-post rotting
   Are the bleaching bones of the old grey horse.

## A Friendly Game of Football

We were challenged by The Dingoes—they're the pride of Squatter's
     Gap—
To a friendly game of football on the flat by Devil's Trap.
And we went along on horses, sworn to triumph in the game,
For the honour of Gyp's Diggings, and the glory of the same.

And we took the challenge with us. It was beautiful to see,
With its lovely, curly letters, and its pretty filagree.
It was very gently worded, and it made us all feel good,
For it breathed the sweetest sentiments of peace and brotherhood.

We had Chang, and Trucker Hogan, and the man who licked The Plug,
Also Heggarty, and Hoolahan, and Peter Scott, the pug;
And we wore our knuckle-dusters, and we took a keg on tap
To our friendly game of football with The Dingoes at The Gap.

All the fellows came to meet us, and we spoke like brothers dear.
They'd a tip-dray full of tucker, and a waggon load of beer,
And some lint done up in bundles; so we reckoned there'd be fun
Ere our friendly game of football with the Dingo Club was done.

Their umpire was a homely man, a stranger to the push,
With a sweet, deceitful calmness, and a flavour of the bush.
He declared he didn't know the game, but promised on his oath
To see fair and square between the teams, or paralyse them both.

Then we bounced the ball and started, and for twenty minutes quite
We observed a proper courtesy and a heavenly sense of right,
But Fitzpatrick tipped McDougal in a handy patch of mud,
And the hero rose up, chewing dirt, and famishing for blood.

Simple Simonsen, the umpire, sorted out the happy pair,
And he found a pitch to suit them, and we left them fighting there;
But The Conqueror and Cop-Out met with cries of rage and pain,
And wild horses couldn't part those ancient enemies again.

So the umpire dragged them from the ruck, and pegged them off a
     patch,
And then gave his best attention to the slugging and the match.
You could hardly wish to come across a fairer-minded chap
For a friendly game of football than that umpire at The Gap.

In a while young Smith, and Henty, and Blue Ben, and Dick, and
     Blake,
Chose their partners from The Dingoes, and went pounding for the
     cake.
Timmy Hogan hit the umpire, and was promptly put to bed
'Neath the ammunition waggon, with a bolus on his head.

Feeling lonely-like, Magee took on a local star named Bent,
And four others started fighting to avoid an argument:
So Simonsen postponed the game, for fear some slight mishap
Might disturb the pleasant feeling then prevailing at The Gap.

Sixty seconds later twenty lively couples held the floor,
And the air was full of whiskers, and the grass was tinged with gore,
And the umpire kept good order in the interests of peace,
Whilst the people, to oblige him, sat severely on the p'lice.

Well, we fought the friendly game out, but I couldn't say who won;
We were all stretched out on shutters when the glorious day was done;
Both the constables had vanished; one was carried off to bunk,
And the umpire was exhausted, and the populace was drunk.

But we've written out a paper, with good Father Feeley's aid,
Breathing brotherly affection; and the challenge is conveyed
To the Dingo Club at Squatter's, and another friendly game
Will eventuate at this end, on the flat below the claim.

We have pressed The Gap to bring their central umpire if they can—
Here we honestly admire him as a fair and decent man—
And we're building on a pleasant time beside the Phoenix slums,
For The Giant feels he's got a call to plug him if he comes.

# C. J. DENNIS

*The Martyred Democrat*
A RECITATION (WITH DIRECTIONS)

*(Begin breezily)*
In Lady Lusher's drawing-room, where float the strains of Brahms,
While cultured caterpillars chew the leaves of potted palms—
In Lady Lusher's drawing-room, upon a summer's day,
The Democrats of Toorak met to pass an hour away.
They listened to a speech by Mister Grabbit, MLC,
While Senator O'Sweatem passed around the cakes and tea.
And all the brains and beauty of the suburb gathered there,
In Lady Lusher's drawing-room—Miss Fibwell in the chair.

*(With increasing interest)*
Ay, all the fair and brave were there—the fair in charming hats;
The brave in pale mauve pantaloons and shiny boots, with spats.
But pride of all that gathering, a giant 'mid the rest,
Was Mr Percy Puttipate, in fancy socks and vest.
Despite his bout of brain-fag, plainly showing in his eyes—
(Contracted while inventing something new in nobby ties)—
He braved the ills—the draughts and chills, damp table-cloths and
    mats—
Of Lady Lusher's drawing-room: this prince of Democrats.

*(Resume the breeze)*
Upon a silken ottoman sat Willie Dawdlerich,
Who spoke of democratic things to Mabel Bandersnitch;
And likewise there, on couch and chair, with keen, attentive ears,
Sat many sons and daughters of our sturdy pioneers—
Seed of our noble squatter-lords—those democrats of old—
Who hold of this fair land of ours as much as each can hold;
Whose motto is, and ever was, despite the traitor's gab:
'Australia for Australians—who've learned the art of grab.'

Good Mr Grabbit spoke his piece 'mid glad 'Heah, heahs' and claps,
And Willie Dawdlerich declared he was the best of chaps.
Then the lady organizer, dear Miss Fibwell, rose to speak.

A fighter she, tho' of the sex miscalled by men 'the weak'.
And, tho' they hailed her there and then as Queen of Democrats,
They privily agreed that she was something choice in 'cats'.
She was, in truth, a shade passé, a trifle frayed, but still,
She was an earnest Democrat who owned a sturdy will.

*(In cultured tones)*
'Deah friends,' began Miss Fibwell, 'you—ah—understand ouah
    league
Is formed to stand against that band of schemers who intrigue—
That horrid band of Socialists who seek to wrest ouah raights,
And with class legislation straive to haunt ouah days and naights.
They claim to be the workers of the land, but Ai maintain
That, tho' they stand for horny hands, we represent the bwain.
Are not bwain-workers toilers too, who labah without feah?'
(The fashioner of fancy ties: 'Heah, heah! Quaite raight! Heah, heah!')

'They arrogate unto themselves the sacred name of Work;
But still, Ai ask, where is the task that we've been known to shirk?
We're toilahs, ev'ry one of us, altho' they claim we're not.'
(The toiler on the ottoman: 'Bai jove, thet's bally rot!')
'Moahovah, friends, to serve theah ends, they're straiving, maight and
    main,
To drag down to theah level folk who work with mind and bwain!
They claim we do not earn ouah share, but Ai maintain we do!'
(The grafter in the fancy socks: 'They're beastly rottahs, too!')

*(With rising inflexion)*
'Yes, friends, they'll drag us down and down, compelling us to live
Just laike themselves, the selfish elves, on what *they* choose to give!
Nay, moah, they'll make us weah theah clothes—plain working-
    clothes, forsooth!
Blue dungarees in place of these ...' *'Mai Gahd! Is this the truth?'*

*(With fine dramatic force)*
A gurgling scream ... A sick'ning thud ... a flash of fancy socks—
And Percy Puttipate went down, felled like a stricken ox—
Crashed down thro' cakes and crockery, and lay 'mid plate and spoon,
In Lady Lusher's drawing-room one summer afternoon.

*(With a rush of emotion)*
A scream from Mabel Bandersnitch broke thro' the ev'ning calm.
(The cultured grubs, alone unmoved, still chewed the potted palm);
Strong men turned white with sudden fright; girls fell in faint and
    swoon
In Lady Lusher's drawing-room that summer afternoon.

*(With tears in the voice)*
But Puttipate? . . . Ah, what of him—that noble Democrat,
As he lay there with glassy stare upon the Persian mat?
What cares he now for nobby ties, and what for fancy socks,
As he lies prone, with cake and cream smeared on his sunny locks?

*(With appropriate mournfulness)*
Good Mr Grabbit took his head, O'Sweatem seized his feet,
They bore him to an ambulance that waited in the street.
Poor Mabel Bandersnitch sobbed loud on Dawdlerich's vest;
And lo, a pall fell over all—Miss Fibwell and the rest.
A settled gloom o'erspread the room as shades of ev'ning fell,
And, one by one, they left the place till none was left to tell
The tale of that dire tragedy that broke the summer calm—
Except the apathetic grubs, who went on chewing palm.

*(Suggestive pause, then with fresh interest)*
There still be men, low common men, who sneer at Toorak's ways,
And e'en upon poor Puttipate bestow but grudging praise.
But when you hear the vulgar sneer of some uncultured bore

*(With fine dramatic intensity)*
Point to that pallid patriot who weltered in his gore!
Point to that daring Democrat, who, with a gurgling scream
And flashing socks, dropped like an ox into the clotted cream!
Point to that hero stricken down for our great Party's sake,
His sunny locks, his fiery socks mixed up with fancy cake.

*(With bitter contempt)*
Then lash with scorn the carping wretch who sullies his fair fame,
Who, moved by fear, attempts to smear the lustre of that name.

Great Puttipate! The Democrat! Who perished all too soon
In Lady Lusher's drawing-room, one summer afternoon.

*(Finish with a noble gesture, expressing intense scorn, bow gracefully, and
retire amidst great applause)*

# VICTOR DALEY

## Tall Hat

Who rules the world with iron rod?―
    The person in the Tall Silk Hat.
He is its sordid lord and god―
    Self-centred in a Shrine of Fat.

He keeps the Hoi Polloi in peace,
    With opiates of Kingdom Come:
His is the Glory that is Grease,
    The Grandeur that is Rum.

He sends the nations forth to fight,
    The war-ships grim across the foam:
They battle for the right―*his* right―
    A mortgage over hearth and home.

## When London Calls

They leave us―artists, singers, all―
    When London calls aloud,
Commanding to her Festival
    The gifted crowd.

She sits beside the ship-choked Thames,
    Sad, weary, cruel, grand;
Her crown imperial gleams with gems
    From many a land.

From overseas, and far away,
  Come crowded ships and ships—
Grim-faced she gazes on them; yea,
  With scornful lips.

The garden of the earth is wide;
  Its rarest blooms she picks
To deck her board, this haggard-eyed
  Imperatrix.

Sad, sad is she, and yearns for mirth;
  With voice of golden guile
She lures men from the ends of earth
  To make her smile.

The student of wild human ways
  In wild new lands; the sage
With new great thoughts; the bard whose lays
  Bring youth to age;

The painter young whose pictures shine
  With colours magical;
The singer with the voice divine—
  She lures them all.

But all their new is old to her
  Who bore the Anakim;
She gives them gold or Charon's fare
  As suits her whim.

Crowned Ogress—old, and sad, and wise—
  She sits with painted face
And hard, imperious, cruel eyes
  In her high place.

To him who for her pleasure lives,
  And makes her wish his goal,
A rich Tarpeian gift she gives—
  That slays his soul.

The story-teller from the Isles
   Upon the Empire's rim,
With smiles she welcomes—and her smiles
   Are death to him.

For Her, whose pleasure is her law,
   In vain the shy heart bleeds—
The Genius with the Iron Jaw
   Alone succeeds.

And when the Poet's lays grow bland,
   And urbanised, and prim—
She stretches forth a jewelled hand
   And strangles him.

*    *    *

She sits beside the ship-choked Thames
   With Sphinx-like lips apart—
Mistress of many diadems—
   Death in her heart!


### Lachesis

Over a slow-dying fire,
   Dreaming old dreams, I am sitting;
The flames leap up and expire;
   A woman sits opposite knitting.

I've taken a Fate to wife;
   She knits with a half-smile mocking
Me, and my dreams, and my life,
   All into a worsted stocking.

## MARY GILMORE

### Nationality

I have grown past hate and bitterness,
I see the world as one;
But though I can no longer hate,
My son is still my son.

All men at God's round table sit,
And all men must be fed;
But this loaf in my hand,
This loaf is my son's bread.

### Eve-song

I span and Eve span
A thread to bind the heart of man;
But the heart of man was a wandering thing
That came and went with little to bring:
Nothing he minded what we made,
As here he loitered, and there he stayed.

I span and Eve span
A thread to bind the heart of man;
But the more we span the more we found
It wasn't his heart but ours we bound.
For children gathered about our knees:
The thread was a chain that stole our ease.
And one of us learned in our children's eyes
That more than man was love and prize.
But deep in the heart of one of us lay
A root of loss and hidden dismay.

He said he was strong. He had no strength
But that which comes of breadth and length.
He said he was fond. But his fondness proved
The flame of an hour when he was moved.

He said he was true. His truth was but
A door that winds could open and shut.

And yet, and yet, as he came back,
Wandering in from the outward track,
We held our arms, and gave him our breast,
As a pillowing place for his head to rest.
I span and Eve span,
A thread to bind the heart of man!

## The Tenancy

I shall go as my father went,
A thousand plans in his mind,
With something still held unspent,
When death let fall the blind.

I shall go as my mother went,
The ink still wet on the line;
I shall pay no rust as rent,
For the house that is mine.

## Heritage

Not of ourselves are we free,
Not of ourselves are we strong;
The fruit is never the tree,
Nor the singer the song.

Out of temptation old, so old
The story hides in the dark Untold,
In some far, dim, ancestral hour
There is our root of power.

The strength we give is the strength we make;
And the strength we have is the strength we take,
Given us down from the long-gone years,
Cleansed in the salt of others' tears.

The fruit is never the tree,
    Nor the singer the song;
Not of ourselves are we free,
    Not of ourselves are we strong.


### The Myall in Prison

Lone, lone, and lone I stand,
    With none to hear my cry,
As the black feet of the night
    Go walking down the sky.

The stars they seem but dust
    Under those passing feet,
As they, for an instant's space,
    Flicker and flame, and fleet.

So, on my heart, my grief
    Hangs with the weight of doom,
And the black feet of its night
    Go walking through my room.


### Fourteen Men

Fourteen men,
And each hung down
Straight as a log
From his toes to his crown.

Fourteen men,
Chinamen they were,
Hanging on the trees
In their pig-tailed hair

Honest poor men,
But the diggers said 'Nay!'
So they strung them all up
On a fine summer's day.

There they were hanging
As we drove by,
Grown-ups on the front seat,
On the back seat I.

That was Lambing Flat,
And still I can see
The straight up and down
Of each on his tree.

## 'E'

### Stupidity

Stupidity achieves the crime
Not less than sheer malevolence;
Praying for virtue time and time,
Pray too for *sense*.

I fear the dullard, for the knave
One's own quick wit can circumvent,
But how beware the fool that has,
No ill intent?

### Martyr

Scourge deep, and quick be done,
Dislodge the marrowed bone:
He did not wince or shake,
Nor did that rack his noble silence break.

Three hundred years ago!
But Life still has it so—
Tests for the splendid blood,
And martyrdom for regal hardihood.

Mouth-deep amid the tide,
She strove, and saved, and died,
Giving the stranger place,
Though waves climbed upward o'er her shining face.


### The Farmer

He went into his harvest barn,
And from his plump and yellowed wheat
Four pairs of eyes looked down on him,
Immensely seeing, and discreet.

Ready to run or keep their place
At the appointed midnight meal;
He stood, a witness in the gloom,
And watched the furry robbers steal.

And so they ate, and so he stood
Less farmer than philosopher;
These were the native of the Land
When the wild grains invested her.

A space he stood his heart bewrayed
By all the strange primeval past;
Why should these creatures be denied?
That he should feast why should they fast?

Still nothing solved he left them there
And moved towards that lighted pane
Past which She slept and all their brood . . .
Next day the miller had the grain.


### A Man's Sliding Mood

Ardent in love and cold in charity,
Loud in the market, timid in debate:
Scornful of foe unbuckled in the dust,
At whimper of a child compassionate,

A man's a sliding mood from hour to hour,
Rage, and a singing forest of bright birds,
Laughter with lovely friends, and loneliness,
Woe with her heavy horn of unspoke words.

What is he then this heir of heart and mind?
Is this the man with his conflicting moods,
Or is there in a deeper dwelling place
Some stilly shaping thing that bides and broods?


*Ninety*

Love essential unto youth
Is almost unto age
A spectacle that's unobserved
From a contracting cage.

The rout is unessential—
Irrelevant to calm—
And even children's voices
Muddle the faded psalm.

She, seated in her cushions,
Has neither book nor thread,
A frail mortality
Not yet accounted dead.

A little sheaf of spirit
Held by a crooked bone:
Amongst the sapless flesh,
Lives dimly on alone.

# CHRISTOPHER BRENNAN

## from *The Wanderer*

When window-lamps had dwindled, then I rose
and left the town behind me; and on my way
passing a certain door I stopt, remembering
how once I stood on its threshold, and my life
was offer'd to me, a road how different
from that of the years since gone! and I had but
to rejoin an olden path, once dear, since left.
All night I have walk'd and my heart was deep awake,
remembering ways I dream'd and that I chose,
remembering lucidly, and was not sad,
being brimm'd with all the liquid and clear dark
of the night that was not stirr'd with any tide;
for leaves were silent and the road gleam'd pale,
following the ridge, and I was alone with night.
But now I am come among the rougher hills
and grow aware of the sea that somewhere near
is restless; and the flood of night is thinn'd
and stars are whitening. O, what horrible dawn
will bare me the way and crude lumps of the hills
and the homeless concave of the day, and bare
the ever-restless, ever-complaining sea?

        *     *     *

Each day I see the long ships coming into port
and the people crowding to their rail, glad of the shore:
because to have been alone with the sea and not to have known
of anything happening in any crowded way,
and to have heard no other voice than the crooning sea's
has charmed away the old rancours, and the great winds
have search'd and swept their hearts of the old irksome thoughts:
so, to their freshen'd gaze, each land smiles a good home.
Why envy I, seeing them made gay to greet the shore?
Surely I do not foolishly desire to go
hither and thither upon the earth and grow weary
with seeing many lands and peoples and the sea:
but if I might, some day, landing I reck not where

have heart to find a welcome and perchance a rest,
I would spread the sail to any wandering wind of the air
this night, when waves are hard and rain blots out the land.

*　　*　　*

Once I could sit by the fire hourlong when the dripping eaves
sang cheer to the shelter'd, and listen, and know that the woods drank
  full,
and think of the morn that was coming and how the freshen'd leaves
would glint in the sun and the dusk beneath would be bright and cool.

Now, when I hear, I am cold within: for my mind drifts wide
where the blessing is shed for naught on the salt waste of the sea,
on the valleys that hold no rest and the hills that may not abide:
and the fire loses its warmth and my home is far from me.

*　　*　　*

How old is my heart, how old, how old is my heart,
and did I ever go forth with song when the morn was new?
I seem to have trod on many ways: I seem to have left
I know not how many homes; and to leave each
was still to leave a portion of mine own heart,
of my old heart whose life I had spent to make that home
and all I had was regret, and a memory.
So I sit and muse in this wayside harbour and wait
till I hear the gathering cry of the ancient winds and again
I must up and out and leave the embers of the hearth
to crumble silently into white ash and dust,
and see the road stretch bare and pale before me: again
my garment and my home shall be the enveloping winds
and my heart be fill'd wholly with their old pitiless cry.

*　　*　　*

The land I came thro' last was dumb with night,
a limbo of defeated glory, a ghost:
for wreck of constellations flicker'd perishing
scarce sustain'd in the mortuary air,
and on the ground and out of livid pools
wreck of old swords and crowns glimmer'd at whiles;
I seem'd at home in some old dream of kingship:
now it is clear grey day and the road is plain,
I am the wanderer of many years

who cannot tell if ever he was king
or if ever kingdoms were: I know I am
the wanderer of the ways of all the worlds,
to whom the sunshine and the rain are one
and one to stay or hasten, because he knows
no ending of the way, no home, no goal,
and phantom night and the grey day alike
withhold the heart where all my dreams and days
might faint in soft fire and delicious death:
and saying this to myself as a simple thing
I feel a peace fall in the heart of the winds
and a clear dusk settle, somewhere, far in me.

from *The Quest of Silence*

Fire in the heavens, and fire along the hills,
and fire made solid in the flinty stone,
thick-mass'd or scatter'd pebble, fire that fills
the breathless hour that lives in fire alone.

This valley, long ago the patient bed
of floods that carv'd its antient amplitude,
in stillness of the Egyptian crypt outspread,
endures to drown in noon-day's tyrant mood.

Behind the veil of burning silence bound,
vast life's innumerous busy littleness
is hush'd in vague-conjectured blur of sound
that dulls the brain with slumbrous weight, unless
some dazzling puncture let the stridence throng
in the cicada's torture-point of song.

*Because She Would Ask Me Why I Loved Her*

If questioning could make us wise
no eyes would ever gaze in eyes;
if all our tale were told in speech
no mouths would wander each to each.

Were spirits free from mortal mesh
and love not bound in hearts of flesh
no aching breasts would yearn to meet
and find their ecstasy complete.

For who is there that lives and knows
the secret powers by which he grows?
Were knowledge all, what were our need
to thrill and faint and sweetly bleed?

Then seek not, sweet, the *If* and *Why*
I love you now until I die:
For I must love because I live
And life in me is what you give.


BERNARD O'DOWD

from *The Bush*

To other eyes and ears you are a great
    Pillared cathedral tremulously green,
An odorous and hospitable gate
    To genial mystery, the happy screen
Of truants or of lovers rambling there
'Neath sun-shot boughs o'er miles of maidenhair.
Wee rubies dot the leaflets of the cherries,
    The wooing wagtails hop from log to bough,
The bronzewing comes from Queensland for the berries,
    The bell-bird by the creek is calling now.

And you can ride, an Eastern queen, they say,
    By living creatures sumptuously borne,
With all barbaric equipages gay,
    Beneath the torrid blue of Capricorn.
That native lotus is the very womb
That was the Hindoo goddess' earthly tomb.

The gang-gang screams o'er cactus wildernesses,
  Palm trees are there, and swampy widths of rice,
Unguents and odours ooze from green recesses,
  The jungles blaze with birds of Paradise.
. . .
Ye, who would challenge when we claim to see
  The bush alive with Northern wealth of wings,
Forget that at a common mother's knee
  We learned, with you, the lore of Silent Things.
There is no New that is not older far
Than swirling cradle of the first-born star:
Our youngest hearts prolong the far pulsation
  And churn the brine of the primordial sea:
The foetus writes the précis of Creation:
  Australia is the whole world's legatee.


## URUMBULA SONG

*The Urumbula Song*[1]

The narrowing sea embraces it forever,—
Its welling waves embrace it forever.

The sea, ever narrowing, forever embraces it,—
The great beam of The Milky Way.

Its embracing arms forever tremble about it,—
The great beam of The Milky Way.

Set in the bosom of the sea it stands,
Reverberating loudly without a pause.

Set in the bosom of the sea it stands,
Sea-flecked with drifts of foam.


[1] Translated from the Aranda by T. G. H. Strehlow

The tnatantja pole, flecked with drifts of foam,—
The tnatantja pole casts off its foamy covering.

The tnatantja pole strips itself bare like a plain,—
The tnatantja pole untwists and frees itself from its covering.

The tnatantja pole rises into the air,—
The great beam of The Milky Way.

The kauaua pole rises into the air,—
The great beam of The Milky Way.

The great mulga beam rises into the air,—
The great beam of The Milky Way.

It showers sparks like burning mulga grass,—
The great beam of The Milky Way.

The great beam of The Milky Way
Gleams and shines forever.

The great beam of The Milky Way
Casts a flickering glow over the sky forever.

The great beam of The Milky Way
Burns bright crimson forever.

The great beam of The Milky Way
Trembles with deep desire forever.

The great beam of The Milky Way
Quivers with deep passion forever.

The great beam of The Milky Way,
Trembles with unquenchable desire.

The great beam of The Milky Way
Draws all men to itself by their forelocks.

The great beam of The Milky Way
Unceasingly draws all men, wherever they may be.

# RODERIC QUINN

## *The Fisher*

All night a noise of leaping fish
   Went round the bay,
And up and down the shallow sands
   Sang waters at their play.

The mangroves drooped on salty creeks,
   And through the dark,
Making a pale patch in the deep,
   Gleamed, as it swam, a shark.

In streaks and twists of sudden fire
   Among the reeds
The bream went by, and where they passed
   The bubbles shone like beads.

All night the full deep drinking-song
   Of Nature stirred,
And nought beside, save leaping fish
   And some forlorn night-bird.

No lost wind wandered down the hills
   To tell of wide
Wild waterways; on velvet moved
   The silky, sucking tide.

Deep down there sloped in shadowy mass
   A giant hill,
And midway, mirrored in the tide,
   The stars burned large and still.

The fisher, dreaming on the rocks,
   Heard Nature say
Strange, secret things that no one hears
   Upon the beaten way;

And whisperings and wonder stirred,
　　And hopes and fears,
And sadness touched his heart, and filled
　　His eyes with star-stained tears:

And so, thrilled through with joy and love
　　And sweet distress,
He stood entranced, enchained by her
　　Full-breasted loveliness.


## 'WILLIAM BAYLEBRIDGE'

### *Love Redeemed*

#### CVII

The quiet moon, immaculate of face,
Her silver pours—it floods the solemn fields;
The glimmering pastures lengthen into space;
The gums, and ghostly those, are all this yields.
This roof, that in the exotic shade retires,
Forlorn, phantasmal, seems—not built with hands
To shield the quick moods human truth requires.
Still every pulse, with its assurance, stands.
No bird, no creeping thing, makes any sound.
A breath—the bamboos tremble as in fear;
Then, in the abysmal silence, that is drowned.
Might Solitude not seat his kingdom here?
　　Yet my desire—a flame to shake his throne—
　　So senses you, none breathes who's less alone!

# ZORA CROSS

## *Love Sonnets*

### XLIX

In me there is a vast and lonely place,
Where none, not even you, have walked in sight.
A wide, still vale of solitude and light,
Where Silence echoes into ebbing space.
And there I creep at times and hide my face,
While in myself I fathom wrong and right,
And all the timeless ages of the night
That sacred silence of my soul I pace.

And when from there I come to you, love-swift,
My mouth hot-edged with kisses fresh as wine,
Often I find your longings all asleep
And unresponsive from my grasp you drift.
Ah, Love, you, too, seek solitude like mine,
And soul from soul the secret seems to keep.

### LIV

What have you more than I, who crave you so?
Have I not hands and feet and thoughts to tell?
All my sweet senses and fine dreams that swell
Rich with contentments that the star-winds blow?
Yet do I need you everywhere I go,
As if you held me in some stinging spell;
And nothing living but yourself could quell
The conscious longings that tumultuous flow.

I am myself; and yet I cannot move
Hand, foot or eye but I am drawn to you.
I want you all—dreams, kisses, thoughts and eyes.
Dearest, it seems, my very wants would prove
I am yourself, dreaming we measure two;
And lack myself, that which yourself supplies.

# LEON GELLERT

### House-Mates

Because his soup was cold, he needs must sulk
From dusk till dark, and never speak to her;
And all the time she heard his heavy bulk
Blunder about the house, making a stir
In this room and in that. She heard him mutter
His foolish breathless noises, snarling and thick.
She knew the very words he first would utter;
He always said them, and they made her sick—
Those awkward efforts at a gracious peace
And kindly patronage of high-forgiving.
She knew these quarrelling calms would never cease
As long as she could keep his body living;
And so she lay and felt the hours creep by,
Wondering lazily upon her bed,
How cold the world would be if he should die
And leave her weeping for her stupid dead.

### Before Action

We always had to do our work at night.
I wondered why we had to be so sly.
I wondered why we couldn't have our fight
Under the open sky.

I wondered why I always felt so cold.
I wondered why the orders seemed so slow,
So slow to come, so whisperingly told,
So whisperingly low.

I wondered if my packing-straps were tight,
And wondered why I wondered. Sound went wild ...
An order came ... I ran into the night
Wondering why I smiled.

## SHAW NEILSON

*The Soldier is Home*

Weary is he, and sick of the sorrow of war,
   Hating the shriek of loud music, the beat of the drum;
Is this the shadow called glory men sell themselves for?
   The pangs in his heart they have paled him and stricken him dumb!
         Oh! yes, the soldier is home!

Still does he think of one morning, the march and the sun!
   A smoke, and a scream, and the dark, and next to his mind
Comes the time of his torment, when all the red fighting was done!
   And he mourned for the good legs he left in the desert behind.
         Oh! yes, the soldier is home!

He was caught with the valour of music, the glory of kings,
   The diplomats' delicate lying, the cheers of a crowd,
And now does he hate the dull-tempest, the shrill vapourings—
   He who was proud, and no beggar now waits for his shroud!
         Oh! yes, the soldier is home!

Now shall he sit in the dark, his world shall be fearfully small—
   He shall sit with old people, and pray and praise God for fine
     weather;
Only at times shall he move for a glimpse away over the wall,
   Where the men and the women who make up the world are striving
     together!
         Oh! yes, the soldier is home!

Simple, salt tears, full often will redden his eyes;
   No one shall hear what he hears, or see what he sees;
He shall be mocked by a flower, and the flush of the skies!
   He shall behold the kissing of sweethearts—close by him, here,
     under the trees—
         Oh! yes, the soldier is home!

## Take Down the Fiddle, Karl!

Men openly call you the enemy, call you the swine,
But all that they say to me never can make you a foeman of mine.
The rain has come over the mountains, the gullies have faded away;
Take down the fiddle, Karl! the little old impudent fiddle: the work is
    all done for the day.

The ganger sits down in the bar-room with money to spend,
And many will laugh at his loudness, and many will hail him as friend.
How strong the mist settles! it sinks in the souls of us all.
Take down the fiddle, Karl! the little old impudent fiddle that hangs on
    the peg on the wall.

We are tired of the jack-hammers' clatter, the rattle of stone,
The many who boast of their travels, the many who moan;
We are tired of the spoil and the spoilers, the lifting of clay:
Take down the fiddle, Karl! the little old impudent fiddle: the work is
    all over today.

Your fiddle will show me your father, the hunt of the boar;
How dark were the forests! but fairies were seen at the door;
And in the stone chapel the neighbours bareheaded they came in to
    pray:
Take down the fiddle, Karl! the little old impudent fiddle: the work is
    all over today.

The fiddle is old but the things it is saying will ever be young;
It goes out and tries to be saying what cannot be sung.
The speech that you have, Karl, to me it means nothing at all:
Take down the fiddle, Karl! the little old impudent fiddle that hangs on
    the peg on the wall.

The fiddle can give us no more than the drinking of wine;
It brings up a world of good fellows to your eyes and mine.
The ganger, poor man, is misguided, his world is so grey:
Take down the fiddle, Karl! the little old impudent fiddle: the work is
    all done for the day.

*The Sundowner*

I know not when this tiresome man
With his shrewd, sable billy-can
And his unwashed Democracy
His boomed-up Pilgrimage began.

Sometimes he wandered far outback
On a precarious Tucker Track;
Sometimes he lacked Necessities
No gentleman would like to lack.

Tall was the grass, I understand,
When the old Squatter ruled the land.
Why were the Conquerors kind to him?
Ah, the Wax Matches in his hand!

Where bullockies with oaths intense
Made of the dragged-up trees a fence,
Gambling with scorpions he rolled
His Swag, conspicuous, immense.

In the full splendour of his power
Rarely he touched one mile an hour,
Dawdling at sunset, History says,
For the Pint Pannikin of flour.

Seldom he worked; he was, I fear,
Unreasonably slow and dear;
Little he earned, and that he spent
Deliberately drinking Beer.

Cheerful, sorefooted child of chance,
Swiftly we knew him at a glance;
Boastful and self-compassionate,
Australia's Interstate Romance.

Shall he not live in Robust Rhyme,
Soliloquies and Odes Sublime?

Strictly between ourselves, he was
A rare old Humbug all the time.

In many a Book of Bushland dim
Mopokes shall give him greeting grim;
The old swans pottering in the reeds
Shall pass the time of day to him.

On many a page our Friend shall take
Small sticks his evening fire to make;
Shedding his waistcoat, he shall mix
On its smooth back his Johnny-Cake.

'Mid the dry leaves and silvery bark
Often at nightfall will he park
Close to a homeless creek, and hear
The Bunyip paddling in the dark.


## The Crane is My Neighbour

The bird is my neighbour, a whimsical fellow and dim;
There is in the lake a nobility falling on him.

The bird is a noble, he turns to the sky for a theme,
And the ripples are thoughts coming out to the edge of a dream.

The bird is both ancient and excellent, sober and wise,
But he never could spend all the love that is sent for his eyes.

He bleats no instruction, he is not an arrogant drummer;
His gown is simplicity—blue as the smoke of the summer.

How patient he is as he puts out his wings for the blue!
His eyes are as old as the twilight, and calm as the dew.

The bird is my neighbour, he leaves not a claim for a sigh,
He moves as the guest of the sunlight—he roams in the sky.

The bird is a noble, he turns to the sky for a theme,
And the ripples are thoughts coming out to the edge of a dream.

### Flowers in the Ward

They speak not of torment,
Nor blackness nor sin.
Quietly as angels come
Do the flowers come in.

Forgetting all frailties
Of humankind,
With sweet scent they give back
Sight to the blind.

See, they come quickly
As rainbows come.
Beckoning they give back
Speech to the dumb.

From green hills they journey,
Where joys first came.
Whispering they give back
Young feet to the lame.

(Unfinished)

### In the Street

The night, the rain, who could forget?—
The grey streets glimmering in the wet:
Wreckers and ruined wreckage met:
    There was no dearth
Of all the unlovely things that yet
    Must plague the earth.

Gloom, and the street's unhallowed joys:
The sly-eyed girls, the jeering boys:
Faint-carolling amid the noise
    A woman worn—
A broken life: a heart, a voice,
    Trembling and torn.

She did not sing of hillside steep,
Of reapers stooping low to reap;
No love-lorn shepherd with his sheep
   Made moan or call:
A mother kissed her child asleep,
   And that was all.

Slowly into our hearts there crept
I know not what: it flamed! it leapt!
Was it God's love that in us slept? . . .
   I saw the mark
Of tears upon her, as she stept
   Into the dark.


### The Orange Tree

The young girl stood beside me. I
   Saw not what her young eyes could see:
—A light, she said, not of the sky
   Lives somewhere in the Orange Tree.

—Is it, I said, of east or west?
   The heartbeat of a luminous boy
Who with his faltering flute confessed
   Only the edges of his joy?

Was he, I said, borne to the blue
   In a mad escapade of Spring
Ere he could make a fond adieu
   To his love in the blossoming?

—Listen! the young girl said. There calls
   No voice, no music beats on me;
But it is almost sound: it falls
   This evening on the Orange Tree.

—Does he, I said, so fear the Spring
   Ere the white sap too far can climb?
See in the full gold evening
   All happenings of the olden time?

Is he so goaded by the green?
　　Does the compulsion of the dew
Make him unknowable but keen
　　Asking with beauty of the blue?

—Listen! the young girl said. For all
　　Your hapless talk you fail to see
There is a light, a step, a call
　　This evening on the Orange Tree.

—Is it, I said, a waste of love
　　Imperishably old in pain,
Moving as an affrighted dove
　　Under the sunlight or the rain?

Is it a fluttering heart that gave
　　Too willingly and was reviled?
Is it the stammering at a grave,
　　The last word of a little child?

—Silence! the young girl said. Oh, why,
　　Why will you talk to weary me?
Plague me no longer now, for I
　　Am listening like the Orange Tree.


*You Cannot Go Down to the Spring*

The song will deceive you, the scent will incite you to sing;
You clutch but you cannot discover: you cannot go down to the Spring.

The day will be painted with summer, the heat and the gold
Will give you no key to the blossom: the music is old.

It is at the edge of a promise, a far-away thing;
The green is the nest of all riddles: you cannot go down to the Spring.

The truth is too close to the sorrow; the song you would sing,
It cannot go into the fever: you cannot go down to the Spring.

# 'FURNLEY MAURICE'

## The Supremer Sacrifice

(In the prisons of England many conscientious objectors have gone gradually insane. Author's note.)

Close now the door; shut down the light:
  Yet can these walls my wrath provoke,
While on the altar of my Right
  My brain burns into smoke?

Close now the door, and lock the chain,
  Men have me judged, and I am glad:
I shall not cry out in my pain,
  I will go slowly mad.

Some drink the dregs of duty's cup,
  Some die, or dare their marvels through,
But I will give my reason up
  For things that I hold true.

The known is merged in the unknown,
  The serpent nestles to the dove,
And I lay all God's beauty down
  For the great God I love.

The fragrant branches wet with rain,
  The babes and bushes by the door,
The dreams that wrack my mortal brain
  Shall trouble me no more.

But I will sit, with a mild stare,
  And count the rain-drips one by one;
I shall not know the sun is there
  When next I see the sun.

## The Team

The wild-eyed team with horned and swaying heads
Goes past; the teamster waves his glad 'Good-day'.
There's load on load of timber at the sheds
And still he would not care to come my way.

While miracles of bush-flowers burst and move
About him, these he will not turn to share.
Yet, like a child eager for things to love
He's hungry to be told what things are fair.

Within him there's a spirit careless, free;
Slow to condemn he is and slow to praise,
Profuse in grumbling generosity,
And drenched at heart with the light of burning days.

And there he strides with all this on his head,
Bawling through dust his blasphemous commands;
The team's his life; he's mountain born and bred;
In death the whip lies in his sunburnt hands.


## The Agricultural Show, Flemington, Victoria

I

The lumbering tractor rolls its panting round,
The windmills fan the blue; feet crush the sand;
The pumps spurt muddy water to the sound,
The muffled thud and blare of a circus band.

II

For this is the other life I know so little of,
A life of fevered effort, of wool and tortured love!
Why didn't somebody tell me ere 'twas too late to learn
This life with its fire and vigour, by brake and anguished burn,
Gorgeous and ghastly and rare,
Flourished out there, out there?

But I just sit in a tram and pay my fare;
Me, an important man in the job I hold.
But there, there are the roots of the hills of gold
That my clawed fingers tell.
Why didn't somebody say before I was old
That there were brumbies to break and these store mobs to muster
When I was bred to the clang of a tram bell,
Answered an 'ad' and took up a shopman's duster?

III

Here is a world that stands upon sun and rain
In a humid odour of wool where the sheafing grain
Falls like pay in the palm.
I but rode out the calm
In a regular job and felt the years fall by
To a pension and senile golf; that's the whole tale;
But there's another world in the white of a bullock's eye
Strained as he horns a rail.

I, with an unshod outlaw between my knees
Dream, but awake to the old 'Fares please, fares please.'
The long low bellowing of yarded herds,
The song of sweating horsemen on the plains,
The outlaw's mating scream,
Drought and the offal-birds,
Yellowing lemons and longed-for rains—
That was the dream.

IV

Here Science like a helpful angel lifts
The drag, straightens the backs and shortens shifts;
While in the town
Men are the engine's slaves
And, drunk with Science, pull the lever down
And stagger into fragmentary graves.

The tractors pant their tract,
The combs of the reapers thrust
Their yielding paths and the stooks are stacked

While clumsy thumbs adjust
The flayer's beating thongs
And evening with tired songs
Sinks down upon the dust.
What load do the geldings carry?
What load do the bullocks drag
Worse than the loads of fear that harry
The city salesman with his bag?
Salesmen and bullocks stagger in the chains
And their red nostrils snuffle at the dust,
Lashed through life and death in the frightful lust
Of urgency that coils in men's mad brains.


V

For there are many worlds to taunt our faith;
The fabled cattle-hills, the green wool-plains;
But fair or fabulous, fact or thin as a wraith
All drift into feverish sums of losses and gains.

Man's god is what he gets his living by;
No doubt this nuzzling litter of auburn swine
Came like an old Venetian argosy
Laden with all the elegant stuffs
For shining hose and scented ruffs,
Its bellying topsails gleaming in the sun
Along the horizon line—
To some bush-whiskered father of a run.

This lustful stallion, Pegasus without wings,
Is a feather-legged temple in a desert place;
This sleek ring-nostrilled bull is King of Kings,
And doe-eyed Jerseys mumble Heaven's grace.

The cloying odour of the milking sheds,
The docking days, the branding days, perchance
The springing pasterns of the thoroughbreds
Are all mere counters of deliverance.

### VI

Many the urgent calls of the cocky's day;
What of his play?
'Within,' the Mongolian Giant is on sight—
And here's his boot to whet the appetite.
The spruiker with his flowery talk enjoins
Me and my likes to view the abortive things
That nestle under the marquee's greasy wings—
A patient, worn-out woman collects the coins.

Not tired snakes nor dancing dogs,
Nor green and human frogs,
Nor ladies bearded or fat,
Nor shark nor seven-teated cow,
Nor feat of horsemanship
Could stir a calm like that,
Put a white tremor on her lip
Or raise the cynically disillusioned brow.
Worn out no doubt is she
With the joy of looking, free,
Too long at each inane monstrosity
Till there's no more wonder
On earth or under
The sea.
But wayback Dan closes a week's carouse
With one long, sixpenny look at a three-tailed mouse.

### VII

I've heard the waggon-wheels grinding by ruts and stumps
Scouring the black night for a possible camp;
I've watched the breeching flop on the horses' rumps
In the green light of a wavering bottle-lamp.
And I have come at last on a sweet home and a bed
And woke to see through the broken blind a munching cow at the bail,
To hear, while the magpies yodelled in the slow dawn's searching
    spread,
The sharp spurt of the milk into the pail.

### VIII

The things of the body pass,
And these are of the day;
The things that nourish
The body flourish
In weather and sun
But soon, like flowers, they're done
And leave no husk.
But the mind's things pass
Not readily away;
The mind goes like a camel in the dusk
Nibbling the grass
Between the stones of the tombs
Or gorging among the sheaves
Of blotted leaves
That fall from the housed looms.
So while the æons run
Hearts leap and brains contrive;
Honey is of the sun
But there's no sun in the hive.

### IX

The morning pastures of the spirit spread
Their dewy carpets for anointed feet,
But the lashed herd and the shearing shed,
These are man's clothes and meat.
For there are many worlds to plague our hopes,
Crumbling owl-haunted belfries of 'perhaps,'
And lantern-lighted alleys whence the stranger gropes
His way to the Andean slopes,
And the old stone stairs of faith scooped out by a myriad feet,
Green at the base, where timeless water laps.
Though there are many worlds, none is complete.

### X

For all the yellowing melons of marvellous size,
And dogs that pen their sheep from the drover's eyes,
And the hew and thew
Of the beanstalk axemen climbing to the blue,

We all turn homeward dusty and overcast
By a sense of cattle-hills without a name;
Carrying bags of samples of the vast
Uncomprehended regions whence they came.
Drenched with the colour of unexperienced days
We go our different ways;
Stallions loose on the plains; apples of Hesperides;
Quiet lakes and milking sheds; 'Fares please, fares please.'


*On a Grey-haired Old Lady Knitting at an Orchestral Concert in the Melbourne Town Hall. Prices, Two and One Plus Tax*

*Cast on 120 stitches,*
*Rep. to the end of the row;*
*Loop the scream of the flying witches*
*And the bassoon moaning low.*

Surely this will be wondrous raiment
With mellow horn-tones woven in,
The clarinet's woodnotes and the clamant
Trombone courting the violin.
Little black dots for the drums, dear lady,
A blue gash for the viola, please;
There's a faun in an afternoon, cool and shady,
And sun on morning seas.
And there's the thin triangle sound—
Can you snare, do you think,
The bell-bird clink
Like fairy jewellers that tap
On silver anvils in the trees?
You will trap, mayhap,
With ease
The procession of chords profound
Purple with passion that sweep
Across the bass viols murmuring deep;
Can you capture those, do you think?
And weave them into your garment's shape,
O feverish finger loom!

So tone and measure shall never escape
The mesh of their woolly doom?

*    *    *

All this comes from the magic wand
Beckoning harmony from beyond,
Of the oil-haired, hollow-backed baton-waver
Who swoops and flogs like a galley-slaver;
So weave them, lady, weave them in,
Horror and sunshine, laughter and sin.
Not words, not words, but moods and measures
Out from the vast's unnameable treasures.
Till through your quiet thread there runs
The unspeakable heat of the suns,
And your deft loopings hold
Space's unspeakable cold,
Till the norms of your rhythms exceed
A constellation's flashing speed.

> *K. 1 purl to the last stitch, K.*
> *Rep. to the end 2 tog. and spurn*
> *The passages where mad brasses bray*
> *And turn, lady, turn.*

A quiet of babies in their beds
Breaks to the drums and the cymbals flashing gold;
An angry gale has torn the clouds to shreds,
A naked moon is shivering in the cold,
O knit and weave your warp and woof
Under the candelabraed roof
That, melting in music, opens wide
On the uncounted stars outside.

Flutter on, fingers, fetch and fend;
How do you know you are venturing where
The phantoms of old desires contend
With spectres of young despair?
How will you know what spells are caught
In the nooses of endless thread?
How will you govern this wild thing fraught
With the abracadabra of dread?

Is it garb for sages, garb for youth?
How much terror, how much truth?
Here all the howling fates are loosed;
Know you what things your chains have noosed?
Here all Christ's miracles are freed
And groping in a hopeless need,
Have a care, lady, oh, have care—
How can you will what you will not snare?

*K. 1 purl to your heart's content,*
*Rep. to the end 2 tog. and spurn*
*The baton waving its last lament*
*And turn, lady, turn.*


## Upon a Row of Old Boots and Shoes in a Pawnbroker's Window

Ah! no!
You are not a soldierly upright row!
In wearisome disillusionment
Brooding on newness spent.
Your uppers might keep one's instep free from rain,
And should these leak, the overflow could drain,
I maintain,
Through the holes
In the soles.
But this isn't poetry, is it? No!
And yet there's an ode here somewhere; how should it go?
Poverty, plenty; joy and woe;
How should it go?

The gruesome samples here displayed
Make me afraid.
Whose the bluchers and whose
The golden couple next to the two outsizes?
But I'm not weaving sentimental stories
About these boots and their departed glories.
Up to blue heaven my entreaty rises
For food, for shelter, and not to pawn my shoes.

Abashed, not gaily
My puzzled vision scans
The bulging outlines of my trusty tans
Which so worthily plod
These pavements daily.
The toecaps take my stony stare
As I mutter, 'There ...
There but for the grace of God ...'
I think my shoe-tongues understood;
They said, 'Touch wood, touch wood.'
'Far, far from here,' says my loved Matthew A.,
'The Adriatic breaks in a warm bay.'

Yet the eternal shuffle of well-booted feet
Disturbs my wanton musing in the street.
Brushing shoulders with sweet and twenty,
Here's poverty, there's plenty.

A chemist's sign is rolling eternally over;
'I wonder,' a flapper squeals, 'what's on to-night.'
Limbs loaded like fat bees from plundered clover,
The women emerge through doors of living light
From the emporiums where joy is sold
For bogus promises to pay in gold.

The spruiker spruiks; your fortune told; three courses; bob the lot.
(A rotten game, the spruiker's, but it's a job he's got.)
The flappers flap in cocktail juice; the saucepan's cold on the hob;
'Lone Pine was hell!' the diggers yell; 'but, Christ! it was a *job*!'
The high signs twinkle, and squat trams trot blithely up and down;
The bootpawner plays hidies in the alleys of the town.

Sometimes he stands and stares
At the beautiful, useless wares
In the windows' taunting displays,
At the signs that flicker and leer and variously rehearse
Methods and schemes and plots,
Registers, carriers, slots;
Loud ways and low ways
To drain the pedestrian's purse.

Gorgeous effects of electric illumination
That might have been a poet's inspiration
Grown common by incessant imitation.
Cascading streams of colour fall
From the shoulders of the divinely tall
Alluring but somewhat unresponsive models that
Proclaim a frock, a corset, some particular hat.

But Hunger has its vision
Of gorging in realms Elysian.
One day, as a bootpawner passed, a model turned;
He paused and gazed till the eyes of the model grew dim,
The lids dropped slowly and he knew she burned
With a terrible love for him.
He resolved to return at dusk and in tones expressive
Demand more liberal terms, as the price was excessive;
But when he got back in the gloaming and found her cut off at the
        waist
He retreated in haste
To the dark
And slept alone in the park.

One night, from a culvert arch,
When the moon was a wind-blown husk,
I heard the mumbling march
Of the bootpawners spoil the dusk.
Their hollow entrails made
A noise like drums in the shade.
It seemed they walked on grass,
So soft the footfalls fell.
The cushioned heels fell soft
As I listened and watched them pass.

I caught a rhythm, a word,
As they sang and spat and coughed.
How shall I ever tell
The terrible things I heard?
Their lips were white and blue
(Could any words mean what their eyes mean?);

The words were bitter, mournful or true—
Most, nearly obscene.

The bitumen peels
Our naked heels;
No work, no work;
No wages, no wages;
No foil to burk
The southerly's rages;
No crust to thrust
Down ravenous gullets,
Though windows are crammed
With succulent pullets.

Be damned, be damned,
You delicatessen!
We've burned and learned
Our terrible lesson.
Guts ache, hearts break,
But never the glass—
We yearn, we burn;
We pass, we pass.

'Far, far from here,' let Matthew Arnold say,
'The Adriatic breaks in a warm bay.'
But not so far from here,
O Matthew dear,
The knots of slimy eels writhe under the rustic bridge,
The sunbeams burrow among the quivering elms,
The tufts of cloud throw shade on the level lawns,
Where a world is green and clean.
The pods fall ceaselessly the whole night through;
The roaring bees
Worry and tear at the throats of the swaying poppies;
The wind's an invisible cloud of scented wool,
Stroking us, patting us, lifting the leaves to the sun;
And all the way from Caulfield station to town
The encroaching pigface pours
Its molten magenta down the sides of the cuttings.

The towers of Melbourne have been wrought
From rock and trouble and grumbling toil,
Or out of the sliding slush the churning concrete-mixer
Spews into a hideous iron-befangled mould.
But watch those towers from the St Kilda Road;
Their windows ablaze in the sunset,
The floating towers with their bases muffled in trees
And the trees cooling their feet in the water,
And behind, long splashes of cloud.

Gaze from the footings up, gaze from the summit down;
Over the river the trees, and over the trees
A wonder of drifting towers
Awash in the evening's dusky gold
Backed by an opal sky whose clouds
Are gashed with enormous wounds of crimson light.

All so complete, so quiet; all so true.
Why, then, debase this vision with old rue?
Are our devisers less, then, than the dreamers who begot
Camelot? O Camelot!
Although those towers are gold and green,
Or spread with a thousand blended hues,
It's little all that would mean
To the fellows who pawned these shoes.

Some pair among the drab and crooked row
May once have trod the lawns of the riverside
Or danced at a Lord Mayor's show.
But the last remnant of hope, happiness, pride
Seems to have gone; they've grown so desolate
Since they crunched gravel by some moonlit gate.
They meet my look with a groggy, shamefaced leer,
And muse on mountains that have known their stride,
Or rocky steeps defied;
They have gone brushing and rustling through
The warm grass and the dew,
Been yellowed with pollen and petals of maimed flowers,
In paddocks of shadows and showers,
Far, far from here.

# LESBIA HARFORD

## Experience

I must be dreaming through the days
And see the world with childish eyes
If I'd go singing all my life,
And my songs be wise.

And in the kitchen or the house
Must wonder at the sights I see.
And I must hear the throb and hum
That moves to song in factory.

So much in life remains unsung,
And so much more than love is sweet;
I'd like a song of kitchenmaids
With steady fingers and swift feet.

And I could sing about the rest
That breaks upon a woman's day
When dinner's over and she lies
Upon her bed to dream and pray

Until the children come from school
And all her evening work begins;
There's more in life than tragic love
And all the storied, splendid sins.

## Beauty and Terror

Beauty does not walk through lovely days,
Beauty walks with horror in her hair;
Down long centuries of pleasant ways
Men have found the terrible most fair.

Youth is lovelier in death than life,
Beauty mightier in pain than joy,
Doubly splendid burn the fires of strife
Brighter than the brightness they destroy.

# HUGH McCRAE

## *Song of the Rain*

Night,
And the yellow pleasure of candle-light . . .
Old brown books and the kind fine face of the clock
Fogged in the veils of the fire—its cuddling tock.

The cat,
Greening her eyes on the flame-litten mat;
Wickedly wakeful she yawns at the rain
Bending the roses over the pane,
And a bird in my heart begins to sing
Over and over the same sweet thing—

*Safe in the house with my boyhood's love,*
*And our children asleep in the attic above.*


## *Winds*

The wind takes colour from the trees;
   Through trees the wind grows green;
And, like a blue wave from the seas,
   The ocean wind is seen.

The red road paints the road-wind red,
   And down the ripe gold corn
The chuckling wind with golden head
   Trots merrily at morn.

The black lake gives the black wind birth,
   The brown breeze blows along
The ploughed brown cocked-up smoking earth
   To the tune of a hunting song.

The white wind moves in the white moon's wake,
   With straight white streaming hair,
And ever she wails in words that ache
   The burthen of her despair.

*O gusty soul that lives within,*
  *Why dost thou flush and fade,*
*Wind-like, to flame and icicle—*
  *Red Rahab and white Maid!*

# KENNETH SLESSOR

## Country Towns

Country towns, with your willows and squares,
And farmers bouncing on barrel mares
To public-houses of yellow wood
With '1860' over their doors,
And that mysterious race of Hogans
Which always keeps General Stores . . .

At the School of Arts, a broadsheet lies
Sprayed with the sarcasm of flies:
'The Great Golightly Family
Of Entertainers Here To-night'—
Dated a year and a half ago,
But left there, less from carelessness
Than from a wish to seem polite.

Verandas baked with musky sleep,
Mulberry faces dozing deep,
And dogs that lick the sunlight up
Like paste of gold—or, roused in vain
By far, mysterious buggy-wheels,
Lower their ears, and drowse again . . .

Country towns with your schooner bees,
And locusts burnt in the pepper-trees,
Drown me with syrups, arch your boughs,
Find me a bench, and let me snore,
Till, charged with ale and unconcern,
I'll think it's noon at half-past four!

### A Bushranger

Jackey Jackey gallops on a horse like a swallow
Where the carbines bark and the blackboys hollo.
When the traps give chase (may the Devil take his power!)
He can ride ten miles in a quarter of an hour.

Take a horse and follow, and you'll hurt no feelings;
He can fly down waterfalls and jump through ceilings,
He can shoot off hats, for to have a bit of fun,
With a bulldog bigger than a buffalo-gun.

Honeyed and profound is his conversation
When he bails up Mails on Long Tom Station,
In a flyaway coat with a black cravat,
A snow-white collar and a cabbage-tree hat.

Flowers in his button-hole and pearls in his pocket,
He comes like a ghost and he goes like rocket
With a lightfoot heel on a blood-mare's flank
And a bagful of notes from the Joint Stock Bank.

Many pretty ladies he could witch out of marriage,
Though he prig but a kiss in a bigwig's carriage;
For the cock of an eye or the lift of his reins,
They would run barefoot through Patrick's Plains.

### North Country

North Country, filled with gesturing wood,
With trees that fence, like archers' volleys,
The flanks of hidden valleys
Where nothing's left to hide

But verticals and perpendiculars,
Like rain gone wooden, fixed in falling,
Or fingers blindly feeling
For what nobody cares;

Or trunks of pewter, bangled by greedy death,
Stuck with black staghorns, quietly sucking,
And trees whose boughs go seeking,
And trees like broken teeth

With smoky antlers broken in the sky;
Or trunks that lie grotesquely rigid,
Like bodies blank and wretched
After a fool's battue,

As if they've secret ways of dying here
And secret places for their anguish
When boughs at last relinquish
Their clench of blowing air—

But this gaunt country, filled with mills and saws,
With butter-works and railway-stations
And public institutions,
And scornful rumps of cows,

North Country, filled with gesturing wood—
Timber's the end it gives to branches,
Cut off in cubic inches,
Dripping red with blood.


*South Country*

After the whey-faced anonymity
Of river-gums and scribbly-gums and bush,
After the rubbing and the hit of brush,
You come to the South Country

As if the argument of trees were done,
The doubts and quarrelling, the plots and pains,
All ended by these clear and gliding planes
Like an abrupt solution.

And over the flat earth of empty farms
The monstrous continent of air floats back
Coloured with rotting sunlight and the black,
Bruised flesh of thunderstorms:

Air arched, enormous, pounding the bony ridge,
Ditches and hutches, with a drench of light,
So huge, from such infinities of height,
You walk on the sky's beach

While even the dwindled hills are small and bare,
As if, rebellious, buried, pitiful,
Something below pushed up a knob of skull,
Feeling its way to air.

### William Street

The red globes of light, the liquor-green,
The pulsing arrows and the running fire
Spilt on the stones, go deeper than a stream;
You find this ugly, I find it lovely.

Ghosts' trousers, like the dangle of hung men,
In pawnshop-windows, bumping knee by knee,
But none inside to suffer or condemn;
You find this ugly, I find it lovely.

Smells rich and rasping, smoke and fat and fish
And puffs of paraffin that crimp the nose,
Or grease that blesses onions with a hiss;
You find it ugly, I find it lovely.

The dips and molls, with flip and shiny gaze
(Death at their elbows, hunger at their heels)
Ranging the pavements of their pasturage;
You find it ugly, I find it lovely.

## from *Out of Time*

Leaning against the golden undertow,
Backward, I saw the birds begin to climb
With bodies hailstone-clear, and shadows flow,
Fixed in a sweet meniscus, out of Time,

Out of the torrent, like the fainter land
Lensed in a bubble's ghostly camera,
The lighted beach, the sharp and china sand,
Glitters and waters and peninsula—

The moment's world, it was; and I was part,
Fleshless and ageless, changeless and made free.
'Fool, would you leave this country?' cried my heart,
But I was taken by the suck of sea.

The gulls go down, the body dies and rots,
And Time flows past them like a hundred yachts.

## *Five Bells*

*Time that is moved by little fidget wheels*
*Is not my Time, the flood that does not flow.*
*Between the double and the single bell*
*Of a ship's hour, between a round of bells*
*From the dark warship riding there below,*
*I have lived many lives, and this one life*
*Of Joe, long dead, who lives between five bells.*

Deep and dissolving verticals of light
Ferry the falls of moonshine down. Five bells
Coldly rung out in a machine's voice. Night and water
Pour to one rip of darkness, the Harbour floats
In air, the Cross hangs upside-down in water.

Why do I think of you, dead man, why thieve
These profitless lodgings from the flukes of thought

Anchored in Time? You have gone from earth,
Gone even from the meaning of a name;
Yet something's there, yet something forms its lips
And hits and cries against the ports of space,
Beating their sides to make its fury heard.

Are you shouting at me, dead man, squeezing your face
In agonies of speech on speechless panes?
Cry louder, beat the windows, bawl your name!

But I hear nothing, nothing . . . only bells,
Five bells, the bumpkin calculus of Time.
Your echoes die, your voice is dowsed by Life,
There's not a mouth can fly the pygmy strait—
Nothing except the memory of some bones
Long shoved away, and sucked away, in mud;
And unimportant things you might have done,
Or once I thought you did; but you forgot,
And all have now forgotten—looks and words
And slops of beer; your coat with buttons off,
Your gaunt chin and pricked eye, and raging tales
Of Irish kings and English perfidy,
And dirtier perfidy of publicans
Groaning to God from Darlinghurst.

*Five bells.*

Then I saw the road, I heard the thunder
Tumble, and felt the talons of the rain
The night we came to Moorebank in slab-dark,
So dark you bore no body, had no face,
But a sheer voice that rattled out of air
(As now you'd cry if I could break the glass),
A voice that spoke beside me in the bush,
Loud for a breath or bitten off by wind,
Of Milton, melons, and the Rights of Man,
And blowing flutes, and how Tahitian girls
Are brown and angry-tongued, and Sydney girls
Are white and angry-tongued, or so you'd found.

But all I heard was words that didn't join
So Milton became melons, melons girls,
And fifty mouths, it seemed, were out that night,
And in each tree an Ear was bending down,
Or something had just run, gone behind grass,
When, blank and bone-white, like a maniac's thought,
The naphtha-flash of lightning slit the sky,
Knifing the dark with deathly photographs.
There's not so many with so poor a purse
Or fierce a need, must fare by night like that,
Five miles in darkness on a country track,
But when you do, that's what you think.

*Five bells.*


In Melbourne, your appetite had gone,
Your angers too; they had been leeched away
By the soft archery of summer rains
And the sponge-paws of wetness, the slow damp
That stuck the leaves of living, snailed the mind,
And showed your bones, that had been sharp with rage,
The sodden ecstasies of rectitude.
I thought of what you'd written in faint ink,
Your journal with the sawn-off lock, that stayed behind
With other things you left, all without use,
All without meaning now, except a sign
That someone had been living who now was dead:
'At Labassa. Room 6 × 8
On top of the tower; because of this, very dark
And cold in winter. Everything has been stowed
Into this room—500 books all shapes
And colours, dealt across the floor
And over sills and on the laps of chairs;
Guns, photoes of many differant things
And differant curioes that I obtained ...'


In Sydney, by the spent aquarium-flare
Of penny gaslight on pink wallpaper,
We argued about blowing up the world,

But you were living backward, so each night
You crept a moment closer to the breast,
And they were living, all of them, those frames
And shapes of flesh that had perplexed your youth,
And most your father, the old man gone blind,
With fingers always round a fiddle's neck,
That graveyard mason whose fair monuments
And tablets cut with dreams of piety
Rest on the bosoms of a thousand men
Staked bone by bone, in quiet astonishment
At cargoes they had never thought to bear,
These funeral-cakes of sweet and sculptured stone.

Where have you gone? The tide is over you,
The turn of midnight water's over you,
As Time is over you, and mystery,
And memory, the flood that does not flow.
You have no suburb, like those easier dead
In private berths of dissolution laid—
The tide goes over, the waves ride over you
And let their shadows down like shining hair,
But they are Water; and the sea-pinks bend
Like lilies in your teeth, but they are Weed;
And you are only part of an Idea.
I felt the wet push its black thumb-balls in,
The night you died, I felt your eardrums crack,
And the short agony, the longer dream,
The Nothing that was neither long nor short;
But I was bound, and could not go that way,
But I was blind, and could not feel your hand.
If I could find an answer, could only find
Your meaning, or could say why you were here
Who now are gone, what purpose gave you breath
Or seized it back, might I not hear your voice?

I looked out of my window in the dark
At waves with diamond quills and combs of light
That arched their mackerel-backs and smacked the sand
In the moon's drench, that straight enormous glaze,

And ships far off asleep, and Harbour-buoys
Tossing their fireballs wearily each to each,
And tried to hear your voice, but all I heard
Was a boat's whistle, and the scraping squeal
Of seabirds' voices far away, and bells,
Five bells. Five bells coldly ringing out.

*Five bells.*

## Polarities

Sometimes she is like sherry, like the sun through a vessel of glass,
Like light through an oriel window in a room of yellow wood;
Sometimes she is the colour of lions, of sand in the fire of noon,
Sometimes as bruised with shadows as the afternoon.

Sometimes she moves like rivers, sometimes like trees;
Or tranced and fixed like South Pole silences;
Sometimes she is beauty, sometimes fury, sometimes neither,
Sometimes nothing, drained of meaning, null as water.

Sometimes, when she makes pea-soup or plays me Schumann,
I love her one way; sometimes I love her another
More disturbing way when she opens her mouth in the dark;
Sometimes I like her with camellias, sometimes with a parsley-stalk,
Sometimes I like her swimming in a mirror on the wall;
Sometimes I don't like her at all.

## Beach Burial

Softly and humbly to the Gulf of Arabs
The convoys of dead sailors come;
At night they sway and wander in the waters far under,
But morning rolls them in the foam.

Between the sob and clubbing of the gunfire
Someone, it seems, has time for this,
To pluck them from the shallows and bury them in burrows
And tread the sand upon their nakedness;

And each cross, the driven stake of tidewood,
Bears the last signature of men,
Written with such perplexity, with such bewildered pity,
The words choke as they begin—

'Unknown seaman'—the ghostly pencil
Wavers and fades, the purple drips,
The breath of the wet season has washed their inscriptions
As blue as drowned men's lips,

Dead seamen, gone in search of the same landfall,
Whether as enemies they fought,
Or fought with us, or neither; the sand joins them together,
Enlisted on the other front.

*El Alamein.*


# ROBERT D. FITZGERALD

## Edge

Knife's edge, moon's edge, water's edge,
graze the throat of the formed shape
that sense fills where shape vanishes:
air at the ground limit of steel,
the thin disc in the moon's curve,
land gliding out of no land.

The new image, the freed thought,
are carved from that inert bulk
where the known ends and the unknown
is cut down before it—at the mind's edge,
the knife-edge at the throat of darkness.

## The Face of the Waters

Once again the scurry of feet—those myriads
crossing the black granite; and again
laughter cruelly in pursuit; and then
the twang like a harpstring or the spring of a trap,
and the swerve on the polished surface: the soft little pads
sidling and skidding and avoiding; but soon caught up
in the hand of laughter and put back . . .

There is no release from the rack
of darkness for the unformed shape,
the unexisting thought
stretched half-and-half
in the shadow of beginning and that denser black
under the imminence of huge pylons—
the deeper nought;
but neither is there anything to escape,
or to laugh,
or to twang that string which is not a string but silence
plucked at the heart of silence.

Nor can there be a floor to the bottomless;
except in so far as conjecture must arrive,
lungs cracking, at the depth of its dive;
where downward further is further distress
with no change in it; as if a mile and an inch
are equally squeezed into a pinch,
and retreating limits of cold mind
frozen, smoothed, defined.

Out of the tension of silence (the twanged string);
from the agony of not being (that terrible laughter
tortured by darkness); out of it all
once again the tentative migration; once again
a universe on the edge of being born:
feet running fearfully out of nothing
at the core of nothing:

colour, light, life, fearfully
becoming eyes and understanding: sound becoming ears . . .

For eternity is not space reaching
on without end to it; not time without end to it,
nor infinity working round in a circle;
but a placeless dot enclosing nothing,
the pre-time pinpoint of impossible beginning,
enclosed by nothing, not even by emptiness—
impossible: so wholly at odds with possibilities
that, always emergent and wrestling and interlinking
they shatter it and return to it, are all of it and part of it.
It is your hand stretched out to touch your neighbour's,
and feet running through the dark, directionless like darkness.

Worlds that were spun adrift re-enter
that intolerable centre;
indeed the widest-looping comet
never departed from it;
it alone exists.
And though, opposing it, there persists
the enormous structure of forces, laws,
as background for other coming and going,
that's but a pattern, a phase, no pause,
of ever-being-erected, ever-growing
ideas unphysically alternative
to nothing, which is the quick. You may say hills live,
or life's the imperfect aspect of a flowing
that sorts itself as hills; much as thoughts wind
selectively through mind.

The egg-shell collapses
in the fist of the eternal instant;
all is what it was before.
Yet is that eternal instant
the pinpoint bursting into reality,
the possibilities and perhapses,
the feet scurrying on the floor.

It is the suspense also
with which the outward thrust
holds the inward surrender—
the stresses in the shell before it buckles under:
the struggle to magpie-morning and all life's clamour and lust;
the part breaking through the whole;
light and the clear day and so simple a goal.

## 1918–1941

Not those patient men who knocked and were unheeded
where ignorance impeded like a flat panel swung
before the tower-stair to the dark mind of the young:
another moved beside them on the dais, at the desk—
War in a square cap, gowned and grotesque.

This was the master whose tongue did the talking;
then time became a chalking-off of dates upon the wall—
for no lad chose a calling who heard instead a call,
and just beyond a boy's years (so the lesson ran)
the one work waited fitting for a man.

None grew so tiptoe as to see the plain road, yonder,
at the hour's edge dip under to the leagues of calm before.
It was odd to break step and shamble from the door,
to plough the broad peace, and be older, and learn pride
from the day's task met and the morrow still defied.

Distant the guns are, and no wind veering
has brought them into hearing, nor yet in these lands
do they bawl between hills as between a pair of hands;
but there's what we were bred to . . . and strange it is then
to be lifting our sons up to watch the marching men.

Tattered the bewilderment I pull across my shoulders,
and shamed before beholders in this torn shirt,
like a slave to my shoes I wander unalert,
with eyes but no thought in them to mark the way I tread
and a thought without eyes that runs lost in my head.

from *Essay on Memory*

Rain in my ears: impatiently there raps
at a sealed door the fury of chill drops—
knuckles bared of the flesh come rattling on
vaults that conceal a sorrier skeleton
huddled, unhearing, in a dark so deep
that this clear summons ruffles not calm sleep.

It is the hand of Memory come scratching
on the tomb of carrion buried from mankind—
forgotten by all except this body-snatching
walker of old night and times dropped from mind,
who knows where the slain rots and seeks it yet;
for Memory does not fail though men forget,
but pokes a ghost-finger into all our pies
and jabs out the dead meat, a grim Jack Horner,
mocking the mild dream, half guess, half lies,
of History babbling from his chimney-corner.

Memory is not that picture tacked on thought
among the show-girls and prize-ribbon rams,
wherein is last week's yesterday to be sought,
lens-twisted and fading, and yet somehow caught
in the known gesture, almost at speaking terms;
nor is it the sky-old story which in stone
within baked saurian footmarks prints its own,
as if the mud might soften and recollect
almost our lean beginnings and project
against the background of these days some far
horrible firmament, or show a star
choking with cloud whereunder, oozed from slime,
slow forms are dragging—half-way back through time;
nor is it composite mind whose cells are men
and whose dour genius grafts great stone on stone
by torch-flare lit on torch-flare—till it seems
that the tall topwork of new cornice gleams
in the glow of ancient lore, and sits firm-stayed
in masonry that hands long cold once laid.

Something of all this ... but Memory peers
from the brown mottled ruin, shrieks and gibbers
among the fallen fragments of lost years,
lurks by the lichened archway, frights the neighbours
when a wind shrills about that older house
on which these days have quarried and made levies.
For Memory is the wind's voice in the crevice,
a wild song through those stones and in the boughs
of trees fast-dug in flint-chips of the novice;
it is the count of hooves for ever dinned
in the ears of the world by the hard-ridden wind;
and more than these and more than headlong haste
of events galloping through widening waste
into the cumulative past—to keep
galloping on with never pause nor sleep—
it is the past itself, the dead time's will
poisoning today's pulse and potent still;
it is the ruled heart's heritage, mortmain;
darkness it is and talons of the rain.
. . .

Argument is the blade-bright window-pane
which shears off cleanly the slant sheaf of rain,
and in the room heart's dream and life's desire
are radiance and curled, unfolding fire.
Here thought may ponder in peace or work at will
or take down book from shelf and read his fill;
but though among men's assets he bides long
always his ears are tuned on that same song
of rain outside; for that's the force he knew
which drenched his hands that battled it, breaking through,
while yet he was homeless in the world, unsafe,
wandering in mindless marshes the wind's waif,
and had not learned to build up word; and fix
a house for himself in speech's bonded bricks.
Hearing it he remembers: though large walls
shelter him now, hold out the rain, rain falls.

And ever the untaught earth, comrade of yore,
out there under the dark and dripping leaves,

although its slave-bent back, laid bare, receives
whip-stripes of rain, possesses yet that more,
wisdom and fullness, which thought has not known,
never can reach. For earth, stooped labourer,
treading the furrow of seasons, early astir
and late abed from heavy fields, wild sown,
has wind and sun for sure realities,
endures this lash, too, as a thing plain-shown,
simple as flooded rivers, tumbling seas,
gaunt hills across the sky . . . These are earth's own;
but thought has only sounds and shadows thrown
by hollow powers, obscure immensities,
upon the screen called living. And the good, solid
meat that earth munches, truth, is proved invalid;
thought is unfed—and even thought has grown
a trifle impatient of philosophies . . .
. . .
If, as may seem, fair future spreads unfurrowed
beneath new morning and there writhes and wheels,
a sun-blind sea all silverly tomorrowed,
ruffled by promise and uncut by keels,
and, Dampiers of this dawn, we pull the prow
off-wind and pay out sheet, none tells us now
what bides our choice or if we drown or starve;
and even if the luck holds and we carve
new coasts on gaping latitudes, who traces
the scarless wake of an adventurer, lost,
sows wheat, finds gold, where we found desert places,
gashes with screws wide lanes where, lone, we crossed?

This hour, a gulp in the long throat of the past,
swallows what once was future, but soon spent;
this hour is a touch of hands, an accident
of instants meeting in unechoing vast:
it is a rail that bursts before the flourish
of black manes and time's haste; it fails our need—
now must decision be brief, must jump or perish
under the feet and fury of stampede.
And to this difficult present will succeed

what present, to be lost as this is lost?
for any decision may fall undermost,
and no hand counts the grandsons of its deed.
Foresight is but a bargain that we make,
which, even should life keep it, death will break.
. . .
Who sees this time all edged about with wars
like tiny points of fire along the rim,
stretching to suns then sinking back to stars,
must hold heart-close his love to speak for him
and be his challenge to those rigorous teeth
that devour all, the answer of his faith—
which is towards the green-burst of new spring,
leaf-revelry and flower-strewn roistering,
life-joy and the dear miracle of increase.
Yet who stares forward through the shimmer of peace,
noon-heavy over valleys soaked in health,
and, baulked of sight beyond this burgeoning wealth,
finds only tremor-tapestry, hung haze,
will watch, adread, for the first beaconing blaze.
Or if the only smokes that, serpentine,
encoil the land be stubble-fires that twine
ribbons of incense round a harvest-feast,
still must one fear be troublous, one at least—
a vision of changed scene wherein smokes, black,
crawl venomous from a Gorgon chimney-stack,
with, deep below, all foreign to our ken,
strange engines and strange customs and strange men!
. . .
Whatever the task, it lies in front: we must
build upward though we guess not to what skies,
and though the eruptive Babels that we thrust
vital in air will fritter back to dust;
else we betray the lamp behind our eyes,
the quickening in our veins, both held in trust
since long before the scumming of the germ
upon first seas. We will serve out our term:
not yet the impetus flags whose course began
when at the blank mouth of our stinking lair

we saw night's infinite curtain shake with grey,
and so went forth determined to be Man,
standing at last erect, and watched new day
wrap back the dark and strip the valley bare.


## Bog and Candle

### I

At the end of life paralysis or those creeping teeth,
the crab at lung or liver or the rat in the brain,
and flesh become limp rag, and sense tap of a cane—
if you would pray, brother, pray for a clean death.

For when the work you chip from age-hard earth must pause,
faced with the dark, unfinished, where day gave love and jest,
day and that earth in you shall pit you to their test
of struggle in old bog against the tug of claws.

### II

What need had such a one for light at the night's rim?
Yet in the air of evening till the medley of sound—
children and birds and traffic—settled in the profound
meditation of earth, it was the blind man's whim

to set at his wide window the warm gift of flame
and put a match to wick for sight not like his own—
for his blank eyes could pierce that darkness all have known,
the thought: 'What use the light, or to play out the game?'

Yet could disperse also the fog of that queer code
which exalts pain as evidence of some aim or end
finer than strength it tortures, so sees pain as friend—
good in itself and guiding to great ultimate good.

Then he would touch the walls of the cold place where he sat
but know the world as wider, since here, beside his hand,
this flame could reach out, out, did touch but understand . . .
Life in a man's body perhaps rayed out like that.

So it is body's business and its inborn doom
past will, past hope, past reason and all courage of heart,
still to resist among the roof-beams ripped apart
the putting-out of the candle in the blind man's room.

### Favour

I'll not touch wood nor, fingers crossed,
creep furtively for fear all's lost.
Luck's liquor pounding through the brain
I'll stand on kerbs and bellow
great news at my indifferent kin—
her favour towards this fellow.

Would you treat gently with that rowdy?
Flaunt or you flout her: Luck's no lady.
Yours in the lavish minute while
you take her gifts two-handed,
she'll break your heart for you, and smile,
so soon as she's so minded.

And pick your pocket when she goes . . .
But snap time's tail up: that hour's woes
will not snake round at now, bite back
where a game grip jerks a summons—
Luck loves him longest who can crack
this kind of lash on omens.

## FREDERICK T. MACARTNEY

### No Less Than Prisoners

Dropped petals of a broken lotus-moon
Lay curled and strewn
Upon the sea.

A night-bird whimpered faintly in its tree;
And as we went with lantern swinging
And carried low,
Its light kept fiercely flinging
Our shadows on the jungle like a foe.
The steep path downward twined;
We passed: it seemed to close behind.

Almost in reach,
The tide slept on the bosom of the beach.
We swam, two shapes in one phosphoric trail,
Diffused as when two tellers blur a tale.
Then we stood still, as mangroves do
Awash with quiet currents rippling through.
Smooth water like the blessing of a priest
Flowed tepidly across our clasping hands—
Salt water (such are tears!), the drained and ceased
Adorning sorrow of deserted sands.

That nuptial intonation of the waves
Shall hold us bound no less than prisoners or
Than those whom marriage bitterly enchains,
Though we take separate pathways evermore.

### Early Summer Sea-Tryst

White hummocks here are rounded to a thigh
And knee of naked sand: with stretching limbs
The season wakens full of drowsy whims,
Propped on elbow, a knuckle at each eye.
From the far haze of merging sea and sky
A slow swell comes—a storm asleep—and skims
The sunny shallows to the rippled rims,
There folded like a garment and put by.

I will forswear my spouse, the lawful earth,
Haggling a-kimbo at her harbour gate,
With cranes for arms, and aproned by a quay.

Her household constancy has nothing worth
This exultation when I consummate
The passion of my body for the sea.


## BALGU SONG

*Balgu Song*[1]

She doesn't say a word, concentrating on one thing only.
She pulls out a length of cotton and stitches the dress together.

In the afternoon it's finished, and my word,
what a nice smell the new cloth has.


## ELIZABETH RIDDELL

*Suburban Song*

Now all the dogs with folded paws
Stare at the lowering sky.
This is the hour when women hear
Their lives go ticking by.

The baker's horse with rattling hooves
Upon the windy hill
Mocks the thunder in the heart
Of women sitting still.

The poppies in the garden turn
Their faces to the sand
And tears upon the sewing fall
And on the stranger's hand.

[1] Translated from the Balgu by Clancy McKenna

Flap flap the washing flies
To meet the starting hail.
Close the door on love and hang
The key upon the nail.

### The Soldier in the Park

All day he slept, his mouth on pennyroyal,
His eyelids couched on clover,
His fingers twined around the stems of grass,
Doves near him, and the sun upon his shoulder.
The earth drowsed under him,
And the clouds slid over.
The boats on the bay rocked, the willows sighed.

How long ago was that?

That was in summer, some time before he died.

### The Children March

The children of the world are on the march
From the dangerous cots, the nurseries ringed with fire,
The poisoned toys, the playgrounds pitted
With bomb craters and shrapnel strewn about;
From the whips, the iron bars, the guns' great shout,
The malevolent teachers and the lethal sports
Played on the ruined fields fenced by red wires.

The children of the world are on the march
With the doll and the school-bag to safe quarters,
The temporary haven, the impermanent home;
Nightly turning their thoughts to the forsaken hearth,
The wandering, wondering children of the world
March on the sea and land and crowded air—
The unsmiling sons, the sad bewildered daughters.

# DOUGLAS STEWART

## *Glencoe*

Sigh, wind in the pine;
River, weep as you flow;
Terrible things were done
Long, long ago.

In daylight golden and mild
After the night of Glencoe
They found the hand of a child
Lying upon the snow.

Lopped by the sword to the ground
Or torn by wolf or fox,
That was the snowdrop they found
Among the granite rocks.

Oh, life is fierce and wild
And the heart of the earth is stone,
And the hand of a murdered child
Will not bear thinking on.

Sigh, wind in the pine,
Cover it over with snow;
But terrible things were done
Long, long ago.


from *The Birdsville Track*

### MARREE

Oh the corrugated-iron town
In the corrugated-iron air
Where the shimmering heat-waves glare
To the red-hot iron plain
And the steel mirage beyond:

The blackfellow's squalid shanty
Of rags and bags and tins,
The bright-red dresses of the gins
Flowering in that hot country
Like lilies in the dust's soft pond:

The camels' bones and the bullocks',
The fierce red acre of death
Where the Afghan groans beneath
His monstrous concrete blankets
That peel in the heat like rind:

Where life if it hopes to breathe
Must crawl in the shade of a stone
Like snake and scorpion:
All tastes like dust in the mouth,
All strikes like iron in the mind.

### RUINS

Two golden butterflies mating over the ruins
Of the iron house that is nowhere's dark dead centre
Stark on the rise in the huge hot circle of the plains
All doors and windows gaping for the wind to enter—
Lord, Lord they think that nowhere is all the world
And, so they can dance their golden dance of love,
One hot blue day in the desert more than enough.

And in that same dark house when her husband perished
The woman, they say, lived on so long alone
With what she could think and the household things she cherished,
Staring at that vast island of purple stone
Without one break until the mirage unfurled
Its ocean of steel, it tore a great gap in her mind
Harsh as the loose sheet of iron that bangs in the wind.

## The Silkworms

All their lives in a box! What generations,
What centuries of masters, not meaning to be cruel
But needing their labour, taught these creatures such patience
That now though sunlight strikes on the eye's dark jewel
Or moonlight breathes on the wing they do not stir
But like the ghosts of moths crouch silent there.

Look it's a child's toy! There is no lid even,
They can climb, they can fly, and the whole world's their tree;
But hush, they say in themselves, we are in prison.
There is no word to tell them that they are free,
And they are not; ancestral voices bind them
In dream too deep for wind or word to find them.

Even in the young, each like a little dragon
Ramping and green upon his mulberry leaf,
So full of life, it seems, the voice has spoken:
They hide where there is food, where they are safe,
And the voice whispers, 'Spin the cocoon,
Sleep, sleep, you shall be wrapped in me soon.'

Now is their hour, when they wake from that long swoon;
Their pale curved wings are marked in a pattern of leaves,
Shadowy for trees, white for the dance of the moon;
And when on summer nights the buddleia gives
Its nectar like lilac wine for insects mating
They drink its fragrance and shiver, impatient with waiting,

They stir, they think they will go. Then they remember
It was forbidden, forbidden, ever to go out;
The Hands are on guard outside like claps of thunder,
The ancestral voice says Don't, and they do not.
Still the night calls them to unimaginable bliss
But there is terror around them, the vast, the abyss,

And here is the tribe that they know, in their known place,
They are gentle and kind together, they are safe for ever,

And all shall be answered at last when they embrace.
White moth moves closer to moth, lover to lover.
There is that pang of joy on the edge of dying—
Their soft wings whirr, they dream that they are flying.


### The Garden of Ships

Even so deep in the jungle they were not safe.
The stars still glittered round them like barbed wire
But more than that, fantastic below the cliff
A lantern filled a tree with orange fire
Like a great tropical flower, one window's gleam
With a round yellow eye stared up at them.

If it was another village of the dog-faced people
As seemed most likely, no one ran out to bark;
And the tree seemed bare and tapering, more like a steeple
Where the light like a golden bell rocked in the dark.
Was it the mast of a ship?—impossibly lost
Here in the forest, mile upon mile from the coast?

They could climb down and creep on it through the jungle
For lights meant men, and men meant water and food
And they were thirsty enough, and they were hungry;
But when had the lights of men ever brought them good?
Not in these evil islands, not in these times;
But years ago, it seemed, in the country of dreams.

All night long they talked about it in whispers.
They would have liked to sleep, for they had come far
By burning and naked seas, by sliding rivers,
By islands smouldering still with the smoke of war
Or shrouded in steam, to reach this ridge at last;
But how could they sleep with that strange light on the mast?

And sometimes water glimmered, sometimes it seemed
That ranging away from the lantern, tree by tree

Or mast by mast, whole fleets of vessels gleamed
Faint in the starshine where no ships could be.
And in the morning they were ships indeed!
It was amazing, Marco Polo said,

Speaking of his own travels to that island,
How such a current surged there through the ocean
It seized upon wandering ships and dragged them inland;
And leaping against the hills in white explosion
Tore by their roots the tall trees out of the jungle;
And up the long gulf, in one vast helpless tangle,

Swept them along, tall ships and trees together,
And drove more timber in and piled it up
So they lay locked at the end of the gulf for ever
While many a merchant mourned his missing ship.
But what was more amazing, though for that matter
Likely enough to happen with trees and water,

Was how while the ships lay still as they did now
High-decked, tall-masted, flotsam from all the seas,
Junks from old China, sampan, Arabian dhow,
Galleon and barque, Dutch, English, Portuguese,
Their anchors green with moss, their sails all furled,
Never again to ride the waves of the world,

That wall of trees, as silt filled up the shallows,
Took root again and stood up tall and green
And taller grew and flung their leafy shadows
From ship to ship with flowering vines between,
Hanging the masts with such enchanting burden
It seemed the fleet was anchored in a garden.

And there were gardeners too—that was the thing,
Piercingly strange, that moved the watchers most;
Far down, unseen, they heard a woman sing,
She might have been a bird there, or a ghost;
But windows opened, plumes of smoke rose up,
Brown men in sarongs walked about each ship

And all the jungle rang with children's laughter;
And they saw too, not least of many solaces,
Where bridges joined the ships across the water,
Bare-breasted girls who walked among the trellises
Or white and golden, fair as waterlilies,
Plunged in the pools and swam with gleaming bodies.

So, ragged and bony, wild-eyed with war and fever,
They came down out of the jungle to the clearing
And truly they thought they could lie down there for ever,
Feasting on fruit, drinking the palm-wine, hearing
The laughter and the music, the lap of the tide
Stealing so far from the sea to the ship's side,

And those soft voices telling the old stories
Of how they had lived on the ships for generations,
And if the dog-faced people on their forays
Chanced on their haven, people of all the nations
Living in peace together untouched by the world,
They lifted up their dog-faced heads and howled

And fled, thinking them spirits. So too, long after
When the war and all their journeying turned to a dream,
Like a wild vision they had seen in their fever,
Even to these two wanderers did they seem;
For calling them always with its clear compulsion
Somewhere over the mountains, across the ocean,

With its broad golden fields, its urgent cities,
Its ports where ships still sailed on whatever venture,
Their homeland lay; and though like waterlilies
The fair girls swam and the birds sang in rapture
And the old ships dreamed in the jungle; even so,
Now they were strong they could reach it, and they must go.

## Two Englishmen

Far, far from home they rode on their excursions
And looked with much amusement and compassion
On Indians and Africans and Persians,
People indeed of any foreign nation
Who milled in mobs completely uninhibited
In the peculiar lands that they inhabited.

But in their own small island crowded thickly,
Each with his pride of self and race and caste,
They could not help but be a little prickly
And in their wisdom they evolved at last
This simple code to save them from destruction—
One did not speak without an introduction.

So naturally when Kinglake on his camel,
Mounted aloft to see the world or take it,
Saw faint against the sky's hard blue enamel
A solar topee, then a shooting jacket,
Then all too clear an Englishman appearing
He found the prospect anything but cheering.

Merely because the distances were wider
One could not speak with every Dick or Harry,
For all he knew some absolute outsider,
Who trotted up upon his dromedary,
And yet he felt, alone and unprotected
On these bare sands some talk might be expected.

Of course, he thought, with spirits briefly lightened,
Though ten to one he did not know the fellow
He might be quite all right; but then he mightn't;
And on he came by sandy hill and hollow—
It was a bit too thick thus to arrive at
The desert's core and then not find it private.

For if for one's own reasons one had ridden
By camel through the empty wastes to Cairo

From Gaza in the distance back there hidden
One did not do the thing to play the hero
Or have some chap come dropping from the sky
To ask what one was doing there, and why.

The sweat lay on his camel dank and soapy
And Kinglake too broke out in perspiration
For close and closer in his solar topee
The stranger came with steady undulation;
One could not hide, for shelter there was none,
Nor yet, however tempting, cut and run.

No, if they met, as meet it seemed they must,
Though heartily he wished him at the devil,
Kinglake decided, halting in the dust,
That if the fellow spoke he must be civil;
But then observed, in ultimate dismay,
He could not think of anything to say.

But he, as it fell out, need not have worried.
It was an English military man
Long years in Burma boiled, in India curried,
Who riding home on some deep private plan
Now sat his camel equally embarrassed
To find himself thus hunted out and harassed;

And while their Arab servants rushed together
With leaps and yells to suit the glad occasion
Each Englishman gazed coolly at the other
And briefly touched his hat in salutation
And so passed by, erect, superb, absurd,
Across the desert sands without a word.

But when they'd passed, one gesture yet endures;
Each turned and waved his hand as if to say,
'Well, help yourself to Egypt'—'India's yours,'
And so continued grandly on his way;
And as they went, one feels that, truth to tell,
They understood each other pretty well.

## At the Entrance

God knows what beat him down into that deadland
Of weed and wild green water; it could have been,
We thought at first when we came round the headland,
The ferry had collided; or, unseen,
Some giant comber from the outer ocean
Swept in and sunk the ship on that bright day;
And huge and high indeed in green commotion
The harbour entrance swirled, and there he lay.

We saw his body floating near the surface,
The waves washed over it and he was dead
And all the sea was filled with planks and corpses
And one swept past us in a mass of weed.
Wreckage and death on that bright water heaving!
Yet he at least still rode his raft of planks
And steadily now through the great waves was moving;
The craft that towed him in had all our thanks—

Though, Lord, he was still no more than food for seagulls!
Still washed by the waves, that long-limbed body lax,
That gaunt white head that might have been beast's or idol's,
Strange, obscure, suffering, like a head of ice,
Stiff and abandoned. The tow-rope through the water
Gleamed straight and gold, hauling with easy speed.
Far, far behind lay all that green disaster,
And now in the last of the swell he moved indeed:

Some stir, some shudder of life was in that body.
We saw his hand move, fumbling the rope that bound him,
The harbour broadening around him, clear and steady;
And hugely, heavily, out of the sea that drowned him,
Warming our hearts as life now warmed his blood,
He clambered, striving to rise, until at last
Upright upon the moving raft he stood,
And on into the distance and the mist.

# JACK DAVIS

## *Day Flight*

I closed my eyes as I sat in the jet
And I asked the hostess if she would let
Me take on board a patch of sky
And a dash of the blue-green sea.

Far down below my country gleamed
In thin dry rivers and blue-white lakes
And most I longed for, there as I dreamed,
A square of the desert, stark and red,
To mould a pillow for a sleepy head
And a cloak to cover me.

# REX INGAMELLS

## from *The Great South Land*

'They made impudent inspection of our Coast,
waving to us,
and calling to us,
as if it were right they should land—
as if it were a thing to be expected—
and as if formality were of no importance;
but we turned our backs on them,
and they returned to the big canoe,
as if they were the aggrieved party.

'In the Bay, though, in the Bay, past Givea,
where they stopped some days with their big canoe,
there was no preventing their aggression.

'We did not like their approach.
They did not stay off-shore quietly in the one place
to await our attention.

'We did not want them anywhere near,
but, had they sat down off-shore,
it would have been proper in us
to accord them the privilege of strangers.

'Their coming was arrogant and hostile,
as if the Law were nothing and did not exist.

'When they brought their big canoe into the Bay,
they did not wait for our acknowledgment;
they climbed into their little canoes without waiting,
and prepared to land.

'Two of our men took up a stand on the beach
to signify taboo against their trespassing,
their act of war against us.

'But the strangers were assertive,
obstinate in bad manners.

'They demanded,
in a very awkward sign-language,
water—
throwing us a number of gifts
that were paltry, insulting barter
for so precious a thing as water.'


from *Memory of Hills*

There are rock-rooted ranges to dominate
the ways of man with peace, enforced but healing;
there are crows settling on the boundary gate,
or poised in the sky, or wheeling.

Slowly the sun moves over the red land, slowly
over the dust-puff silence that never changes
except for crow caws that suddenly, wholly
envelop those random ranges. . .

The old hills are obstinate in my mind,
and I thank them now for the long familiarity.
Merely I shut my eyes to find
their reflex of moonlight, their kind
wrinkled acknowledgement of the moon's clarity.


## KENNETH MACKENZIE

### Heat

'Well, this is where I go down to the river,'
the traveller with me said, and turned aside
out of the burnt road, through the black trees
spiking the slope, and went down, and never
came back into the heat from water's ease
in which he swooned, in cool joy, and died.

Often since then, in brutal days of summer
I have remembered him, with envy too;
thought of him sinking down above his knees
in a cold torrent, senseless of the rumour
of death gone down behind him through the trees,
through the dead grass and bushes he shoved through.

He must have tasted water after walking
miles and miles along that stream of road,
gulping and drooling it out of his mouth
that had for one day been too dry for talking
as we went on through drought into the south
shouldering leaden heat for double load.

Plainly he couldn't bear it any longer.
Like the hand of a bored devil placed
mercilessly upon a man's head,
it maddened him. I was a little stronger
and knew the river, rich with many dead,
lustrous and very cold, but two-faced

like some cold, vigorous, enticing woman
quite at the mercy of her remote source
and past springs. I could not warn him now—
not if he were here now. I could warn no man
while these red winds and summer lightnings blow
frantic with heat across my dogged course

into the south, beside the narrow river
which has that traveller's flesh and bones, and more.
Often I see him walking down that slope
thirsty and mad, never to return, never
quenched quite of his thirst, or of his hope
that heat would be arrested on its shore.

### Autumn Mushrooms

White moons like midnight's in the morning sun
set in the dew among the leaves of grass
are autumn mushrooms, kneecaps of bleached bone
thrown up in the dark with silent speed and grace
by Earth the bounteous—a gesture planned
to teach surprise to men, at so much riches
hushed for a year, then thrust forth unexplained
beyond the limits expectation reaches.
Pausing even with my knife at the smooth flesh
of throat-like stalk, once more I know, I know
(as I knew last year) wonder in a flash
to find these fruits that are so old so new—
    and in each microscopic spore to see
    the enormous pattern of eternity.

### Two Trinities

*Are you ready?* soul said again
smiling deep in the dark
where mind and I live passionately
grain rasping across grain

in a strangled question-mark
—or so we have lived lately.

I looked through the hollow keyhole
at my wife not young any more
with my signature on her forehead
and her spirit hers and whole
unsigned by me—as before
we knew each other, and wed.

I looked at my grown daughter
cool and contained as a flower
whose bees I shall not be among—
vivid as white spring water
full of womanish power
like the first phrases of a song.

I looked at my son, and wept
in my mouth's cave to see
the seed ready for sowing
and the harvest unready to be reaped—
green fruit shocked from the tree,
the bird killed on the wing.

*Well?* soul said and I said,
Mind and I are at one
to go with you now—finally
joined now to be led—
for our place here is gone:
we are not among those three.

Soul said, *Now come with me.*


### God! How I Long for You ...

God! how I long for you, sealed up in night,
when in the lonely darkness of this bed
I lie awake with shut eyes, shut mind

enclosing your white image, shut ears
tormented by the echo of your voice.
This is not love. This is timeless torment—
a cruelty of the gods, who let you rob me
of my old easy unconsciousness of time,
and weight each second with your heavy memory—
each minute a thick coin stamped with your face,
each hour intolerable, each day a nightmare
of speechless, frightened, desperate anticipation,
and every night a sepulchre containing
my murdered body and your body's ghost.


*Caesura*

Sometimes at night when the heart stumbles and stops
a full second endless the endless steps
that lead me on through this time terrain
without edges and beautiful terrible
are gone never to proceed again.

Here is a moment of enormous trouble
when the kaleidoscope sets unalterable
and at once without meaning without motion
like a stalled aeroplane in the middle sky
ready to fall down into a waiting ocean.

Blackness rises. Am I now to die
and feel the steps no more and not see day
break out its answering smile of hail all's well
from east full round to east and hear the bird
whistle all creatures that on earth do dwell?

Not now. Old heart has stopped to think of a word
as someone in a dream by far too weird
to be unlikely feels a kiss and stops
to praise all heaven stumbling in all his senses . . .
and suddenly hears again the endless steps.

### The Hospital—Retrospections

#### NEW ARRIVAL

Burgess was drunk when he was admitted
   not with alcohol—with pain.
The wailing ambulance that brought him
   grumbled and growled away again.

Pain was the brilliant light the smell
   of nurse and surgeon the strange faces
swimming in bluish air then gone:
   but he had been in stranger places—

but never strangeness and pain together
   never the incurious wish to die
that squeezed his mind like the white fingers
   probing his pelvis ribs and thigh.

Transported, drunk with so much anguish,
   Burgess observed the ceiling part
To show him heaven and hell united
   ready to fall upon his heart.

Each of his wounds cried out against it
   voiceless and twisted mouths of blood.
Clasped in a cruel consciousness
   he closed his lips on the sacred flood

of revelation that welled up in him.

   The needle lying within the vein
sobered and then annihilated
   Burgess the faces the light the pain.

#### MATRON

Trailing the incense of many thousand Masses
caught in her grey hair which the kerchief hides
the Matron, the unmated mother of the hospital,
of all here, and many more besides,
salutes each bed.

Morning through the open windows watches her
move in the wards, never forgetting a name,
though names mean nothing to her as she passes
serenely on, almost the grand dame,
her almost-holy head
bent gravely in something not quite surprise
to find each bed is still inhabited
by unredeemed expectant flesh that lies
attentive to the recognition bred
by habit in her eyes.

*And how are you today? . . . You're looking better.*
The faith-inducing words float smoothly free
from her well-disciplined and chiselled lips
but no one would say what her grave eyes see
beneath the brows beneath the brow beneath
the banded veil,
too stiff to rustle, that implacably
turns when she turns to go, and keeps
its virgin counsel
like the command of god upon her breath
asking again *And how are you today?*
And like smooth beads in her rosary of faith,
again *You're looking better . . . That's good. Good . . .*
the mindless words come soft and worn and wise
almost with faint surprise:
but coming from her lips not from her eyes.

For she has seen always
through the pervasive anaesthetic haze
the casting of accounts the even and the odd
additions summed up between man and man
and sometimes man and god.
Librae sestertii denarii
play with her dreams a ghastly hide-and-seek:
must into can't goes can—
or please explain it to the secretary,
the man of secrets, at the end of the week
before he meets the board.

So in a rage
of wordless godless desperate jealousy
against the world, the healthy and the sick,
she'll take a broom and sweep a length of passage
with downward lids and menial energy
as though to clear some passage in her mind
towards what she cannot find—
the door marked *End of Conflict: Ladies Rest Room.*
No matriarchate had such to take her in
and shut outside her womanly sense of sin
and free her from the soul-devouring womb
ambition's generator, fear's old incubator,
passion's and pain's and penitence's begetter.
Her eyes above her lips above her breast
above sedately folded fingers know all this
but admit nothing, nothing, all is peace,
all is better, better, better and better . . .

She is the Matron. This is her hospital
a projection of herself body and soul
where bodies are made whole
as in the woman bodies are made, whole.


## Earth Buried

Let me be buried as flesh, not burned, I say;
lie in time as bones among all my bones
in good loam soil, to grow fat blue cabbages
with the aid of autumn's rain; not in clay
nor near streets or fields of underground stones
but in a place whence occasional messages—
sudden memoranda of the good things known—
may reach the light as living leaves
telling you we are well enough there below,
lest any at all, recalling me, may grieve.

In my time I have turned and loved much soil,
found flints and shards, and broken glass, and tin,

like stops among the steady life beneath
the floor of light and air; but for all my toil
I never found a skull. Bury me then
somewhere likely, so perhaps some gardener
working like me, most of the time for love,
may, after the pleasant sweating pause for breath,
turn up my brain-case, the pitted, knitted warden
of what I knew, what I died thinking of.
Let him unearth my house, thoughtless of death,
and guess at who I was, and what my faith,
and put me back into the earth again,
later planting his seed firmly and well
so that once more in what had been my brain
life glorious and unconquerable may swell.

Let me by all means be buried as flesh,
not burned. There's little nourishment in ashes.

A. D. HOPE

*Imperial Adam*

Imperial Adam, naked in the dew,
Felt his brown flanks and found the rib was gone.
Puzzled he turned and saw where, two and two,
The mighty spoor of Jahweh marked the lawn.

Then he remembered through mysterious sleep
The surgeon fingers probing at the bone,
The voice so far away, so rich and deep:
'It is not good for him to live alone.'

Turning once more he found Man's counterpart
In tender parody breathing at his side.
He knew her at first sight, he knew by heart
Her allegory of sense unsatisfied.

The pawpaw drooped its golden breasts above
Less generous than the honey of her flesh;
The innocent sunlight showed the place of love;
The dew on its dark hairs winked crisp and fresh.

This plump gourd severed from his virile root,
She promised on the turf of Paradise
Delicious pulp of the forbidden fruit;
Sly as the snake she loosed her sinuous thighs,

And waking, smiled up at him from the grass;
Her breasts rose softly and he heard her sigh—
From all the beasts whose pleasant task it was
In Eden to increase and multiply

Adam had learned the jolly deed of kind:
He took her in his arms and there and then,
Like the clean beasts, embracing from behind,
Began in joy to found the breed of men.

Then from the spurt of seed within her broke
Her terrible and triumphant female cry,
Split upward by the sexual lightning stroke.
It was the beasts now who stood watching by:

The gravid elephant, the calving hind,
The breeding bitch, the she-ape big with young
Were the first gentle midwives of mankind;
The teeming lioness rasped her with her tongue;

The proud vicuña nuzzled her as she slept
Lax on the grass; and Adam watching too
Saw how her dumb breasts at their ripening wept,
The great pod of her belly swelled and grew,

And saw its water break, and saw, in fear,
Its quaking muscles in the act of birth,
Between her legs a pigmy face appear,
And the first murderer lay upon the earth.

## The Martyrdom of St Teresa

There was a sudden croon of lilies
Drifting like music through the shop;
The bright knives flashed with heavenly malice,
The choppers lay in wait to chop;

And Jesus with his crown of briar
Worn like a little hat in *Vogue*
Picked up her soul of ruby fire
And popped it in his shopping bag.

She was so small a saint, a holy
Titbit upon the butcher's block—
Death chose the cuts with care and slowly
Put on his apron, eyed the clock

And sitting down serenely waited
Beside the plump brown carcass there,
Which kings had feared and the popes hated,
Which had known neither hate nor fear;

While through all Spain mysterious thunder
Woke cannibal longings in the blood,
Inviting man to put asunder
The flesh that had been joined with God.

The little nuns of her foundation
Arrived on foot, by mule or cart,
Each filled with meek determination
To have an elbow, or the heart.

Death with a smile expertly slices
A rib for one, for one the knee,
Cuts back a breast, cuts deeper, prises
Out the raw heart for all to see;

In Sister Philomena's basket
Safe for St Joseph's lies an arm;

The saw shrills on a bone, the brisket
Becomes a miracle-working charm;

At five to six Death drops his cleaver:
The sunset, as the crowd goes home,
Pours down on every true believer
The mystic blood of martyrdom.

### On an Engraving by Casserius
For Dr John Z. Bowers

Set on this bubble of dead stone and sand,
Lapped by its frail balloon of lifeless air,
Alone in the inanimate void, they stand,
These clots of thinking molecules who stare
Into the night of nescience and death,
And, whirled about with their terrestrial ball,
Ask of all being its motion and its frame:
This of all human images takes my breath;
Of all the joys in being a man at all,
This folds my spirit in its quickening flame.

Turning the leaves of this majestic book
My thoughts are with those great cosmographers,
Surgeon adventurers who undertook
To probe and chart time's other universe.
This one engraving holds me with its theme:
More than all maps made in that century
Which set true bearings for each cape and star,
De Quiros' vision or Newton's cosmic dream,
This reaches towards the central mystery
Of whence our being draws and what we are.

It came from that great school in Padua:
Casserio and Spiegel made this page.
Vesalius, who designed the *Fabrica*,
There strove, but burned his book at last in rage;
Fallopius by its discipline laid bare

The elements of this humanity,
Without which none knows that which treats the soul;
Fabricius talked with Galileo there:
Did those rare spirits in their colloquy
Divine in their two skills the single goal?

'One force that moves the atom and the star,'
Says Galileo; 'one basic law beneath
All change!' 'Would light from Achernar
Reveal how embryon forms within its sheath?'
Fabricius asks, and smiles. Talk such as this,
Ranging the bounds of our whole universe,
Could William Harvey once have heard? And once
Hearing, strike out that strange hypothesis,
Which in *De Motu Cordis* twice recurs,
Coupling the heart's impulsion with the sun's?

Did Thomas Browne at Padua, too, in youth
Hear of their talk of universal law
And form that notion of particular truth
Framed to correct a science they foresaw,
That darker science of which he used to speak
In later years and called the Crooked Way
Of Providence? Did *he* foresee perhaps
An age in which all sense of the unique,
And singular dissolves, like ours today,
In diagrams, statistics, tables, maps?

Not here! The graver's tool in this design
Aims still to give not general truth alone,
Blue-print of science or data's formal line:
Here in its singularity he has shown
The image of an individual soul;
Bodied in this one woman, he makes us see
The shadow of his anatomical laws.
An artist's vision animates the whole,
Shines through the scientist's detailed scrutiny
And links the person and the abstract cause.

Such were the charts of those who pressed beyond
Vesalius their master, year by year
Tracing each bone, each muscle, every frond
Of nerve until the whole design lay bare.
Thinking of this dissection, I descry
The tiers of faces, their teacher in his place,
The talk at the cadaver carried in:
'A woman—with child!'; I hear the master's dry
Voice as he lifts a scalpel from its case:
'With each new step in science, we begin.'

Who was she? Though they never knew her name,
Dragged from the river, found in some alley at dawn,
This corpse none cared, or dared perhaps, to claim;
The dead child in her belly still unborn,
Might have passed, momentary as a shooting star,
Quenched like the misery of her personal life,
Had not the foremost surgeon of Italy,
Giulio Casserio of Padua,
Bought her for science, questioned her with his knife,
And drawn her for his great *Anatomy*;

Where still in the abundance of her grace,
She stands among the monuments of time
And with a feminine delicacy displays
His elegant dissection: the sublime
Shaft of her body opens like a flower
Whose petals, folded back expose the womb,
Cord and placenta and the sleeping child,
Like instruments of music in a room
Left when her grieving Orpheus left his tower
Forever, for the desert and the wild.

Naked she waits against a tideless shore,
A sibylline stance, a noble human frame
Such as those old anatomists loved to draw.
She turns her head as though in trouble or shame,
Yet with a dancer's gesture holds the fruit
Plucked, though not tasted, of the Fatal Tree.

Something of the first Eve is in this pose
And something of the second in the mute
Offering of her child in death to be
Love's victim and her flesh its mystic rose.

No figure with wings of fire and back-swept hair
Swoops with his: Blessed among Women!; no sword
Of the spirit cleaves or quickens her; yet there
She too was overshadowed by the Word,
Was chosen, and by her humble gift of death
The lowly and the poor in heart give tongue,
Wisdom puts down the mighty from their seat;
The vile rejoice and rising, hear beneath
Scalpel and forceps, tortured into song,
Her body utter their magnificat.

Four hundred years since first that cry rang out:
Four hundred years, the patient, probing knife
Cut towards its answer—yet we stand in doubt:
Living, we cannot tell the source of life.
Old science, old certainties that lit our way
Shrink to poor guesses, dwindle to a myth.
Today's truths teach us how we were beguiled;
Tomorrow's how blind our vision of today.
The universals we thought to conjure with
Pass: there remain the mother and the child.

Loadstone, loadstar, alike to each new age,
There at the crux of time they stand and scan,
Past every scrutiny of prophet or sage,
Still unguessed prospects in this venture of Man.
To generations, which we leave behind,
They taught a difficult, selfless skill: to show
The mask beyond the mask beyond the mask;
To ours another vista, where the mind
No longer asks for answers, but to know:
What questions are there which we fail to ask?

Who knows, but to the age to come they speak
Words that our own is still unapt to hear:
'These are the limits of all you sought and seek;
More our yet unborn nature cannot bear.
Learn now that all man's intellectual quest
Was but the stirrings of a foetal sleep;
The birth you cannot haste and cannot stay
Nears its appointed time; turn now and rest
Till that new nature ripens, till the deep
Dawns with that unimaginable day.'


## The Double Looking Glass

See how she strips her lily for the sun:
The silk shrieks upward from her wading feet;
Down through the pool her wavering echoes run;
Candour with candour, shade and substance meet.

From where a wet meniscus rings the shin
The crisp air shivers up her glowing thighs,
Swells round a noble haunch and whispers in
The dimple of her belly . . . Surely eyes

Lurk in the laurels, where each leafy nest
Darts its quick bird-glance through the shifting screen.
. . . Yawn of the oxter, lift of liquid breast
Splinter their white shafts through our envious green

Where thuds this rage of double double hearts.
. . . My foolish fear refracts a foolish dream.
Here all things have imagined counterparts:
A dragon-fly dim-darting in the stream

Follows and watches with enormous eyes
His blue narcissus glitter in the air.
The flesh reverberates its own surprise
And startles at the act which makes it bare.

Laced with quick air and vibrant to the light,
Now my whole animal breathes and knows its place
In the great web of being, and its right;
The mind learns ease again, the heart finds grace.

I am as all things living. Man alone
Cowers from his world in clothes and cannot guess
How earth and water, branch and beast and stone
Speak to the naked in their nakedness.

... A silver rising of her arms, that share
Their pure and slender crescent with the pool
Plunders the braided treasure of her hair.
Loosed from their coils uncrowning falls the full

Cascade of tresses whispering down her flanks,
And idly now she wades a step, and stays
To watch the ripples widen to the banks
And lapse in mossy coves and rushy bays.

Look with what bliss of motion now she turns
And seats herself upon a sunny ledge,
Leans back, and drowsing dazzles, basking burns.
Susannah! ... what hiss, what rustle in the sedge;

What fierce susurrus shifts from bush to bush?
... Susannah! Susannah, Susannah! ... Foolish heart,
It was your own pulse lisping in a hush
So deep, I hear the water-beetle dart

And trace from bank to bank his skein of light,
So still the sibilance of a breaking bud
Speaks to the sense; the hairy bee in flight
Booms a brute chord of danger in my blood.

What danger though? The garden wall is high
And bolted and secure the garden door;
The bee, bold ravisher, will pass me by
And does not seek my honey for his store;

The speckled hawk in heaven, wheeling slow
Searches the tufts of grass for other prey;
Safe in their sunny banks the lilies grow,
Secure from rough hands for another day.

Alert and brisk, even the hurrying ant
Courses these breathing ranges unafraid.
The fig-tree, leaning with its leaves aslant,
Touches me with broad hands of harmless shade.

And if the urgent pulses of the sun
Quicken my own with a voluptuous heat,
They warm me only as they warm the stone
Or the thin liquid paddling round my feet.

My garden holds me like its private dream,
A secret pleasure, guarded and apart.
Now as I lean above the pool I seem
The image of my image in its heart.

In that inverted world a scarlet fish
Drifts through the trees and swims into the sky,
So in the contemplative mind a wish
Drifts through its mirror of eternity.

A mirror for man's images of love
The nakedness of woman is a pool
In which her own desires mount and move,
Alien, solitary, purposeful

Yet in this close were every leaf an eye,
In those green limbs the sap would mount as slow.
One with their life beneath an open sky,
I melt into the trance of time, I flow

Into the languid current of the day
... The sunlight sliding on a breathing flank
Fades and returns again in tranquil play;
Her eyelids close; she sleeps upon the bank.

Now, now to wreak upon her Promised Land
The vengeance of the dry branch on the bud.
Who shall be first upon her? Who shall stand
To watch the dragon sink its fangs in blood?

Her ripeness taunts the ignominy of age;
Seethes in old loins with hate and lust alike.
Now in the plenitude of shame and rage
The rod of chastisement is reared to strike.

And now to take her drowsing; now to fall
With wild-fire on the cities of the plain;
Susannah! . . . Yet once more that hoarse faint call,
That rustle from the thicket comes again?

Ah, no! Some menace from the edge of sleep
Imposes its illusion on my ear.
Relax, return, Susannah; Let the deep
Warm tide of noonday bear you; do not fear,

But float once more on that delicious stream.
Suppose some lover watches from the grove;
Suppose, only suppose, those glints, the gleam
Of eyes; the eyes of a young man in love.

Shall I prolong this fancy, now the sense
Impels, the hour invites? Shall I not own
Such thoughts as women find to recompense
Their hidden lives when secret and alone?

Surprise the stranger in the heart, some strong
Young lion of the rocks who found his path
By night, and now he crouches all day long
Beside the pool to see me at my bath.

He would be there, a melancholy shade
Caught in the ambush of his reckless joy,
Afraid to stir for fear I call, afraid
In one unguarded moment to destroy

At once the lover and the thing he loves.
Who should he be? I cannot guess; but such
As desperate hope or lonelier passion moves
To tempt his fate so far, to dare so much;

Who having seen me only by the way,
Or having spoken with me once by chance,
Fills all his nights with longing, and the day
With schemes whose triumph is a casual glance.

Possessed by what he never can possess,
He forms his wild design and ventures all
Only to see me in my nakedness
And lurk and tremble by the garden wall.

He lives but in my dream. I need repel
No dream for I may end it when I please;
And I may dream myself in love as well
As dream my lover in the summer trees,

Suppose myself desired, suppose desire,
Summon that wild enchantment of the mind,
Kindle my fire at his imagined fire,
Pity his love and call him and be kind.

Now think he comes, and I shall lie as still
As limpid waters that reflect their sun,
And let him lie between my breasts and fill
My loins with thunder till the dream be done.

The kisses of my mouth are his; he lies
And feeds among the lilies; his brown knees
Divide the white embraces of my thighs.
Wake not my love nor stir him till he please,

For now his craft has passed the straits and now
Into my shoreless sea he drives alone.
Islands of spice await his happy prow
And fabulous deeps support and bear him on.

He rides the mounting surge, he feels the wide
Horizon draw him onward mile by mile;
The reeling sky, the dark rejoicing tide
Lead him at last to this mysterious isle.

In ancient woods that murmur with the sea,
He finds once more the garden and the pool.
And there a man who is and is not he
Basks on the sunny margin in the full

Noon of another and a timeless sky,
And dreams but never hopes to have his love;
And there the woman who is also I
Watches him from the hollow of the grove;

Till naked from the leaves she steals and bends
Above his sleep and wakes him with her breast
And now the vision begins, the voyage ends,
And the great phoenix blazes in his nest.

... Ah, God of Israel, even though alone,
We take her with a lover, in the flush
Of her desires. SUSANNAH! ... I am undone!
What beards, what bald heads burst now from the bush!


### Moschus Moschiferus
#### A SONG FOR ST CECILIA'S DAY

In the high jungle where Assam meets Tibet
The small Kastura, most archaic of deer,
Were driven in herds to cram the hunters' net
And slaughtered for the musk-pods which they bear;

But in those thickets of rhododendron and birch
The tiny creatures now grow hard to find.
Fewer and fewer survive each year. The search
Employs new means, more exquisite and refined:

The hunters now set out by two or three;
Each carries a bow and one a slender flute.
Deep in the forest the archers choose a tree
And climb; the piper squats against the root.

And there they wait until all trace of man
And rumour of his passage dies away.
They melt into the leaves and, while they scan
The glade below, their comrade starts to play.

Through those vast listening woods a tremulous skein
Of melody wavers, delicate and shrill:
Now dancing and now pensive, now a rain
Of pure, bright drops of sound and now the still,

Sad wailing of lament; from tune to tune
It winds and modulates without a pause;
The hunters hold their breath; the trance of noon
Grows tense; with its full power the music draws

A shadow from a juniper's darker shade;
Bright-eyed, with quivering muzzle and pricked ear,
The little musk-deer slips into the glade
Led by an ecstasy that conquers fear.

A wild enchantment lures him, step by step,
Into its net of crystalline sound, until
The leaves stir overhead, the bowstrings snap
And poisoned shafts bite sharp into the kill.

Then, as the victim shudders, leaps and falls,
The music soars to a delicious peak,
And on and on its silvery piping calls
Fresh spoil for the rewards the hunters seek.

But when the woods are emptied and the dusk
Draws in, the men climb down and count their prey,
Cut out the little glands that hold the musk
And leave the carcasses to rot away.

A hundred thousand or so are killed each year;
Cause and effect are very simply linked:
Rich scents demand the musk, and so the deer,
Its source, must soon, they say, become extinct.

Divine Cecilia, there is no more to say!
Of all who praised the power of music, few
Knew of these things. In honour of your day
Accept this song I too have made for you.


## JOHN MANIFOLD

*Garcia Lorca Murdered in Granada*

Night by nightfall more benighted
Folds the gypsy city under;
Desolation gives a mongrel's
Homeless tongue to the horizon.

In that skull where lemons ripened,
Children sang, and water bubbled,
In that fount of golden numbers
They have set their leaden silence.

They whose bullets he attracted—
Devotees of *rigor mortis*,
Black, and lecherous for blackness—

Could not cosset their deformity
Save in a Granada lacking
Federico Garcia Lorca.

## Fife Tune

For Sixth Platoon, 308th ITC

One morning in spring
We marched from Devizes
All shapes and all sizes
Like beads on a string,
But yet with a swing
We trod the bluemetal
And full of high fettle
We started to sing.

She ran down the stair
A twelve-year-old darling
And laughing and calling
She tossed her bright hair;
Then silent to stare
At the men flowing past her—
There were all she could master
Adoring her there.

It's seldom I'll see
A sweeter or prettier;
I doubt we'll forget her
In two years or three,
And lucky he'll be
She takes for a lover
While we are far over
The treacherous sea.

## Making Contact

Crazy as hell and typical of us:
The blackout bus-light stippling the passengers' shoulders,
Rumbling through darkness, and a whistling behind me smoulders
Into recognition—'Comrade'—like that, in the bus.

So that minutes later I am talking across a table
At a tall girl laughing with friendliness and relief—
Soldier with pickup? Not likely. Nothing so brief.
I have found my footing, that's all; I am standing stable.

Oh, I was hungry for this! I needed reminding
What countless comrades are mine for the seeking and finding.
The numbness of isolation falls off me like sleep,

Something a light wind or a word could abolish;
And the girl comrade smiles, disclaiming the knowledge
That at any moment I could put my head in her lap and weep.

### The Deserter

Born with all arms, he sought a separate peace.
Responsibilities loomed up like tanks,
And since his manhood marked him of our ranks
He threw it off and scrambled for release.

His power of choice he thrust on the police
As if it burnt his hands; he gave the banks
His power to work; then he bestowed with thanks
His power to think on Viscount Candlegrease.

Claiming the privileges of the dead
Before his time—the heart no blood runs through,
The undelighted hands, the rotting head—

Strong in his impotence he can safely view
The battlefield of men, and shake his head
And say, 'I know. But then what can I do?'

## The Tomb of Lt John Learmonth, AIF

*'At the end on Crete he took to the hills, and said he'ld fight it out with only a revolver. He was a great soldier . . .' One of his men in a letter.*

This is not sorrow, this is work: I build
A cairn of words over a silent man,
My friend John Learmonth whom the Germans killed.

There was no word of hero in his plan;
Verse should have been his love and peace his trade,
But history turned him to a partisan.

Far from the battle as his bones are laid
Crete will remember him. Remember well,
Mountains of Crete, the Second Field Brigade!

Say Crete, and there is little more to tell
Of muddle tall as treachery, despair
And black defeat resounding like a bell;

But bring the magnifying focus near
And in contempt of muddle and defeat
The old heroic virtues still appear.

Australian blood where hot and icy meet
(James Hogg and Lermontov were of his kin)
Lie still and fertilise the fields of Crete.

\*     \*     \*

Schoolboy, I watched his ballading begin:
Billy and bullocky and billabong,
Our properties of childhood, all were in.

I heard the air though not the undersong,
The fierceness and resolve; but all the same
They're the tradition, and tradition's strong.

Swagman and bushranger die hard, die game,
Die fighting, like that wild colonial boy—
Jack Dowling, says the ballad, was his name.

He also spun his pistol like a toy,
Turned to the hills like wolf or kangaroo,
And faced destruction with a bitter joy.

His freedom gave him nothing else to do
But set his back against his family tree
And fight the better for the fact he knew

He was as good as dead. Because the sea
Was closed and the air dark and the land lost,
'They'll never capture me alive,' said he.

      \*     \*     \*

That's courage chemically pure, uncrossed
With sacrifice or duty or career,
Which counts and pays in ready coin the cost

Of holding course. Armies are not its sphere
Where all's contrived to achieve its counterfeit;
It swears with discipline, it's volunteer.

I could as hardly make a moral fit
Around it as around a lightning flash.
There is no moral, that's the point of it,

No moral. But I'm glad of this panache
That sparkles, as from flint, from us and steel,
True to no crown nor presidential sash

Nor flag nor fame. Let others mourn and feel
He died for nothing: nothings have their place.
While thus the kind and civilised conceal

This spring of unsuspected inward grace
And look on death as equals, I am filled
With queer affection for the human race.

## Fencing School

White to the neck he glides and plunges
But black above, no human foe
Pity for whom could rob my lunges
Of their direction. Faceless, so,

He is no fellow but a show
Of motion purposed to withstand
The blade that sets my nerves aglow
And sings exultant in the hand.

Thus each withdrawn and wide alert,
Focussed on self from hilt to heel,
Nothing breaks in to controvert

The single aim. I only feel
The sinews of my wrist assert
The tremor of engaging steel.

## L'Embarquement pour Cythère

Watteau was slightly silly to equip
His voyagers as for a minuet.
Panniers and pumps and pose of hand on hip
Will have to be discarded. Else I bet

We'll hear these passionate pilgrims in a sweat
Call on the captain to reverse the ship,
Claiming with hypocritical regret
They're not in trim to go ashore this trip.

Once through that surf, where earlier wreckage swarms,
And up the beach you're in a land as wild
As Crusoe's. Violent electric storms

Flare up at night. Fever and agues dwell
In the dense bush; and old, unreconciled
Blood-rites of pagan sanctity as well.

## Makhno's Philosophers

Back in *tachanka*[1] days, when Red and Green
Pursued in turn each other and the White,
Out on the steppe, I'm told, there could be seen
A novel sight.

Professors of philosophy, whom war
From some provincial faculty dismissed
To seek new pasture on the Black Sea shore,
Fell in with Makhno—anarchist,

Terrorist, bandit, call him what you will—
Who spared their lives and, either for a laugh
Or from some vague respect for mental skill,
Attached them to his staff.

Their duties were not hard. For months or years,
Lacking a porch in which to hold debate,
These peripatetics, ringed by Cossack spears,
Had leisure to discuss The State.

With flashing pince-nez, while the sabres flashed,
They sat berugged in carts and deep dispute,
Or in some plundered village hashed and thrashed
The nature of The Absolute.

Bergsonians quite enjoyed it: from the first
They'd known Duration to depend on Space.
But Nietzscheans found their values arsy-versed
By Supermen of unfamiliar race.

And, whereas Platonists got mulligrubs,
Cynics were cheerful—though I'll not deny
They grumbled when obliged to share their tubs
With hogs from Epicurus' sty.

[1] A light horse-drawn gun-carrier used by the Greens (the Anarchists) in the Russian Revolution.

On quiet nights, bandits would form a ring
And listen with amazed guffaws
As syllogisms flew, and pillaging
Was reconciled with Universal Laws.

Symposia were held, whereat the host
(Taught by Hegelians of the Left)
In stolen vodka would propose a toast
To Proudhon's dictum: Property is Theft!

How did this idyll end? There's some confusion.
Makhno, I fear, was caught—
Perhaps he let his native resolution
Get sicklied o'er with other people's thought.

But what of his philosophers? I feel
Certain they reached an Academe at last
Where each in his own manner might conceal
His briefly bandit past.

To fool the OGPU or the C.I.A.
Would not be hard for any skilled expounder
Of Substance and Illusion, growing grey
But ever metaphysically sounder.

Yet each might feel at times old memories stir,
And know himself, as ever, set apart:
Once, among bandits, a philosopher;
Now, among academics, Green at heart.

In fact—I've wondered—take Professor X—
Mightn't his arid manner be a blind?
Are those lack-lustre eyes, behind those specs,
Truly the mirror of his mind?

Or is the real man, far away
From Kantian imperatives, once more
Roaming the steppe, not as a waif and stray
But waging revolutionary war?

Although his tongue belabours
The stony boundaries of a bloodless creed,
His soul is back again among the sabres
Yelling, 'The Deed! The Deed!'


### Assignation with a Somnambulist

Walk in your sleep beyond Yeppoon
Out to the islands. Fear no wrong.
From cone-shell, stonefish, or the prong-
ed lightning presaging the monsoon.

Call it a dream, and watch the moon
Casting your shadow straight along
With that of she-oaks. You belong
To silence, night and the lagoon.

Walk in your summer sleep. You know
There's nowhere that you cannot go
When you go thus. But understand

On the last island, there am I
Beyond the combers, high and dry,
Shaping our burrow in the sand.


## JAMES McAULEY

### Jesus

Touching Ezekiel his workman's hand
Kindled the thick and thorny characters;
And seraphim that seemed a thousand eyes,
Flying leopards, wheels and basilisks,
Creatures of power and of judgment, soared
From his finger-point, emblazoning the skies.

Then turning from the book he rose and walked
Among the stones and beasts and flowers of earth;
They turned their muted faces to their Lord,
Their real faces, seen by God alone;
And people moved before him undisguised;
He thrust his speech among them like a sword.

And when a dove came to his hand he knew
That hell was opening behind its wings.
He thanked the messenger and let it go;
Spoke to the dust, the fishes and the twelve
As if they understood him equally,
And told them nothing that they wished to know.

### from *A Letter to John Dryden*

Dear John, whoever now takes pen to write
Or at the keys tap-taps through half the night
To give a new *Religio Laici*
Or *Hind and Panther* to this vacant sly
Neurotic modern world, must first take note
That things are not the same as when you wrote.
The Modern Mind was then scarce embryonic
Which now stands forth loud, indistinct, moronic.
The great Unculture that you feared might be
'Drawn to the dregs of a democracy'
Is full upon us; here it sours and thickens
Till every work of art and honour sickens.

You chose for your attempt a kind of verse
Well-bred and easy, energetic, terse;
Reason might walk in it, or boldly fence,
And all was done with spirit and with sense.
But who cares now for reason?—when we see
The very guardians of philosophy
Conceive it as their task to warn the youth
Against the search for philosophic truth;
Rather to keep a vacuum in their head

Wherein *opinions* may, at most, be bred,
Such as excite or soothe or subtly flatter,
And at the lightest change of feeling, scatter,
But never principles, never proofs—these do not matter.
How would you go about it, John, I ask,
What means and metres summon to your task,
What motives find of credibility
In such a fog of insipidity?
Perhaps you'd choose T. Eliot's mighty line,
To drift, and flutter, hesitate, opine,
Hint at a meaning, murmur that God knows,
And gently settle in a soup of prose.
Or would you use the old means, and reach out
To bang the heads of philosophic doubt
Between two rhymes, and knock the feathers out?


### Merry-Go-Round

Bright-coloured, mirror-plated, strung with lights,
With swan-shaped cars and prancing wooden horses,
The silent waiting merry-go-round invites
A swarm of eager riders for its courses.

It moves: a painted miniature cosmos, turning
With planetary music blaring loud.
The riders lean intent, lips parted, faces burning;
Brief smiles float out towards the watching crowd.

On their brass poles the horses rise and fall
In undulant flight; the children ride through dreams.
How faery-bright to them, how magical,
The crude and gaudy mechanism seems!

Almost I see the marvel that they see,
And hear like them the music of the spheres;
They smile out of the enchanted whirl to me.
The lights and colours suddenly dim with tears.

But now their turning world is slowing, slowing;
Horses and music stop: how brief the ride!
New-comers clamber on as these are going
Reluctantly to join the crowd outside.

### Pietà

A year ago you came
Early into the light.
You lived a day and night,
Then died; no-one to blame.

Once only, with one hand,
Your mother in farewell
Touched you. I cannot tell,
I cannot understand

A thing so dark and deep,
So physical a loss:
One touch, and that was all

She had of you to keep.
Clean wounds, but terrible,
Are those made with the Cross.

### In the Huon Valley

Propped boughs are heavy with apples,
Springtime quite forgotten.
Pears ripen yellow. The wasp
Knows where windfalls lie rotten.

Juices grow rich with sun.
These autumn days are still:
The glassy river reflects
Elm-gold up the hill,

And big white plumes of rushes.
Life is full of returns;
It isn't true that one never
Profits, never learns:

Something is gathered in,
Worth the lifting and stacking;
Apples roll through the graders,
The sheds are noisy with packing.


## Because

My father and my mother never quarrelled.
They were united in a kind of love
As daily as the *Sydney Morning Herald*,
Rather than like the eagle or the dove.

I never saw them casually touch,
Or show a moment's joy in one another.
Why should this matter to me now so much?
I think it bore more hardly on my mother,

Who had more generous feeling to express.
My father had dammed up his Irish blood
Against all drinking praying fecklessness,
And stiffened into stone and creaking wood.

His lips would make a switching sound, as though
Spontaneous impulse must be kept at bay.
That it was mainly weakness I see now,
But then my feelings curled back in dismay.

Small things can pit the memory like a cyst:
Having seen other fathers greet their sons,
I put my childish face up to be kissed
After an absence. The rebuff still stuns

My blood. The poor man's curt embarrassment
At such a delicate proffer of affection
Cut like a saw. But home the lesson went:
My tenderness thenceforth escaped detection.

My mother sang *Because*, and *Annie Laurie*,
*White Wings*, and other songs; her voice was sweet.
I never gave enough, and I am sorry;
But we were all closed in the same defeat.

People do what they can; they were good people,
They cared for us and loved us. Once they stood
Tall in my childhood as the school, the steeple.
How can I judge without ingratitude?

Judgment is simply trying to reject
A part of what we are because it hurts.
The living cannot call the dead collect:
They won't accept the charge, and it reverts.

It's my own judgment day that I draw near,
Descending in the past, without a clue,
Down to that central deadness: the despair
Older than any hope I ever knew.

## Convalescence

Coffee and jasmine on a tray.
The stair resounds with feet to school,
Then fills with silence like a pool.
The world outside is windy grey.

A girl was strangled at Thirroul;
The market steadied yesterday.
I try to read, I ought to pray,
But lie and think how wonderful

To lift the phone or write a letter.
As I get well I grow more sure
*(Erbarme dich, du heiliger Retter)*

There's no relief or natural cure.
I drown in silence and endure
The thought of never getting better.


## 'ERN MALLEY'

### *Dürer: Innsbruck, 1495*

I had often, cowled in the slumberous heavy air,
Closed my inanimate lids to find it real,
As I knew it would be, the colourful spires
And painted roofs, the high snows glimpsed at the back,
All reversed in the quiet reflecting waters—
Not knowing then that Dürer perceived it too.
Now I find that once more I have shrunk
To an interloper, robber of dead men's dream,
I had read in books that art is not easy
But no one warned that the mind repeats
In its ignorance the vision of others. I am still
The black swan of trespass on alien waters.


## ROSEMARY DOBSON

### *In a Café*

She clasps the cup with both her hands,
Over the rim her glance compels;
(A man forgets his hat, returns,
The waitress leans against the shelves.)

And Botticelli, painting in the corner,
Glances absorbed across a half-turned shoulder
Thinking of lilies springing where she walks
As now she rises, moves across the room,

(The yawning waitress gathers up the stalks,
The ash, the butt-ends and the dregs of tea.)
Pausing between the gesture and the motion,
Lifting her hand to brush away her hair,
He limns her in an instant, always there
Between the doorway and the emphatic till
With waves and angels, balanced on a shell.

### The Bystander

I am the one who looks the other way,
In any painting you may see me stand
Rapt at the sky, a bird, an angel's wing,
While others kneel, present the myrrh, receive
The benediction from the radiant hand.

I hold the horses while the knights dismount
And draw their swords to fight the battle out;
Or else in dim perspective you may see
My distant figure on the mountain road
When in the plains the hosts are put to rout.

I am the silly soul who looks too late,
The dullard dreaming, second from the right.
I hang upon the crowd, but do not mark
(Cap over eyes) the slaughtered Innocents,
Or Icarus, his downward-plunging flight.

Once in a Garden—back view only there—
How well the painter placed me, stroke on stroke,
Yet scarcely seen among the flowers and grass—
I heard a voice say, 'Eat,' and would have turned—
I often wonder who it was that spoke.

## Child with a Cockatoo

PORTRAIT OF ANNE, DAUGHTER OF THE EARL OF BEDFORD, BY S. VERELST

'Paid by my lord, one portrait, Lady Anne,
Full length with bird and landscape, twenty pounds
And framed withal. I say received. Verelst.'

So signed the painter, bowed, and took his leave.
My Lady Anne smiled in the gallery
A small, grave child, dark-eyed, half turned to show
Her five bare toes beneath the garment's hem,
In stormy landscape with a swirl of drapes.
And, who knows why, perhaps my lady wept
To stand so long and watch the painter's brush
Flicker between the palette and the cloth
While from the sun-drenched orchard all the day
She heard her sisters calling each to each.
And someone gave, to drive the tears away,
That sulphur-crested bird with great white wings,
The wise, harsh bird—as old and wise as Time
Whose well-dark eyes the wonder kept and closed.
So many years to come and still, he knew,
Brooded that great, dark island continent
Terra Australis.

                    To those fabled shores
Not William Dampier, pirating for gold,
Nor Captain Cook his westward course had set
Jumped from the longboat, waded through the surf,
And clapt his flag ashore at Botany Bay.
Terra Australis, unimagined land—
Only that sulphur-crested bird could tell
Of dark men moving silently through trees,
Of stones and silent dawns, of blackened earth
And the long golden blaze of afternoon.
That vagrant which an ear-ringed sailor caught
(Dropped from the sky, near dead, far out to sea)
And caged and kept, till, landing at the docks,
Walked whistling up the Strand and sold it then,

The curious bird, its cynic eyes half-closed,
To the Duke's steward, drunken at an inn.
And he lived on, the old adventurer,
And kept his counsel, was a sign unread,
A disregarded prologue to an age.
So one might find a meteor from the sun
Or sound one trumpet ere the play's begun.

### Being Called For

Come in at the low-silled window,
Enter by the door through the vine-leaves
Growing over the lintel. I have hung bells at the
Window to be stirred by the breath of your
Coming, which may be at any season.

In winter the snow throws
Light on the ceiling. If you come in winter
There will be a blue shadow before you
Cast on the threshold.

In summer an eddying of white dust
And a brightness falling between the leaves.

When you come I am ready: only, uncertain—
Shall we be leaving at once on another journey?
I would like first to write it all down and leave the pages
On the table weighted with a stone,
Nevertheless I have put in a basket
The coins for the ferry.

# MARIA VALLI

### The Crows[1]

Gentle footsteps on the sand
After sunset.
*What will the weather be like tomorrow?*
The stroll under the airy starlit sky
To drive away the nagging thought.
The meeting, as in a dream,
With two lads and a girl.
Without seeing them I turned round in the darkness
At the sound of the girl's voice,
Longing for what I was about to lose again.
And the lump in my throat
Rose up to the crows
And melted away in their cries.


# ROLAND ROBINSON

### from *The Wanderer*

I reached that waterhole, its mud designed
by tracks of egret, finch, and jabiru,
while in the coming night the moon declined:
a feather floating from a cockatoo.

Ten paces more and there, in painted mime,
against the mountain like a stone-axe dropped,
the spirit-trees stood stricken from the time
the song-sticks, song-man, and the drone-pipe stopped.

Some thrust their arms and hands out in the air,
and some were struck, contorted, on their knees:

[1] Translated from the Italian by A. G. E. Speirs

and deep and still the leaves like unbound hair
lay over limbs and torsos of those trees.

Over their limbs their night still tresses slept;
faint in the stars a wandering night bird creaked.
Then, as towards their company I stepped,
the whole misshapen tribe awoke and shrieked.

And, beating from limbs and leaves, white birds,
like spirits in a terror of strange birth,
streamed out with harsh and inarticulate words
above the mountains, trees, and plains of earth.


### from *Deep Well*

I am at Deep Well where the spirit-trees
writhe in cool white limbs and budgerigar—
green hair along the watercourse carved out
in deep red earth, a red dry course that goes
past the deep well, past the ruined stone
homestead where the wandering blacks make camp
(their campfire burning like a star at rest
among dark ruins of the fallen stone)
to find the spinifex and ochre-red
sandhills of a land inhabited by those
tall dark tribesmen with long hair, and voices
thin and far and, deepening, like a sea.
I am at Deep Well where the fettlers' car
travels towards the cool blue rising wave,
that is the Ooraminna Range, and starts
those pure birds screaming from the scrub to swerve,
reveal their pristine blush in wings and breasts,
to scatter, settle and flower the desert oak.

Here I have chosen to be a fettler, work
to lay the red-gum sleepers, line and spike
the rails with adze and hammer, shovel and bar,
to straighten up and find my mates, myself

lost in the spinifex flowing down in waves
to meet the shadow-sharpened range, and know
myself grown lean and hard again with toil.
Here, in the valley camp where hills increase
in dark blue depths, the desert hakea stands
holding the restless finches and a single star.


## MILTON LOCKYER

### Dark Mountains[1]

Those dark mountains face to face

There sure was a lot of noisy conversation at Pawirra Pool


## YITYANGU ('NEW') EJONG

### Long Song[2]

Tiny children
tiny ones
right in the water


[1] and [2] Translated from the Yindjibarndi by Frank Wordick

# JUDITH WRIGHT

## Wings

Between great coloured vanes the butterflies
drift to the sea with fixed bewildered eyes.

Once all their world was food; then sleep took over,
dressed them in cloaks and furs for some great lover—

some Juan, some Helen. Lifted by air and dream
they rose and circled into heaven's slipstream

to seek each other over fields of blue.
Impassioned unions waited—can't-come-true

images. Blown, a message or a kiss,
earth sent them to the sun's tremendous Yes.

Once met and joined, they sank; complete and brief
their sign was fastened back upon the leaf;

empty of future now, the wind turned cold,
their rich furs worn, they thin to membraned gold.

Poor Rimbauds never able to return
out of the searing rainbows they put on,

their wings have trapped them. Staring helplessly
they blow beyond the headland, to the sea.


## Bullocky

Beside his heavy-shouldered team,
thirsty with drought and chilled with rain,
he weathered all the striding years
till they ran widdershins in his brain:

Till the long solitary tracks
etched deeper with each lurching load
were populous before his eyes,
and fiends and angels used his road.

All the long straining journey grew
a mad apocalyptic dream,
and he old Moses, and the slaves
his suffering and stubborn team.

Then in his evening camp beneath
the half-light pillars of the trees
he filled the steepled cone of night
with shouted prayers and prophecies.

While past the campfire's crimson ring
the star-struck darkness cupped him round,
and centuries of cattlebells
rang with their sweet uneasy sound.

Grass is across the waggon-tracks,
and plough strikes bone beneath the grass,
and vineyards cover all the slopes
where the dead teams were used to pass.

O vine, grow close upon that bone
and hold it with your rooted hand.
The prophet Moses feeds the grape,
and fruitful is the Promised Land.

from *The Blind Man*

COUNTRY DANCE

The dance in the township hall is nearly over.
Hours ago the stiff-handed wood-cheeked women
got up from the benches round the walls
and took home their aching eyes and weary children.

Mrs McLarty with twenty cows to milk
before dawn, went with the music stinging
like sixty wasps under her best dress.
Eva Callaghan whose boy died in the army
sat under the streamers like a house to let
and went alone, a black pot brimming with tears.
'Once my body was a white cedar, my breasts the buds on the
    quince-tree,
that now are fallen and grey like logs on a cleared hill.
Then why is my blood not quiet? what is the good
of the whips of music stinging along my blood?'


The dance in the township hall is nearly over.
Outside in the yard the fire like a great red city
eats back into the log, its noisy flames fallen.
Jimmy Dunn has forgotten his camp in the hills
and sleeps like a heap of rags beside a bottle.
The young boys sit and stare at the heart of the city
thinking of the neon lights and the girls at the corners
with lips like coals and thighs as silver as florins.
Jock Hamilton thinks of the bally cow gone sick
and the cockatoos in the corn and the corn ready to pick
and the wires in the thirty-acre broken.
Oh, what rats nibble at the cords of our nerves?
When will the wires break, the ploughed paddocks lie open,
the bow of the fiddle saw through the breast-bone,
the dream be done, and we waken?


Streamers and boughs are falling, the dance grows faster.
Only the lovers and the young are dancing
now at the end of a dance, in a trance or singing.
Say the lovers locked together and crowned with coloured paper,
'The bit of black glass I picked up out of the campfire
is the light the moon puts on your hair.'
'The green pool I swam in under the willows
is the drowning depth, the summer night of your eyes.'
'You are the death I move to.' 'O burning weapon,
you are the pain I long for.'

Stars, leaves and streamers fall in the dark dust
and the blind man lies alone in his sphere of night.

Oh, I,
red centre of a dark and burning sky,
fit my words to music, my crippled words to music,
and sing to the fire with the voice of the fire.
Go sleep with your grief, go sleep with your desire,
go deep into the core of night and silence.
But I hold all of it, your hate and sorrow,
your passion and your fear; I am the breath
that holds you from your death.
I am the voice of music and the ended dance.

### Woman to Man

The eyeless labourer in the night,
the selfless, shapeless seed I hold,
builds for its resurrection day—
silent and swift and deep from sight
foresees the unimagined light.

This is no child with a child's face;
this has no name to name it by:
yet you and I have known it well.
This is our hunter and our chase,
the third who lay in our embrace.

This is the strength that your arm knows,
the arc of flesh that is my breast,
the precise crystals of our eyes.
This is the blood's wild tree that grows
the intricate and folded rose.

This is the maker and the made;
this is the question and reply;
the blind head butting at the dark,
the blaze of light along the blade.
Oh hold me, for I am afraid.

## Eli, Eli

To see them go by drowning in the river—
soldiers and elders drowning in the river,
the pitiful women drowning in the river,
the children's faces staring from the river—
that was his cross, and not the cross they gave him.

To hold the invisible wand, and not to save them—
to know them turned to death, and yet not save them;
only to cry to them and not to save them,
knowing that no one but themselves could save them—
this was the wound, more than the wound they dealt him.

To hold out love and know they would not take it,
to hold out faith and know they dared not take it—
the invisible wand, and none would see or take it,
all he could give, and there was none to take it—
thus they betrayed him, not with the tongue's betrayal.

He watched, and they were drowning in the river;
faces like sodden flowers in the river—
faces of children moving in the river;
and all the while, he knew there was no river.

## Request to a Year

If the year is meditating a suitable gift,
I should like it to be the attitude
of my great-great-grandmother,
legendary devotee of the arts,

who, having had eight children
and little opportunity for painting pictures,
sat one day on a high rock
beside a river in Switzerland

and from a difficult distance viewed
her second son, balanced on a small ice-floe,
drift down the current towards a waterfall
that struck rock-bottom eighty feet below,

while her second daughter, impeded,
no doubt, by the petticoats of the day,
stretched out a last-hope alpenstock
(which luckily later caught him on his way).

Nothing, it was evident, could be done;
and with the artist's isolating eye
my great-great-grandmother hastily sketched the scene.
The sketch survives to prove the story by.

Year, if you have no Mother's day present planned;
reach back and bring me the firmness of her hand.


from *Habitat*

IV

Furniture: humble, dependent,
asking for nothing
except to be there, to be used,
to be let stay around,
like an ageing aunt
waiting to hold the new baby.

Once in a street
I saw two old chairs
put out for the rubbish-collector.
They were shamed; their patches and stains
like age-spots and tear-tracks,
their bony legs
thin and bowed, their laps
suddenly empty.

Furniture likes its own place,
wears its way into carpets.
Move it around, even,
it looks dispossessed.
People are all it has left
of forests, of living and growing,
which is why furniture likes us,
can be betrayed.

Mirrors: cool ones.
Too quick on the uptake,
they've got all the snap answers before you.
They follow you round
and observe you.
They remember you instantly
like clever policemen,
and keep on reminding you
how you looked ten years ago.

Mirrors lie waiting in tombs.
Etruscan ladies
tried to take them along;
but glibly and faithlessly
they answer the tomb-robber.
They wait smooth and calm in the night
utterly certain
daylight will come back and find them
contemporary,
relevant,
quite up on the issues.

Mirrors repeat and repeat
that we're vain and ugly,
but will always need mirrors.
Only the final bomb
will melt the last mirror
with the last face.

What will the last face
look like?
Mirrors know.
It will contain all faces, all
human history
(which mirrors remember).

Shatter them: every knife-sharp bit
is a mirror, cursing you
seven years long.
Even their wooden frames
wince back, sensitive
as fingernails clipped too close,
from their ice-blink.

Mirrors reverse us.
Mirrors are mathematics,
reason, logic.
They stare at each other and demonstrate
Infinite Regress:
Reductio ad Absurdum:
Eternity: Zero:
the Cyclical Theory:
Vanitas Vanitatum.

Furniture wears out and dies.
Mirrors
never.

### VI

The charity lotteries for Dream Houses
will always succeed.
They build on a deep base.
Women are always dreaming
about houses.

My own are always large,
faintly decaying,
with some rooms empty.

Their shadowy corridors
hide more than spiders.
Their front rooms are handsome,
but the action goes on at the back.

No one I know
lives in them.
They're occupied and guarded
by inner familiars:
the Two Black Villains,
the Handsome Man,
the Idiot Boy.
It's the women I know best:
the very old lady,
the child who follows me,
the Guide with Brown Hair
and the rest of the cast.

Heraldic animals
stand at the garden entrance.
My snakes are at home there.
We all play in difficult dramas
I can't quite interpret.

What's cooking in the kitchen?
Who's crying in the passage?
I wake and worry
but don't find the answers.

And outside—ah, outside!
The juggernaut machines,
the blue drifting gases,
the crashing aircraft!
Even a dream-house
can be a refuge.

But who wants them modern?
I'm happy with dust in the corners
and the old cast
to rehearse with.

## Tableau

Bent over, staggering in panic or despair
from post to parking-meter in the hurried street,
he seemed to gesture at me,
as though we had met again; had met somewhere
forgotten, and now for the last time had to meet.

And I debated with myself; ought I to go
over the road—since no one stopped to ask
or even stand and look—
abandon my own life awhile and show
I was too proud to shirk that ant-like task?

And finally went. His almost vanished voice
accepted me; he gave himself to my hold,
*(pain, cancer—keep me still).*
We leaned on a drinking-fountain, fused in the vice
of a double pain; his sweat dropped on me cold.

Holding him up as he asked till the ambulance came,
among the sudden curious crowd, I knew
his plunging animal heart,
against my flesh the shapes of his too-young bone,
the heaving pattern of ribs. As still I do.

Warding the questioners, bearing his rack of weight,
I drank our strange ten minutes of embrace,
and watched him whiten there,
the drenched poverty of his slender face.
We could have been desperate lovers met too late.

## Australia 1970

Die wild country, like the eaglehawk,
dangerous till the last breath's gone,
clawing and striking. Die
cursing your captor through a raging eye.

Die like the tigersnake
that hisses such pure hatred from its pain
as fills the killer's dreams
with fear like suicide's invading stain.

Suffer, wild country, like the ironwood
that gaps the dozer-blade.
I see your living soil ebb with the tree
to naked poverty.

Die like the soldier-ant
mindless and faithful to your million years.
Though we corrupt you with our torturing mind,
stay obstinate; stay blind.

For we are conquerors and self-poisoners
more than scorpion or snake
and dying of the venoms that we make
even while you die of us.

I praise the scoring drought, the flying dust,
the drying creek, the furious animal,
that they oppose us still;
that we are ruined by the thing we kill.


# KATH WALKER

*We are Going*
For Grannie Coolwell

They came in to the little town
A semi-naked band subdued and silent,
All that remained of their tribe.
They came here to the place of their old bora ground
Where now the many white men hurry about like ants.
Notice of estate agent reads: 'Rubbish May Be Tipped Here'.

Now it half covers the traces of the old bora ring.
They sit and are confused, they cannot say their thoughts:
'We are as strangers here now, but the white tribe are the strangers.
We belong here, we are of the old ways.
We are the corroboree and the bora ground,
We are the old sacred ceremonies, the laws of the elders.
We are the wonder tales of Dream Time, the tribal legends told.
We are the past, the hunts and the laughing games, the wandering
    camp fires.
We are the lightning-bolt over Gaphembah Hill
Quick and terrible,
And the Thunderer after him, that loud fellow.
We are the quiet daybreak paling the dark lagoon.
We are the shadow-ghosts creeping back as the camp fires burn low.
We are nature and the past, all the old ways
Gone now and scattered.
The scrubs are gone, the hunting and the laughter.
The eagle is gone, the emu and the kangaroo are gone from this place.
The bora ring is gone.
The corroboree is gone.
And we are going.'

### Dawn Wail for the Dead

    Dim light of daybreak now
    Faintly over the sleeping camp.
    Old lubra first to wake remembers:
    First thing every dawn
    Remember the dead, cry for them.
    Softly at first her wail begins,
    One by one as they wake and hear
    Join in the cry, and the whole camp
    Wails for the dead, the poor dead
    Gone from here to the Dark Place:
    They are remembered.
    Then it is over, life now,
    Fires lit, laughter now,
    And a new day calling.

# BRALGU SONG

## *Djalbarmiwi's Song*[1]

Ah, the blowfly is whining there, its maggots are eating the flesh.
The blowflies buzz, their feet stray over the corpse.
The buzzing goes on and on.
Who is it, eating there, whose flesh are they eating?
Ah, my daughter, come back to me here!
Ah, our daughter was taken ill—
You didn't sing for her as a father should.
You are foolish and silly, you sing only to please the ears of women.
You like to lie close to a young girl, a virgin, and give her a child.
You will not stay in one place;
Here and there, all over the place, you go among the camps,
You go walking hither and thither, looking for sweethearts.
Ah, before it was here that you used to stay.
You should be ashamed to do that before all these strangers!
Presently I will take up a knife and cut you!
(*Banggalawi says:* 'This is all that I do: I get food to eat and tobacco to
    smoke.')
No, you go to sit down beside some woman,
You sit close, close beside her . . .
Ah, my lost sick child—ah, the blowflies.
Soon I will hit that woman of yours, that Yandin. She is rubbish
    that woman of yours, her face is ugly, she smells like an
    evil spirit. Presently when she is pregnant, I won't look
    after her! You, Banggalawi, you her husband, you indeed,
    all by yourself, you can help her in childbirth!

[1] Translated from the Djambarbingu dialect by Catherine Berndt

## LIAGARANG

### Snails[1]

Sound of snails—crying,
Sound drifting through the bush, sound of crying.
Slime of snails, dragging themselves
Along the low-lying plain, crying;
Snails with their slime, crying.
Sound drifting through the bush: dragging themselves along,
        crying,
Snails, their sound blowing overhead from among the bushes.


## DAVID CAMPBELL

### Ariel

Frost and snow, frost and snow:
The old ram scratches with a frozen toe
At silver tussocks in the payable mist
And stuffs his belly like a treasure chest.

His tracks run green up the mountainside
Where he throws a shadow like a storm-cloud's hide;
He has tossed the sun in a fire of thorns,
And a little bird whistles between his horns.

'Sweet-pretty-creature!' sings the matchstick bird,
And on height and in chasm his voice is heard;
Like a bell of ice or the crack of the frost
It rings in the ears of his grazing host.

'Sweet-pretty-creature!' While all is as still
As the bird on the ram on the frozen hill,
O the wagtail warms to his tiny art
And glaciers move through the great beast's heart.

[1] Translated from the Dharlwangu dialect by Ronald M. Berndt

## Night Sowing

O gentle, gentle land
Where the green ear shall grow,
Now you are edged with light:
The moon has crisped the fallow,
The furrows run with night.

This is the season's hour:
While couples are in bed,
I sow the paddocks late,
Scatter like sparks the seed
And see the dark ignite.

O gentle land, I sow
The heart's living grain.
Stars draw their harrows over,
Dews send their melting rain:
I meet you as a lover.

## On Frosty Days

On frosty days, when I was young,
I rode out early with the men
And mustered cattle till their long
Blue shadows covered half the plain;

And when we turned our horses round,
Only the homestead's point of light,
Men's voices, and the bridles' sound,
Were left in the enormous night.

And now again the sun has set
All yellow and a greening sky
Sucks up the colour from the wheat—
And here's my horse, my dog and I.

## Pallid Cuckoo

Alone the pallid cuckoo now
Fills his clear bottles in the dew:
Four five six seven—climb with him!
And eight brings morning to the brim.

Then from green hills in single file
My ewes and lambs come down the scale:
Four three two one—the matrons pass
And fill their bellies up with grass.

But in the evening light the lambs
Forget their hillward-munching dams;
To cuckoo pipes their dances start
And fill and overflow the heart.

## Fox

When a green fox looks
Into a still pool
Creek stones look back
At the fox looking in.

When I look in the pool
Of her green eyes
I catch a man
Bathing naked.

Shedding disguises
In her clear eyes
I rest as still
As stones in a pool.

And the little green fox
Looks down at me
Where I lie in the bed
Of her still eyes.

## The Australian Dream

The doorbell buzzed. It was past three o'clock.
The steeple-of-Saint-Andrew's weathercock
Cried silently to darkness, and my head
Was bronze with claret as I rolled from bed
To ricochet from furniture. Light! Light
Blinded the stairs, the hatstand sprang upright
I fumbled with the lock, and on the porch
Stood the Royal Family with a wavering torch.

'We hope,' the Queen said, 'we do not intrude.
The pubs were full, most of our subjects rude.
We came before our time. It seems the Queen's
Command brings only, "Tell the dead marines!"
We've come to you.' I must admit I'd half
Expected just this visit. With a laugh
That put them at their ease, I bowed my head.
'Your Majesty is most welcome here,' I said.
'My home is yours. There is a little bed
Downstairs, a boiler-room, might suit the Duke.'
He thanked me gravely for it and he took
Himself off with a wave. 'Then the Queen Mother?
She'd best bed down with you. There is no other
But my wide bed. I'll curl up in a chair.'
The Queen looked thoughtful. She brushed out her hair
And folded up *The Garter* on a pouf.
'Distress was the first commoner, and as proof
That queens bow to the times,' she said, 'we three
Shall share the double bed. Please follow me.'

I waited for the ladies to undress—
A sense of fitness, even in distress,
Is always with me. They had tucked away
Their state robes in the lowboy; gold crowns lay
Upon the bedside tables; ropes of pearls
Lassoed the plastic lampshade; their soft curls
Were spread out on the pillows and they smiled.
'Hop in,' said the Queen Mother. In I piled

Between them to lie like a stick of wood.
I couldn't find a thing to say. My blood
Beat, but like rollers at the ebb of tide.
'I hope your Majesties sleep well,' I lied.
A hand touched mine and the Queen said, 'I am
Most grateful to you, Jock. Please call me Ma'am.'


### Mr Hughes

When my grandmother left the races with Mr Hughes,
She left at the same time eight children and a husband
The committee deeply loved. She waved a hand
And Mr Hughes was dressed in purples and blues.
He kissed the hand and listened to her views
Which did not surprise him. He bought newspapers and
Confectionery and said in yellow grand-
Mother looked delightful. He was a goose;
And she never regretted leaving the maids, the flies,
The paddocks and the children—not to mention
That house and its verandahs. Throwing up her eyes,
There was the ferry greening into Mosman—
So convenient. Her rooms were bright if snug.
Mr Hughes smiled like a tiger from the rug.


### Ulinda

There was a duck egg as green as the evening sky.
Trout hovered in the horse-trough. The road was white
And vanished like a headache in sheets of light
And pale blue mountains. The homestead creek was dry
And warm with pebbles. Grandfather said that *Why?*
Was a crooked letter. His beard got in his plate.
'Milk grandfather. Sugar grandfather.' 'Now that
Is just what I can't have.' And he winked the bluest eye.
It was like the duck egg. We were only playing a game,
But mother left the table; so we ran along.
One sundown they butchered a pig and I saw it scream.
I held my ears and it went on screaming. 'What's wrong?'
They said. 'It's only a dream.' But I sang in my dream:
'Grandfather's dying. He's going to die,' I sang.

## JOHN BLIGHT

### *The Gate's Open*

The paddock's a lonely space to stay inside
when the gate's open to the whole world wide.
I'd step outside, were I Macpherson's bull,
and bluff the world at large. How wonderful
to bail up Jock Macpherson on the road,
make him remember God and all Jock owed,
then stamp the mushrooms after August rain
like organ stops, hear early thunder, plain;
and roar and scrape the dust and bust a fence
to raise the cost of beef and—damn expense!

Always a quiet flat where clover, late
in the winter, blossoms with an earthy spate
of scent and discontent for cows—ah, cows!
the women that I love! forget the vows,
devotion to the breed cooped at the stud,
and let us mix a little earth with blood.


### *Down from the Country*

When we came down from the country, we were strangers to the sea.
The rise and fall of waters without rain,
the lunglike breathing of the estuary
caused our amazement; and the white stain
of salt on the rocks, when the tide receded,
where we were used to dark mud that a flood leaves behind,
held us enthralled; and we needed
some mental adjustment which people noticed. When the mind
is confronted by such magnitudes of sight and sound
there is no mask for refuge in frown or grimace;
but the face looks blank, as if it were dragged up, drowned.

How much loneliness is there in a different place,
out of one's shell, out of all knowledge, to be caught
out of the dullness of self by such alien thought?

## Cormorants

The sea has it this way: if you see
cormorants, they are the pattern for the eye.
In the sky, on the rocks, in the water—shags!
To think of them every way: I see them, oily rags
flung starboard from some tramp and washed
on to rocks, flung up by the waves, squashed
into sock-shapes with the foot up; sooty birds
wearing white, but not foam-white; swearing, not words.
but blaspheming with swastika-gesture, wing-hinge to nose;
ugly grotesqueries, all in a shag's pose.
And beautifully ugly for their being shags,
not partly swans. When the eye searches for rags,
it does not seek muslin, white satin; nor,
for its purpose, does the sea adorn shags more.

## Death of a Whale

When the mouse died, there was a sort of pity:
the tiny, delicate creature made for grief.
Yesterday, instead, the dead whale on the reef
drew an excited multitude to the jetty.
How must a whale die to wring a tear?
Lugubrious death of a whale: the big
feast for the gulls and sharks; the tug
of the tide simulating life still there,
until the air, polluted, swings this way
like a door ajar from a slaughterhouse.
Pooh! pooh! spare us, give us the death of a mouse
by its tiny hole; not this in our lovely bay.
—Sorry we are, too, when a child dies;
but at the immolation of a race who cries?

## Pearl Perch

There are those fish that swim ever in the dim
recesses of the reef. A visit near
the surface means their swift demise. They can rise,

but never high as flying-fish that skim
across the seas, fleeing from deeper fear.

Yet I have ever marvelled at their eyes
when I have hauled a specimen aboard,
upon the deck have seen their gaze despise
our meaner air, and stigmatise our skies
by dying; seeing nothing to accord
with their deep consciousness—no Lord,
no Saviour? No Saviour! Have I, too, seen amiss
the airy vacuum of heaven where
these eyes at last leak out their dying stare?


### Morgan

More than Morgan, I desire to eat people,
wondering in a frenzy—are there any
white-skinned cannibals remaining?
        It must take place now in the very high
buildings. I have seen hawks there.
There are just bones of people, clothes picked
to rags ... their eyes, pools of blood ... some
in the cramped pose of old clothes thrown down
in a bundle awaiting their collection
        by the in city police at nine-o'clock
when the white cars prowl again near
the odd parks and places. It is enough
now to lift my eyes, because I see it
all again—the wild hide-out, Morgan would
        have accepted.


### Evolution

Remember, while you are sleeping here, offshore
in the night, less than a suburb away, more
than a suburb of people in numbers, the fish
are awake and swimming much as they wish.

For they had their design to evolve as fish; just
as your ancestors escaped from the primal dust
to be sportive in trees, and walk on the earth.

Remember the incidence of birth
which made them fish, you man? Yet can you
take comfort from your shape as man; or do
you wake in the night with them, hear swish
and slap of a tide; knowing to have your wish
again, to evolve as angel now, you must do these things;
don sheets, wear stars in your hair, fix tinsel wings?


### The Letter

Better one thin frail line of friendship in a letter
lonely as a lost white glove, than never
knowing your whereabouts; in which poxed port
of travel guessing you ailed in fetter
of fever, hunger, or anguish of ever
finding your way to return. Resort
to pen and paper leaves not much more
than a pale white dream of doubt—much as I said,
your lost white glove; but in my hand
a dream of substance, form that you once wore.
It fitted your slight hand; and from it sped
like a white bird of welcome to this land
—much as I said, like a lost white glove.
I have it pressed to me, this hour, with love.


### Tenant at Number 9

Predicament: a corner of
a room in which my woman smokes
but is terrified of mice and
there's a mouse shuttling the skirting-
boards between her and the door. So
late, so slow a strain to lay her

on my bed . . . now to unload her
I have to slay a mouse.

                     God!
she is standing on my pallet,
naked as Venus though she's far
as Saturn from such perfections
of sightliness. A minority
of hands—two; insufficient to
cover all points and parts.

                    Standing
(I remind you) on my pallet near
an uncurtained window across
which I've hastily draped only
my shirt. They'll see her torso with
the arms snapped off to outside eyes
and gasp at the latest vitals
of the new de Milo.

                  Curse mice
for living in holes.

                 Fatigued as
a spavined cart-horse in a race,
I'd rather not this hurdle to
front up. Now, if my landlady's
returning from the food-mart with
fruit: lemons and . . .
whatever over-ripe fruit she
may scrounge; their reds, their yellows
will change to the dirty grey of my
blankets (mould in the streets).

                  She'll
rush indoors and bang on mine—her
tenant in number 9, her free
guest, her have-you-to-myself
lover.

Oh, the miserly nibbling of
mice! I feel the darkness creeping
out of their holes, filling the room
like a flood and flushing me out.


## J.  R.  ROWLAND

### A Traveller

Here the round begins again
A bed, a mirror, and four walls
An empty wardrobe and a chair.

Lift from its case your folded life
Secured beneath that hard dry skin
Shake it and hang it up to air:

Through much compression and long use
The creases will not leave the stuff
All have their habits in the layer

Sooner or later they expect
To fall in their accustomed place
Within the shell, to reappear

Where other mirrors will reflect
A bending figure, or a hand
Sifting through hair as if through sand.


### London

As if some irremediable poison
Were secretly destroying sight, and you stood to watch,
Without even horror, the development of blindness,
The quiet approach of the horizon

Fading towards you in perpetual twilight—
So this city and season circumscribe the stranger
With a mild prison of blues and greys, where darkness
Is always implied in light

No view is long, and nothing is sharp or dry:
A foreshortened landscape, limited by forests
Of elegant trees or chimneys, formal patterns
Dovegrey in a dovelike sky.

In the web of a breathing noon,
The neutrality of a dying world, the streets
And shadows are elusive as ghosts, and a low infernal
Sun swims, round as the moon

Till evening in a denser net
Gathers up sight and sound, soon leaving only
A bombed wall darkening, and a swollen treetrunk
Poisonously green and bursting with the wet.


## DOROTHY AUCHTERLONIE

### *Waiting for the Post*

No black and swirling cloak, no faceless grin,
No poised and shining scythe, no hour-glass . . .
Death has a freckled nose and wears a khaki shirt,
And rides a bicycle. I watch him pass

Day after day, climbing the same hill—
The housewives time him by their kitchen-clocks.
Today I see him pause, undo his bag,
And drop a letter in my box.

I hear it fall, and hear the whistle blow
Its shrill parody as he walks on up the hill.
I hold my doomed love in my trembling hand:
The earth turns over, though the street is still.

## Meditation of a Mariner

When you scuttled the ship, the shore was still in sight,
You were in good fettle, swimming strongly, the enemy withdrawn
For a moment, perhaps discouraged and in full flight;
The sea was clear, slow-moving, flowing east to the dawn.

And it was a fine piece of driftwood came floating past,
Buoyant and hard, just as your arms began to fail.
You could hang on now for hours, days, weeks, perhaps, till at last
You caught a glimpse of smoke to windward, or was it a sail?

It was then that the unsuspected foe struck from the smiling sea
And took the fingers of your right hand at a blow,
The red stump trailed in the water uselessly,
Inviting a second monster from the depths below.

The sail has hardly moved—no doubt a painted illusion,
Born of solitude and the sea's immensity, and pain.
The remaining fingers still hold on, in deep confusion,
While the enemy bides his moment and will strike again.

Why do you will them to hold, those cold, cold fingers?
Loosen their grip and put an end to doubt and death!
Is it that hope of touching land still lingers,
Or mere joy of breathing, while you still have breath?
Is hand simply to hold, to grip: is that the whole story,
The last affirmation, the only deed of glory?


## DIMITRIS TSALOUMAS

from *A Rhapsody of Old Men*[1]
VII

They brought him one morning
O unbearable beauty
of my mornings

[1] Translated from the Greek by Margaret Carroll

poppies still stain with blood
the floors of memory
and daisies untrodden
cover with gentle white
the paths of death.

Erect and sinless I
on the edge of vineyards
touched by vine shoots—
and suddenly his eyes
demented,
glance of a frightened hare
indelibly upon me.

They hurried him past,
he in the middle,
and above the uphill road
and the dust of wheels
the shouting of gendarmes
and unseemly laughter
on the birthday of my immortality.

And they handed him over in
the wilderness of prickly pear
beyond the barricade of cicadas
where the mind smashes
like a pigeon against a door-pane
falling
with a blood clot on its beak.

Later, poets came
weaving wreaths of barbed wire
and threnodies of song,
and I was left alone with my nights
to fight, indestructible,
the look of his necessity
and the stigma of my shame.

# DAVID ROWBOTHAM

## *Mullabinda*

A fig-tree, a falling woolshed, a filled-in well:
The acute corners of one man's figure of hell . . .
When the tree was young and the well deep and the shed
Mullabinda, these three and Campbell's sheep
Were Campbell's pride—before this northern sweep
Of channelling shallows marked the Queensland-side;
Before death speared and drained the day to dark,
And Campbell, riding home, heard no dog bark.

His broad and glaring mare snorted at the ford
And splashed cold fear into his eyes and beard
With hooves restlessly obedient and ominous.
Upstream, on the highest bank, through the blowing rows
Of wind-break coolabahs, the cypress pine
Of Mullabinda, slabbed between the shine
And pillared strength of bloodwood, rose a violence,
A smokeless shock of fortress stormed by silence.

He heeled the mare to the gallop in his heart.
'Keep clear of the trees, close to the house. At night
Bar the door and open to no stranger,'
He had said, then kissed away the rape of danger
In her eyes, and (gently), 'Take the gun to the well
And when you water the fig.' A voice replied, 'I will . . .'
Inside the coolabahs the broad mare shied,
And a wind struck through and broke down Campbell's pride.

'I found my wife murdered at the well,
The boy with a bucket in his hand and a spear
In his back beside the fig, the girl on a chair
In the house, clubbed like a little animal.
I beg Your Excellency's kind permission to kill.
I remain Your Excellency's humble servant—Campbell.'
The graves were heaped, and the special licence came,
And Mullabinda Campbell rode after game.

The target-circles of black breasts, glistening, hung
Thick-nipple-centred over the billabong,
And paddling and playing in pools of water and sun,
The piccaninnies turned plump bellies to the gun,
Teasing the tiny apex of the steely sight ...
The legends ricochetted with each report;
Till stone thoughts filled the well of his heart, and age
Made a crumbling woolshed of his slab-hard rage.

Time grooved him like the bloodwood; but deep in the dried
And channelled country of his being where pride
Once flooded to the full, whispered and grew the fig-tree,
Fruitless, but a wild, green and rooted memory,
Growing on, long after the vengeful spear,
Thumping his shoulders out of the quiet air,
Acquitted him of hate, and of tree, shed, well—
Mullabinda Campbell's estimate of hell.


### Prey to Prey

The birds come like fishes out of the air
And fishes out of the encountering sea, like birds,
And meet in the murderous limit that they share,
Fins and wings thunderous, without words.

And fishes into the air, birds into the sea,
Die, and the wind and water scatter their death;
And whatever in nature made them enemy
Made them as prey to prey, without wrath.

And this is the cold compulsion to be feared
If men as heirs to these should likewise meet,
Humanity to nature nothing or unheard,
The hunger total, battering without retreat,

With none from the encounter as none even here
Being borne back though the world they inhabited wait,
But all in their own wounds and the floundering air
Sea-dead, having died so without even hate.

# GEOFFREY DUTTON

### The Stranded Whales
for Maggie Matison

There were the whales, six of them,
    Stranded like panting mothers
On the amiable, deadly sand,
    And the word soon got around
In the deadly weekend town
    So the aniline Holdens and Datsuns
Disgorged all ages and sizes
    Thick as whitebait on the sand
Softly golden under the blueblack whales.
    They ran up the sides of the gasping creatures
That had been three days dying already
    And had two more days to live.
They came armed with domestic weapons,
    Curved pruning saws, axes, kitchen knives,
Workshop hacksaws, some even with ladders,
    And these do-it-yourself amiable weekend people
Climbed up on the heaving whales and chopped out
    Bloody gussets of blubber and tossed them down to the kids
While the dying whales shook out slack spouts of bubbling breath.
    One lad with long blond hair, wobbling on a ladder,
Scooped out a whale's eye with a trowel
    And stuffed it down the front of his girlfriend's jeans,
While a leathery home carpenter of fifty,
    With separate hairs greased down across his skull,
Levered open the living jaws the size of his front door
    And with a hacksaw cut out a couple of teeth.
One man amiably fervid with patriotism
    Stuck a pole flying the Southern Cross
Straight down a whale's shuddering blowhole,
    And a lady teacher with a knowledge of biology
Succeeded at last in slicing, though slippery with blood,
    And giggly, a complete anterior fin,
Which will reveal, when cleaned down to the skeleton,
An arm, a hand and five fingers, just like a human's.

At the end of the weekend, after five days,
   The whales were at last, though not moving,
Going from dying to dead.
   Only their blood had found the way back to the sea
Down the little ripply side channels
   Beyond the emerald shallows to stain the deep sapphire
Till the deadly hunters came after the treasure of blood,
   Beating the water into a pink froth of frustration.
The weekenders gouging their black mountains grew nervous,
   Slid down with their trophies and went off homewards.

So the whales died, and putrefied, and quarrelling over their carcases
   The District Council said they had come from the sea
And thus were not a Council responsibility,
   While the Marine and Harbours Board said they had died on land
And thus were not a Marine and Harbours responsibility.

   No one wanted the whales at all.
Only the fire, when they were bulldozed into heaps
   And burnt, lovingly stayed with them
For as many days as they had taken to die.

## Time of Waiting

He will sit at the bare table, reading a dictionary,
Glancing at his watch, waiting for time to begin,
As it has already, on some heat-struck pavement
Contradicted by a cool summer dress
Disguising an urgency of limbs, till at last
Through the heavy semi-silence of the city
Breaks her light step along the empty corridor
And words and minutes fall like clothing to the floor.

# RAY MATHEW

### Lover's Meeting

Why is it,
that even with the cicadas' shrilling sound
so locust-loud it seems that heat has found
a voice, the land stays silent, the waters of its bay
stainless steel, and its trees quiet?

It is because there is nothing to say,
because there is nothing to be said.

Why is it,
that even with sunlight losing light
to the leaves in water-turn of bright unbright,
the leaves seem silent, and the crow-call far away,
mere hovering on the land's quiet?

It is because there is nothing to say,
because there is nothing to be said.

Why is it,
that even with the heart so loud with love
the rock so cool to hold the sky above
so frail to touch the light so fluid to stay,
that tongue makes words, but heart is quiet?

It is because there is nothing to say,
because there is nothing to be said.

### A Good Thing

But this fruit-dish (I suppose it is for fruit;
The reason for its being never was)
Was made by human hands. You see the dent.
The maker trembled and the shape was lost,
Or found; you can determine which: I can't

Insist but this bowl seems to me
Most perfect imperfection. It seems good.
Besides it has a story, has some point—
As human things must have if they are true.
The girl that made it was a girl I loved.
And she loved me, while she was making this.
You see her fingers trembled, made a dent
That gathered all the glaze and ruined it
For those that want the smoothness of machines.
I wanted love, and found the whole thing good.

And later, when the girl and I were mad,
Our sensible arrangement fallen true,
Shouting at one another in a little room
As though we stood a block or two apart,
Calling each other stranger, stronger, and destroyer—
As though the words might somehow say our thought—
Nothing the world held in that crowded room,
Not bed nor desk, not talk, not thought, not self
Had any truth or being; nothing real:
The whole thing stagy, someone's clever book.
Only this bowl that she made with her hands
Seemed real enough to make our hatred false.
So real she lifted it to smash but said,
My God, it's good! And we both laughed. And so
The dish survived. And later, as two sane
Intelligences should, we parted; no bitterness, no smash.
She left the bowl with me. And that is that.


### Wynyard Sailor

Sailor, we all stare at you.
Not because we are laughing;
nor that we envy
the bottle on your hip
(beer as we know should be cold),
and that girl with her grip
monkey-tight in your pocket
(better the blondes that grow old).

Sailor, we all stare at you.
Not because we are laughing,
although your wide trousers
go flippety-flap
(we have worn clothes as odd),
and, if your hat
makes a sailor-suit boy of you—
they say it's the young who are God.

Sailor, we all stare at you,
because you are mystery:
one who has walked
on the dark of the green,
while we were afraid to be drowned;
one who has been
with the seas of great silence,
and now touches ground.

Sailor, we all stare at you,
because death has been under you;
days have been seas;
you have cast off from land,
and now you've no home.
While we who have manned
this old coffin earth
have never, will never
face death having known.


FRANCIS  WEBB

*This Runner*

This runner on his final lap
Sucks wildly for elusive air;
Space is a vortex, time's a gap,
Seconds are shells that hiss and flare
Between red mist and cool white day
Four hundred throttling yards away.

Each spike-shod muscle, yelping nerve,
Worries, snaps at his stumbling weight;
He goes wide on this floating curve,
Cursing with crazy, hammering hate
A rival glued to inside ground
Who flogs his heart, forces him round.

Friends, here is your holiday;
Admire your image in this force
While years, books, flesh and mind give way
To the sheer fury of the source.
Here is your vicious, central shape
That has no need of cheer or tape.

## The Sea

Mile and mile and mile; but no one would gather
That we are running from something; peremptory hours
Examine, order, condemn; all the stars patter together,
A heathen tongue, while our homesick storytelling fires
Are Hellas mouthing, burning;
Little dangerous men attack without warning;
We loot and kill, singing hopelessly in the foreign morning.

And the guide from Gymnias—none of us trusts him, but here
We kick anthills, villages tickling his queasy city;
At fear's uplifted finger, fear ravages fear.
Ghosts of an army, of a people, how might we have pity?
Pity is none of our pain
As, dutifully, dully, we prod blaze for bone.
Talents wink witlessly as we shamble on.

And counterfeit silver on the dry salt leaves of his promise;
Still, in profile, he is our medal of the kill.
See, the sun's withers, letting blood, inform us
Of frightened villages past this giant hill.
—But new rioting overhead:
The little dangerous men? Let us double up to our dead
As the tail of the serpent lashes back to his battered head.

Chorus, tempest, O canting heavy cruse of oil . . .
The sea! And this bay, a carved golden gymnasium
With alarums of the coastal birds that dip and wheel:
Famous, jockeying, muscular, the waves come
Putting their silver weights
Of spray so vehemently. Genesis of lights!
Odysseus begs and prays his passage through the gates.

We call, we fall on our knees, and we embrace.
But Zeus, but Zeus, it is lungs, a living tongue:
These years are resolved in the shapely lips of peace.
Dead men of Melos enter, carefree and young,
To wash all blood from our hands.
We raise an altar of stones; the chanting winds
Fret godly cliff-face for yellow coin of sands.

And our guide? stockstill, the half-smile, the dumb anger.
Something is lost to him, finding itself at the breast.
But something makes obeisance with rings for that thin finger.
A horse, a goblet, money. Something may not rest:
Tatterdemalion—see—
Ten thousand ghosts flutter after him. And we
Turn again to our mother, our revels. The sea, the sea!


### The Gunner

When the gunner spoke in his sleep the hut was still,
Uneasily strapped to the reckless wheel of his will;
Silence, humble, directionless as fog.
Lifted, and minutes were rhythmical on the log;

While slipstream plucked at a wafer of glass and steel,
Engines sliced and scooped at the air's thin wall,
And those dim spars dislodged from the moon became
Red thongs of tracer whipping boards aflame.

Listening, you crouched in the turret, watchful and taut
—*Bogey two thousand, skipper, corkscrew to port*—
Marvellous, the voice: driving electric fires
Through the panel of sleep, the black plugs, trailing wires.

The world spoke through its dream, being deaf and blind,
Its words were those of the dream, yet you might find
Forgotten genius, control, alive in this deep
Instinctive resistance to the perils of sleep.

## Airliner

I am become a shell of delicate alleys
Stored with the bruit of the motors, resolute thunders
And unflagging dances of the nerves.
Beneath me the sad giant frescoes of the clouds:
Towerings and defiles through intense grey valleys,
Huge faces of kings, queens, castles—travelling cinders,
And monuments, and shrouds.
A fortress crammed with engines of warfare swerves

As we bank into it, and all the giant sad past
Clutches at me swimming through it: here
Is faith crumbling—here the engines of war
In sleek word and sad fresco of print,
Landscapes broken apart; and here at last
Is home all undulant, banners hanging drear
Or collapsing into chaos, burnt.
And now we are through, and now a barbarous shore

Grimaces in welcome, showing all its teeth
And now the elder sea all wrinkled with love
Sways tipsily up to us, and now the swing
Of the bridge; houses, islands, and many blue bushlands come.
Confine me in Pinchgut, bury me beneath
The bones of the old lag, analyse me above
The city lest I drunkenly sing
Of wattles, wars, childhoods, being at last home.

## Ward Two

### 1. PNEUMO-ENCEPHALOGRAPH

Tight scrimmage of blankets in the dark;
Nerve-fluxions, flints coupling for the spark;
Today's guilt and tomorrow's blent;
Passion and peace trussed together, impotent;
Dilute potage of light
Dripping through glass to the desk where you sit and write;
Hour stalking lame hour . . .
May my every bone and vessel confess the power
To loathe suffering in you
As in myself, that arcane simmering brew.

Only come to this cabin of art:
Crack hardy, take off clothes, and play your part.
Contraband enters your brain;
Puckered guerilla faces patrol the vein;
The spore of oxygen passes
Skidding over old inclines and crevasses,
Hunting an ancient sore,
Foxhole of impulse in a minute cosmic war.
Concordat of nature and desire
Was revoked in you; but fire clashes with fire.

Let me ask, while you are still,
What in you marshalled this improbable will:
Instruments supple as the flute,
Vigilant eyes, mouths that are almost mute,
X-rays scintillant as a flower,
Tossed in a corner the plumes of falsehood, power?
Only your suffering.
Of pain's amalgam with gold let some man sing
While, pale and fluent and rare
As the Holy Spirit, travels the bubble of air.

### 2. HARRY

It's the day for writing that letter, if one is able,
And so the striped institutional shirt is wedged
Between this holy holy chair and table.

He has purloined paper, he has begged and cadged
The bent institutional pen,
The ink. And our droll old men
Are darting constantly where he weaves his sacrament.

Sacrifice? Propitiation? All are blent
In the moron's painstaking fingers—so painstaking.
His vestments our giddy yarns of the firmament,
Women, gods, electric trains, and our remaking
Of all known worlds—but not yet
Has our giddy alphabet
Perplexed his priestcraft and spilled the cruet of innocence.

We have been plucked from the world of commonsense,
Fondling between our hands some shining loot,
Wife, mother, beach, fisticuffs, eloquence,
As the lank tree cherishes every distorted shoot.
What queer shards we could steal
Shaped him, realer than the Real:
But it is no goddess of ours guiding the fingers and the thumb.

She cries: *Ab aeterno ordinata sum.*
He writes to the woman, this lad who will never marry.
One vowel and the thousand laborious serifs will come
To this pudgy Christ, and the old shape of Mary.
Before seasonal pelts and the thin
Soft tactile underskin
Of air were stretched across earth, they have sported and are one.

Was it then at this altar-stone the mind was begun?
The image besieges our Troy. Consider the sick
Convulsions of movement, and the featureless baldy sun
Insensible—sparing that compulsive nervous tic.
Before life, the fantastic succession,
An imbecile makes his confession,
Is filled with the Word unwritten, has almost genuflected.

Because the wise world has for ever and ever rejected
Him and because your children would scream at the sight

Of his mongol mouth stained with food, he has resurrected
The spontaneous thought retarded and infantile Light.
Transfigured with him we stand
Among walls of the no-man's-land
While he licks the soiled envelope with lover's caress

Directing it to the House of no known address.

### 3. OLD TIMER

I have observed even among us the virus
Eating its way, lipping, complaining
In a multitude of cozening wheedling voices:
O Being is tender and succulent and porous:
Erect your four paternal walls of stone
(Gauleiters with burnished window-badges, no faces):
Checkmate the sun, the cloud, the burning, the raining,
Let deferential stars peep in one by one:
Sit, feed, sleep, have done.

Isolate the Identity, clasp its dwindling head.
Your birth was again the birth of the All,
The Enemy: he treads roads, lumbers through pastures,
Musters the squeaking horde of the countless dead.
To guard your spark borrow the jungle art
Of this hospital yard, stamp calico vestures
For H.M. Government, for your funeral;
And in this moment of beads let nothing start
Old rages leaping in the dying heart.

So we become daily more noncommittal:
This small grey mendicant man must lean
Against his block of wall, old eyes rehearsing time
Whose hanged face he is. I take my fatal vital
Steps to the meal, the toilet, in worse than derision
Of his pipe craving a fill, of his monologue and rhyme:
Children who loved him, Bathurst, Orange, of green
Neighbourlinesses, of the silken and stony vision:
His faith-healing, his compassion.

But some little while ago it was all appalling.
He knew my footstep, even the pipe
Between blackened teeth hissed in its comeliness
As an exotic snake poising itself for the falling
Of heart's-blood, tobacco; an ancient iron of unrest
Melted before his hopeful word of address.
Christ, how I melted! for healing and faith were ripe
As Bathurst opening the gigantic West
Or Orange golden as the breast.


### 4.  WARD TWO AND THE KOOKABURRA

We fingered the World, or watered little cacti of anger.
So broad and shrewd and worshipful, the Wall
Peeped with some reservations at all the riff-raff of hunger
And desire—much as the schooled and tall
Mountain or introvert desert might peep at a city
—The crude etude without art, pandemonium
Of living—and remain dumb:
But at dawn that shiver in the limbs of a eunuch pity.


And then the Yard was empty: snap of the thick thumb
From somewhere, and the moon with the lined face,
Old voyageuse, dined on her continental crumb
And sea-sauce, and then portmanteau'd every trace
Of knick-knacks and a world.
Or, friends, had each of you somehow jerked ajar
The quantum portal, like a star
Erupting into sleep's non-magnetic field?


Today on the sky's porous hulk there is unfurled
Naïve bunting: very discreetly, arms and legs
Of light tread the greying timbers: and now this wild,
This lumbering giant ghost of laughter while the dregs
Of planets are drained, the cup shakes:
His guffaw like some coup of megatons past belief
Shivers our gold and copper grief:
History's bowels roll for breakfast as history wakes.

Our menial hands and trouserlegs sweep in the brief
Gesture, the Fixed Idea; or time's complaint
Flutters in this air-pocket like a leaf.
Arms, legs of man and colour crawl aslant
Unpausing: but the head
Of obsessed ultimate Laughter in ascent
Bulges into testament!
Gape at your porridge, munch it like a god!


### 5. HOMOSEXUAL

To watch may be deadly. There is no judgment, compulsion,
And the object becomes ourselves. That is the terror:
We have simply ceased, are not dead, and have been
And are; only movement—our movement—is relegated,
Only thought, being—our thought, being—are given
Over; and pray God it be simply given.
So, at this man's ending, which is all a watching,
Let us disentangle the disgust and indifference,
Be all a thin hurried magnanimity:
For that is movement, our movement. Let us study
Popular magazines, digests, psychoanalysts:
For that is thought, being, our thought, our being.
I shall only watch. He is born, seized by joy,
I shall not speak of that joy, seeing it only
As the lighted house, the security, the Beginning.
Unselfconscious as the loveliest of flowers
He grows—and here we enter: the house stands yet,
But the joists winge under our footsteps. Now the God,
The Beginning, the joy, give way to boots and footmarks.
Pale glass faces contorted in hate or merriment
Embody him; and words and arbitrary laws.
He is embodied, he weeps—and all mankind,
Which is the face, the glass even, weeps with him.

The first window broken. Something nameless as yet
Resists embodiment. Something, the perennial rebel,
Will not rest. And this, his grandest element,
Becomes his terror, because of the footsteps, us.

I shall not consider sin beginning, our sin,
The images, furtive actions. All is a secret
But to us all is known as on the day of our birth.
He will differ, must differ among all the pale glass faces,
The single face contorted in hate or merriment.

Comes the day when his mother realizes all.
Few questions, and a chaos of silence. Her thin eyes
Are emptied. Doors rattle in the house,
Foundations stagger. The Beginning becomes us;
And he is mulcted of words, remain to him only
The words of sin, escape, which is becoming all of life.
Easier, the talk with his father, rowdy, brief
Thank God, and only the language of the gutter,
He watches the moth pondering the gaslight, love-death,
Offers a wager as to her love or death or both.
His father stops speaking, fingers some papers on the desk.

And now he is here. We had him conveyed to this place
Because our pale glass faces contorted in hate or merriment
Left only sin as flesh, the concrete, the demanded.
He does not speak or hear—perhaps the pox.
But all his compatriots in sin or in other illness
Are flesh, the demanded, silent, watching, not hearing:
It is all he ever sought. Again I am tempted, with the Great,
To see in ugliness and agony a way to God:
Worse, I am tempted to say he has found God
Because we cannot contort our faces in merriment,
And we are one of the Twelve Tribes—he our king.
He has dictated silence, a kind of peace
To all within these four unambiguous walls,
Almost I can say with no answering scuffle of rejection,
He is loving us now, he is loving all.

### 6.  A MAN

He can hardly walk these days, buckling at the knees,
Wrestling with consonants, in raggedy khakis
Faded from ancient solar festivities,

He loiters, shuffles, fingering solid wall:
    *Away down, the roots, away down,*
    *Who said Let there be light?*

The clock in its tower of worked baroque stone
Holds at three o'clock and has always done.
Nothing else shuffles, works, is ended, begun,
There is only the solid air, the solid wall.
    *Away down, the roots, away down,*
    *Who said Let there be light?*

Three weeks under the indigent paid-off clock:
He pulls from his photograph album the heavy chock,
Squats like a king behind a heavy lock,
Niched in and almost part of solid wall.
    *Away down, the roots, away down,*
    *Who said Let there be light?*

Canaries silent as spiders, caged in laws,
Shuffle and teeter, begging a First Cause
That they may tear It open with their claws
And have It hanging in pain from solid wall.
    *Away down, the roots, away down,*
    *Who said Let there be light?*

His King's Cup for swimming, the shimmering girl,
The photogenic light aircraft spin and whirl
Out of the loam, stained by all weathers, hurl
Their petty weight against a solid wall.
    *Away down, the roots, away down,*
    *Who said Let there be light?*

The great goldfish hangs mouthing his glass box
And élite of weeds, like an old cunning fox
Or red-bronze gadfly, hangs in contentment, mocks
All that is cast in air or solid wall.
    *Away down, the roots, away down,*
    *Who said Let there be light?*

But his Cup glitters, the light monoplane bucks
Into the head-wind, girls in panel trucks
Arrive like flowers, and the dry mouth sucks
Deeply, puffs into flesh behind solid wall.
 *Away down, the roots, away down,*
 *Who said Let there be light?*

#### 7. THE OLD WOMEN

From social ellipses, from actual weight and mass
They are disembarking, from age and weight and sex,
Floating among us this Sunday afternoon,
Ugly, vague, tiny as the vagrant island of gas
Embracing, nosing certain unthinkable wrecks,
Sunken faces like the face of the cretin moon.
Son, husband, lover, have spun out of orbit; this place
Holds the fugitive vessel to be kissed; and the rest is space.

They wait in the visitors' room: archaic clothing,
Reading-glass, patois of tin, rigmarole hair.
Men like meteorites enter their atmosphere:
The bombast, the wake of fire, the joy, the nothing,
Known strata of repartee unveiled with care,
Ice Age of the cherished calculated fear.
Gravity bends to an earlier law in this place:
Comes a lifting of heads among grazing herds of space.
The grazing herds are all for a foundering
Old planet borne in the omnibus of the sun
Patchy and coughing in all its wheels and wild
About the roof. They watch her blundering
While gravity pauses, down to clipped hedges, mown
Grasses, ferrying pastries for her child.
So this is earth, the worn stockings in this place
They are chewing and swishing, the startled herds of space.

They have missed her absurd mimesis of cosmic war;
Her rain of trivial shapely missiles; the pimple
Of the megaton explosion upon her brow;
Her deaths by the spadeful; her dancing orator.
Missed the man punchdrunk, grappling with a simple

Colour or stone or song that might disavow
His midget mother tumbling in metre, displace
The ancient entente between earth and space and space.

Giggling, squinting, with laundry, confectioneries,
Old women bear fodder for the universe, add their spark
To a train of time that blows open the infinite.
It is blackness about them discloses our galaxies.
Look on these faces: now look out at the dark:
It was always and must be always the stuff of light.
The decrepit persistent folly within this place
Will sow with itself the last paddock of space.

### 8. WILD HONEY

Saboteur autumn has riddled the pampered folds
Of the sun; gum and willow whisper seditious things;
Servile leaves now kick and toss in revolution,
Wave bunting, die in operatic reds and golds;
And we, the drones, fated for the hundred stings,
Grope among chilly combs of self-contemplation
While the sun, on sufferance, from his palanquin
Offers creation one niggling lukewarm grin.

But today in Sports Day, not a shadow of doubt:
Scampering at the actual frosty feet
Of winter, under shavings of the pensioned blue,
We are the Spring. True, rain is about:
You mark old diggings along the arterial street
Of the temples, the stuttering eyeball, the residue
Of days spent nursing some drugged comatose pain,
Summer, autumn, winter the single sheet of rain.

And the sun is carted off; and a sudden shower:
Lines of lightning patrol the temples of the skies;
Drum, thunder, silence sing as one this day;
Our faces return to the one face of the flower
Sodden and harried by diehard disconsolate flies.
All seasons are crammed into pockets of the grey.
Joy, pain, desire, a moment ago set free,
Sag in pavilions of the grey finality.

Under rain, in atrophy, dare I watch this girl
Combing her hair before the grey broken mirror,
The golden sweetness trickling? Her eyes show
Awareness of my grey stare beyond the swirl
Of golden fronds: it is her due. And terror,
Rainlike, is all involved in the golden glow,
Playing diminuendo its dwarfish rôle
Between self-conscious fingers of the naked soul.

Down with the mind a moment, and let Eden
Be fullness without the prompted unnatural hunger,
Without the doomed shapely ersatz thought: see faith
As all such essential gestures, unforbidden,
Persisting through Fall and landslip; and see, stranger,
The overcoated concierge of death
As a toy for her gesture. See her hands like bees
Store golden combs among certified hollow trees.

Have the gates of death scrape open. Shall we meet
(Beyond the platoons of rainfall) a loftier hill
Hung with such delicate husbandries? Shall ascent
Be a travelling homeward, past the blue frosty feet
Of winter, past childhood, past the grey snake, the will?
Are gestures stars in sacred dishevelment,
The tiny, the pitiable, meaningless and rare
As a girl beleaguered by rain, and her yellow hair?


GWEN HARWOOD

*The Second Life of Lazarus*


Lazarus, kindling at the breath of pain,
    consumed the onrushing stimuli
of light, sound, hospital smells. Could not make plain
    his loss, but knew night's ossuary

held all the earth's dead names. Towards his protecting
  thickness of flesh, faces like flowers,
as blind as flowers, shrill-coloured, thrust expecting
  some news of heavenly powers.

The world lay flat against his field of vision.
  Inward, true roundness rolled apart
from speech. He showed them through what clean incision
  the surgeon had massaged his heart,

but could not utter the pure permanence
  globing his late asylum. Bent
across him, sterile as their own instruments,
  the doctors breathed 'Aphasia'; leant

with gestures as of love towards his clean wound.
  Outside the sober mountain spread
its cardboard backdrop while a sister spooned
  comforting pap, and smoothed his bed,

moved flowers and visitors, whispered that one night,
  not infinite, might well suffice
for resurrection; and put out his light.
  Reborn in flames, pain cried its price.

### At the Sea's Edge

  Sea at this town's neat threshold spills its gloss
  of cold, of distance. Urban colours toss

  in thousand-faceted water. Gulls outrace
  the wavering wind. A crowd comes to this place

  daily, gathers to watch a tame seal fed.
  They smile to see its grave grey-whiskered head

  cruise by the fish-punt, its dense body dive
  with ecstasy of balance through its live

element for scraps. A car stops. One by one
three people step into the lavish sun.

The crowd stirs, looks, and looks away to find
darkness upon the water: one is blind.

And worse than blind; as in a hideous mask
degraded eyelids squint. Young children ask,

'What—?' and are hushed, as the blind woman stands
between a man and woman, with her hands

held gently; neither proud nor humble turns
her ruined face to the oblique wind and learns

what the blind learn from wind. Beyond her night
green beards of seaweed drip, light, light, light, light,

where water sucks and shudders round half-rotten
staves of the wharf, and murmurs long forgotten

furies of wave on rock. Of light no trace
of recollection marks her ravaged face,

only the sea-wind speaks to her. The crowd
melts, lest ill-luck should touch them. A torn cloud

of gulls descends, disputing scraps. The sea
is marked by the wind's tread, that may not be

told or foreseen, but wanders where it will,
speaking its comfort to the spirit still

in darkness. 'Look,' says the man, 'he begs! He shakes
his whiskers like a dog.' Green water flakes

in silver from the seal. The woman cries
'Look! Now he's diving. Look, he's got his eyes

right on that scrap of fish. He never misses!
He goes like a torpedo.' Water hisses

and churns in the seal's wake. As the three stand
silent, the blind one smiles. From hand to hand

a live hope flows. The wind walks on the sea,
printing the water's face with charity.

### In the Park

She sits in the park. Her clothes are out of date.
Two children whine and bicker, tug her skirt.
A third draws aimless patterns in the dirt.
Someone she loved once passes by—too late

to feign indifference to that casual nod.
'How nice,' etcetera. 'Time holds great surprises.'
From his neat head unquestionably rises
a small balloon ... 'but for the grace of God ...'

They stand awhile in flickering light, rehearsing
the children's names and birthdays. 'It's so sweet
to hear their chatter, watch them grow and thrive,'
she says to his departing smile. Then, nursing
the youngest child, sits staring at her feet.
To the wind she says, 'They have eaten me alive.'

### Prize-giving

Professor Eisenbart, asked to attend
a girls' school speech night as an honoured guest
and give the prizes out, rudely declined;
but from indifference agreed, when pressed
with dry scholastic jokes, to change his mind,
to grace their humble platform, and to lend

distinction (of a kind not specified)
to the occasion. Academic dress

became him, as he knew. When he appeared
the girls whirred with an insect nervousness,
the Head in humbler black flapped round and steered
her guest, superb in silk and fur, with pride

to the best seat beneath half-hearted blooms
tortured to form the school's elaborate crest.
Eisenbart scowled with violent distaste,
then recomposed his features to their best
advantage: deep in thought, with one hand placed
like Rodin's Thinker. So he watched the room's

mosaic of young heads. Blonde, black, mouse-brown
they bent for their Headmistress' opening prayer.
But underneath a light (no accident
of seating, he felt sure), with titian hair
one girl sat grinning at him, her hand bent
under her chin in mockery of his own.

Speeches were made and prizes given. He shook
indifferently a host of virgin hands.
'*Music!*' The girl with titian hair stood up,
hitched at a stocking, winked at near-by friends,
and stood before him to receive a cup
of silver chased with curious harps. He took

her hand, and felt its voltage fling his hold
from his calm age and power; suffered her strange
eyes, against reason dark, to take his stare
with her to the piano, there to change
her casual schoolgirl's for a master's air.
He forged his rose-hot dream as Mozart told

the fullness of all passion or despair
summoned by arrogant hands. The music ended,
Eisenbart teased his gown while others clapped,
and peered into a trophy which suspended
his image upside down: a sage fool trapped
by music in a copper net of hair.

## Panther and Peacock

Professor Eisenbart, with grim distaste,
skirted the laughter of a Sunday crowd
circling an ape's gross mimicry of man.
His mistress watched a peacock. He grimaced,
making rude observations on the proud
creature's true centre of that radiant fan.

Raked by the aureoled bird's nerve-twisting cries
they strolled away, affecting noble ease.
A clot of darkness moved in temperate shade:
a jungle climate, favouring decay,
flared through the keyholes of a panther's eyes
to tarnish the gold gauze of sun, and fade

blue from the brilliant air.
                                          'Glutted with leisure
dull-coupled citizens and their buoyant young
gape at your elegant freedom, and my face
closed round the cares of power, see with mean pleasure
age scaling massive temples overhung
with silver mists of hair—that handspan space

corners their destiny: at my word they'll bear
acerebrate hybrid monsters. *Fiat nox!*
Let the dark beast whose cat-light footpads scour
my cortex barren leap from its cage and tear
their feathers out!'
                                His mistress said, 'What shocks
await the bourgeois! In this twilight hour

the earth blooms velvet-soft, while its immense
authority of volume fails and dies
with the clear colours of substantial day.
Now the sharp iconography of sense
declines to vague abstraction, let your eyes
socket the blaze of Venus, through the play

of leaves in the last branch-caught stir of wings.
Rest here.'
　　　　　　She cradled his Darwinian head.
Its intricate landscape of fine lines and scars,
ridges and hollows, veins' meanderings,
grew desolate in sleep. Above them spread
a leaf-divided tissue of space and stars.

He dreamed: he walked at sunset through the same
gardens; safe on his tongue the incredible
formula that, spoken, would impel
prodigious ruin. His mistress called his name.
Feathers sprang from the sutures of his skull.
His hands grew rattling quills. As darkness fell

it circumfused worse darkness, in which prowled
familiar nightmare towards him, cowering, gripped
as always fast in horror. A stale breath
of carrion choked him. Fingerless, dewlap-jowled,
bird-beaked, he screamed in silence, and was ripped
awake still rooted in his dream of death.

His mind deep in the vehemence of shade
groped worldwards. Though his body showed no harm,
stone-still, with sorrow frozen on her face
the young girl bent above him. While they made
this strange *pietà*, feathers glistening warm
with his own heartstain fell through infinite space.


### Carnal Knowledge

Roll back, you fabulous animal
be human, sleep. I'll call you up
from water's dazzle, wheat-blond hills,
clear light and open-hearted roses,
this day's extravagance of blue
stored like a pulsebeat in the skull.

Content to be your love, your fool,
your creature tender and obscene
I'll bite sleep's innocence away
and wake the flesh my fingers cup
to build a world from what's to hand,
new energies of light and space

wings for blue distance, fins to sweep
the obscure caverns of your heart,
a tongue to lift your sweetness close
leaf-speech against the window-glass
a memory of chaos weeping
mute forces hammering for shape

sea-strip and sky-strip held apart
for earth to form its hills and roses
its landscape from our blind caresses,
blue air, horizon, water-flow,
bone to my bone I grasp the world.
But what you are I do not know.


### Suburban Sonnet

She practises a fugue, though it can matter
to no one now if she plays well or not.
Beside her on the floor two children chatter,
then scream and fight. She hushes them. A pot
boils over. As she rushes to the stove
too late, a wave of nausea overpowers
subject and counter-subject. Zest and love
drain out with soapy water as she scours
the crusted milk. Her veins ache. Once she played
for Rubinstein, who yawned. The children caper
round a sprung mousetrap where a mouse lies dead.
When the soft corpse won't move they seem afraid.
She comforts them; and wraps it in a paper
featuring: *Tasty dishes from stale bread.*

## New Music
### to Larry Sitsky

Who can grasp for the first time
these notes hurled into empty space?
Suddenly a tormenting nerve
affronts the fellowship of cells.
Who can tell for the first time
if it is love or pain he feels,
violence or tenderness that calls
plain objects by outrageous names

and strikes new sound from the old names?
At the service of a human vision,
not symbols, but strange presences
defining a transparent void,
these notes beckon the mind to move
out of the smiling context of
what's known; and what can guide it is
neither wisdom nor power, but love.

Who but a fool would enter these
regions of being with no name?
Secure among their towering junk
the wise and powerful congregate
fitting old shapes to old ideas,
rocked by their classical harmonies
in living sleep. The beggars' stumps
bang on the stones. Nothing will change.

Unless, wakeful with questioning,
some mind beats on necessity,
and being unanswered learns to bear
emptiness like a wound that no
word but its own can mend; and finds
a new imperative to summon
a world out of unmeasured darkness
pierced by a brilliant nerve of sound.

### Night Thoughts: Baby & Demon

Baby I'm sick. I need
nursing. Give me your breast.
My orifices bleed.
I cannot sleep. My chest
shakes like a window. Light
guts me. My head's not right.

Demon, we're old, old chap.
Born under the same sign
after some classic rape.
Gemini. Yours is mine.
Sickness and health. We'll share
the end of this affair.

Baby, I'm sick to death.
But I can't die. You do
the songs, you've got the breath.
Give them the old soft shoe.
Put on a lovely show.
Put on your wig, and go.

The service station flags, denticulate
plastic, snap in the wind. Hunched seabirds wait

for light to quench the unmeaning lights of town.
This day will bring the fabulous summer down.

Weather no memory can match will fade
to memory, leaf-drift in the pines' thick shade.

All night salt water stroked and shaped the sand.
All night I heard it. Your bravura hand

chimed me to shores beyond time's rocking swell.
The last cars leave the shabby beach motel.

Lovers and drunks unroofed in sobering air
disperse, ghost-coloured in the streetlight-glare.

Rock-a-bye Baby
   in the motel
Baby will kiss
   and Demon will tell.

One candle lights us. Night's cool airs begin
to lick the luminous edges of our skin.

When the bough bends
   the apple will fall
Baby knows nothing
   Demon knows all.

Draw up the voluptuously crumpled sheet.
In rose-dark silence gentle tongues repeat
the body's triumph through its grand eclipse.
I feel your pulsebeat through my fingertips.

Baby's a rocker
   lost on the shore.
Demon's a mocker.
   Baby's a whore.

World of the happy, innocent and whole:
the body's the best picture of the soul
couched like an animal in savage grace.
Ghost after ghost obscures your sleeping face

My baby's like a bird of day
   that flutters from my side,
my baby's like an empty beach
   that's ravished by the tide.

So fair are you, my bonny lass,
   so sick and strange am I,
that I must lie with all your loves
And suck your sweetness dry.

And drink your juices dry, my dear,
   and grind your bones to sand,

then I will walk the empty shore
   and sift you through my hand.

And sift you through my hand, my dear,
   and find you grain by grain,
and build your body bone by bone
   and flesh those bones again,

with flesh from all your loves, my love,
   while tides and seasons stream,
until you wake by candle-light
   from your midsummer dream,

and like some gentle creature meet
   the huntsman's murderous eye,
and know you never shall escape
   however fast you fly.

Unhoused I'll shout my drunken songs
   and through the streets I'll go
compelling all I meet to toast
   the bride they do not know.

Till all your tears are dry, my love,
   and your ghosts fade in the sun.
Be sure I'll have your heart, my love,
   when all your loving's done.


### Father and Child

#### I. BARN OWL

Daybreak: the household slept.
I rose, blessed by the sun.
A horny fiend, I crept
out with my father's gun.
Let him dream of a child
obedient, angel-mild—

old No-Sayer, robbed of power
by sleep. I knew my prize
who swooped home at this hour
with daylight-riddled eyes
to his place on a high beam
in our old stables, to dream

light's useless time away.
I stood, holding my breath,
in urine-scented hay,
master of life and death,
a wisp-haired judge whose law
would punish beak and claw.

My first shot struck. He swayed,
ruined, beating his only
wing, as I watched, afraid
by the fallen gun, a lonely
child who believed death clean
and final, not this obscene

bundle of stuff that dropped,
and dribbled through loose straw
tangling in bowels, and hopped
blindly closer. I saw
those eyes that did not see
mirror my cruelty

while the wrecked thing that could
not bear the light nor hide
hobbled in its own blood.
My father reached my side,
gave me the fallen gun.
'End what you have begun.'

I fired. The blank eyes shone
once into mine, and slept.
I leaned my head upon
my father's arm, and wept,

owl-blind in early sun
for what I had begun.


II. NIGHTFALL

Forty years, lived or dreamed:
what memories pack them home.
Now the season that seemed
incredible is come.
Father and child, we stand
in time's long-promised land.

Since there's no more to taste
ripeness is plainly all.
Father, we pick our last
fruits of the temporal.
Eighty years old, you take
this late walk for my sake.

Who can be what you were?
Link your dry hand in mine,
my stick-thin comforter.
Far distant suburbs shine
with great simplicities.
Birds crowd in flowering trees,

sunset exalts its known
symbols of transience.
Your passionate face is grown
to ancient innocence.
Let us walk for this hour
as if death had no power

or were no more than sleep.
Things truly named can never
vanish from earth. You keep
a child's delight for ever
in birds, flowers, shivery-grass—
I name them as we pass.

'*Be your tears wet?*' You speak
as if air touched a string
near breaking-point. Your cheek
brushes on mine. Old king,
your marvellous journey's done.
Your night and day are one

as you find with your white stick
the path on which you turn
home with the child once quick
to mischief, grown to learn
what sorrows, in the end,
no words, no tears can mend.


# VINCENT BUCKLEY

*Good Friday and the Present Crucifixion*

Good Friday.  Somewhere a death.
Somewhere a murder has been arranged,
And in each church a ritual.
Spring the bright spring stands for resurrection
But the present days are a sharp autumn.

All down the nave the faces turn
To see who's coming under lowered brows
And hide their souls with a neighbourly sharp look,
The young lit with a faint expectancy,
The old held tense with previous pain,
But all with bodies in antique postures
Before the empty tabernacle
And the lit candles, their tributary fires.

Now if I'm to impersonalize this death
I must fight through these to some abstract symbol,

Some watercourse running blood,
Some hill or slope of dying:
Hard, from slow level to level,
Stopping often, hardly ascending,
Sinews strained absurdly against need
(As though from the deep gut of earth,
Deep from the lassitude of churchy stone)
I, somehow I, climb come
Self-hauled, or
Hauled by a straining bush, by
Sideways flint, by
(Even)
The wind,
Hauled, like a sideways crab, up,
Suddenly to be held
By the catch and terror of new breath

   (The people have humped backs,
   Turning vacantly, or running,
   Or dwindling into a walking stare,
   And the vulture's cocked head
   Swivels, and retches at me)
Eyes held by the shadowless wood,
Mouth held by a soundless cry,
Ears by a rushing wind, hands
Gripping nails to the sweat of palms
Held fast by what they parody.
Here is the rim of it, here's
Body's emergence into light; and nostrils
Smell at last the stink of crucifixion.

The smell of packed bodies.　　Only
This world of flesh is scored with the full meaning.
We go out, in our twos.　　The earth is pallid,
The sun distracted with its three hours' death,
But still in the sibilant air,
Its mottled-with-crimson darkness, hangs
The thong and point of rain.

## Return of a Popular Statesman

Brought back from the tedium of dying,
From the work of holding skin and bone
And memories together, from a life
Pottered at like a never-ending hobby
Down the soft lanes of second childhood, he
Stands a while, head tremulous with events,
Like a boy fetched out of nightmare
Blinking light away in the sudden doorway.
Someone takes his hat, raises his hand
In promise, or blessing, or to gain a respite.
Is it himself, or the People,
Or the bodyguard with the belted coat?
He neither knows nor cares; the grand old man
Blinks on a surfeit of smoky light,
Ducks his head to the tidal wave of cheering.
The armoured cars point away from him;
The committees meet in other rooms;
The pickpockets move among the crowds.

## No New Thing

No new thing under the sun:
The virtuous who prefer the dark;
Fools knighted; the brave undone;
The athletes at their killing work;
The tender-hearts who step in blood;
The sensitive paralysed in a mood;
The clerks who rubber-stamp our deaths,
Executors of death's estate;
Poets who count their dying breaths;
Lovers who pledge undying hate;
The self-made and self-ruined men;
The envious with the strength of ten.

They crowd in nightmares to my side,
Enlisting even private pain

In some world-plan of suicide:
Man, gutted and obedient man,
Who turns his coat when he is told,
Faithless to our shining world.
And hard-faced men, who beat the drum
To call me to this Cause or that,
Those heirs of someone else's tomb,
Can't see the sweeter work I'm at,
The building of the honeycomb.


## Parents

My father asks me how I stand it all,
The work, the debts, the spite.  My mother talks
As though I were a famous man and yet
Unguarded somehow, too fragile to touch.
It's their needs, not mine, that flutter here
In the questions and the anecdotes.  I stare
At the rust encroaching on the walnut branches
Or the pile of litter where the biggest pine tree
Used to stand, before my absence killed it.
Their door has a vine over it; they murmur
Endearments to the animals, and cry
At small wrongs.  Which is the oldest of us three?

Facts sound like charges.  The least important man
Is a legend in his neighbour's living room,
Menacing and remarkable as the lightning
That ran from tree to tree about the house
So lately, like the shining of its ghosts.
I nod, but the names, perils, dates mean nothing,
And where that's true, the deepest bonds are lost.
How will the vine bear this year?  I feel
My heart growing till my thoughts are hoarse
And the old branches pick at the heap of leavings.
There is so much I don't recall.  They stand,
Timid, waving to watch me go, barely
Visible in the window's copper sheen.

# R. F. BRISSENDEN

## Verandahs
### for Monique Delamotte

They don't build houses like that any more—not
With verandahs the way they used to: wide verandahs
Running round three sides of the place, with vines
Growing up the posts and along the eaves—passion-
fruit, grape, wistaria—and maiden-hair fern in pots,
And a waterbag slung from the roof in the shade with the water
Always cool and clean and tasting of canvas.

Comfortable worn cane chairs and shabby lounges,
Beds for the kids to sleep in, a ping-pong table,
A cage for the cockatoo the boys had caught
Twenty years ago by the creek, a box for the cat
And a blanket for the old blind dog to doze on—
There was room for everything and everybody,
And you lived out on the verandah through the summer.

That's where the talking happened—over a cup
Of tea with fresh sponge cake and scones, or a drink
(A beer for the men and a shandy for the girls)
On Sunday afternoons or warm dry evenings:
Do you remember, it always began, do you
Remember?—How it was Grandpa who forged the hook
They used to catch the biggest cod in the Lachlan—

And didn't we laugh when Nell in her English voice
Said: 'Hark at the rain!'—And who was the bloke that married
Great-aunt Edith and drove the coach from Burke?
And weren't they working up Queensland way in that pub
Frank Gardiner ran, and nobody twigged who he was
Even though they called him the Darkie—and they never
Found it, did they, the gold: nobody found it.

And they never will—just like that reef at Wyalong:
Nothing but quartz and mullock. But the fishing

Was good in those days, Tom, they'd say: remember
The ducks, the way we'd watch them in their hundreds
Flying along the billabong at sunset?
You won't see that anymore—they're all fished out,
The waterholes, and the mallee-fowl have gone.

And in the dusk and under a rising moon
The yarning voices would drift and pause like a river
Eddying past the ears of the drowsing children
As they settled down in their beds and watched the possums
Playing high in the branches—and when they opened
Their eyes it would somehow always be morning with sunlight
Flooding level and bright along the verandah.

### Walking down Jalan Thamrin

Jalan Thamrin in Denpasar
Was made by feet—
The feet of men, horses, dogs, pigs, cattle.
Now we walk a narrow dusty strip
Between the open ditch
And the petrol-stinking bitumen
Roaring with motorbikes, bemos, cars.

An old woman
Delicately erect
Balancing a pink rolled mattress
On her head
Threads her way towards us through the traffic.

On her left hand, in the ditch,
Two pigs
Root and snuffle through a heap of garbage.
On her right
A boy
White shirt fresh as a photograph from *Vogue*
Pedals a gleaming bicycle:
On his handlebars
A flower.

# NANCY KEESING

### *Reverie of a Mum*

Here let me rest me feet!
The boys have gone to try
The shooting gallery, the girls
Are off to prospect for boys.
Here let me drop me bundle
Of bulging sample bags,
I was lucky to find this seat
In the shade, away from the noise.
We come on an early bus,
We seen the fruit and the jams,
The handicrafts and the flowers,
Bacon like marble, hams
Big as the side of a palace,
Wheels of golden cheese
Like off one of them olden chariots
From them spectacle films. And Jeez
The cakes done in royal icing!
There was one great galleon—clever!
All icing; sails, decks, ropes,
You could hardly credit. I never
Seen such a cake. It took me
Back to that Spanish Gob
Off the Yankee ship in the war years
And a lying, promising slob
He turned out. Now my eldest, Marie,
Her eyes are funny but,
As hot and black as that little goat's feet
And she's a stuck-up slut.
She's got ideas of the stage now
Since we let her stay on at school
And they chose her for Cleopatra
In that play they done by the pool
In Hyde Park there. It's queer,
You marry and you settle down
Like they say, and you never think

Of the boys who done you brown.
Jeez! When I think of me hair
With frangipanis, and a high
Pompadour style—I used to swing
As if I'd of owned the sky.
There was that night in the Dom.
(I'd tan my kids if they went
Where we used ... War-time, but,)
And all around was the scent
Of gabardine coats and hair-oil
And frangipani in the night—
Whispers, rustling, and the giggles
When one Yank shinned up the light
And took out the bulb ... My God
But those boys knew what they wanted.
The whole world turned on velvet,
The sky came down and panted
Like a dog that's been running. Them fig-trees
Rattled that sky in their leaves.
Well, it isn't like that when you settle.
If my hubby knew! Funny though, I grieves
For them boys. Just sometimes. And the Vice Squad
Out on their surf-boat boots
Treading the Moreton Bay fig-leaves ...
Fig-leaves! We up and we scoots
With my Spanish Yank having zip trouble,
It was funny giving coppers the slip,
The frangipani night laughed with us
As we dodged through the 'Loo to their ship.
We all took a sickie from the factory
When they sailed—'See youse again' ...
Then the grey boys in jungle green come home.
And *that* was my castle in Spain.

# ANNE ELDER

## *School Cadets*

The day of the fête—and what a day for it,
blazing with *bonhomie* and sun. But what a fate
for the dads jam-packed in the hoop-la tent; for Mum
buying back the cakes she sent. The mike
crackles amicably: Your presence is requested,
Ladies and Gentlemen, on the lower field.
'Crikey what a row!' the juniors bawl.
'Only the old Cadets—can't march for nuts!'
But Colonel Bogey, limping a bit, but still
incorruptible, taking fair advantage
of the British Raj and The Bridge on the River Kwai,
draws them by the nose. The chins go up
on the kid sisters, bearded in fairy-floss.
                        Formidable Headmaster,
affecting a walking stick, conversing precisely,
escorts the Mayoress to see how nicely
the Best School teaches the game of War.

They wheel on the green glare of grass
like stripling gods in cohort, and stars
are struck from their brass, the moving frieze
of their bright lives unrolls. The gaiters surge
and ripple as a white wave of the sea.
The tune blurts out and strangles, faltering
to slow march half a tone off key.

'Excuse me—excuse me'—the mothers are shoving
like hooligans. There he is! The short one, third
from the right, sloped in the tango embrace
of the great spiralled horn. Impossible to separate
that agonizing familiar forlorn
lowing practised in bathrooms on holiday.

He is pitiful
as a babe in python coils, they are pitiful

all of them, they are terrible
as Kings in Babylon. The hateful nations
inhabit their slight frames, the future leers
desirous on their wavering formations.
Earnestly they are inflated, diminished . . . and *away* . . .


### Carried Away

The beautiful eyes of the dead,
lambent and sleepless, the curve of flesh,
the pale one unprepared for conformity,
tender of lip, still pouting for a kiss—
these, uncorrupted, embalmed in wishful thinking,
roll in their carriages, clatter away in the clanking
last black boxes shunting to the long goods-train of death.

Surely, we ask, in the beautiful eyes
of our children we shall be remembered,
limned in their curve of flesh?
The children, suddenly dutiful, cry when bereft:
Oh they were beautiful, this and that they said,
let them be praised! They turn to their own children:
Give us your praise then, smother us beneath
the softgoods of wishful thinking,
the last goodies shoved shunting in the last carriages
                    of the black goods-train of death.

But once there were those who said:
Look, we have beautiful eyes, curve of flesh;
and listen, this word how it sings
in the mouth; we hold in the cup of the hand
the babble of eternal springs.
It is in the artefact we shall be remembered.
So they patterned the wall, hammer-hammered the red
lips from the stone, burnished the bright
bronze, wreathed the bright head
of the lyrist, declaimed and postured with their last breath
a beautiful counterpart of the black face of death.

The sands blew over,
the slow green rivers turned to an altered bed.
A man in this field unearthed a perfect vessel
and drank from it. They gaped in the broken temple
and found a stone hand in theirs, and they said:
Look, in those times they had beautiful eyes,
curve of flesh, and listen,
this word on the scroll how it stings
the heart. Oh let me better it!
and seizing a few short years of breath
they bend with vehemence to their artefact,
squeeze the clay, sweep the strings, slash with the brush, inflate
the breast for song, raise the tower and trumpet
and hammer-hammer the beautiful counterfeit black-boxed
    face of death.

Oh let me better it! we cry.
The sweat still rolls on a chiselled passion,
the tear hangs in the stone eye.
It is finished. We limp down to the station,
trembling for the great beauty of the failed artefact,
turn, wave, whisper on a last breath: Remember me?
and die
to the hammer-hammer of the last carriages coupling to the
                    shunting black-boxed goods-train vanishing ...
Ee ... eeeeh!
In our dreams, in our rhymes,
how the whistle screams.


### Farmer Goes Berserk

Perhaps she said, lively at first but once
too often in that softly stubborn voice:
'What kind of a country d'ye call this!'—or
'Pity I can't send for a wee drop of rain
from Home'—and that would be Ballachulish
on Loch Lynne (for the nine hundredth time).

Here, water is khaki and each day a battle
with mouths. Seven, born quick as roses but grown
slowly insupportable with their throats
and itches and grizzles. Two farmed out
(a shame, that) and one in a home,
returned maybe for Christmas and Easter
a frightfully quiet stranger. They kept,
just, the four little girls.
                                    Would that be enough?
Rain at last, too much; the spuds
to be got in, tractor on the blink, more
work than feasible for one man with fear
waiting in unopened bills and no rest.
No rest ever from her soft worrying tongue
and that ultimate gnawed bone, no rest within
except in the grog (money ill spent) but oh
the beautiful glad spurt of the grog
                                    so that he said
'Shut your trap, woman!' Astoundingly.
With the rabbiting gun. And she slumped
open-mouthed all over the bed and then
the four of them, easy! Sleeping easy
in their bright blood *and* the bloody dog
                                    and the excitement
of no fear for the crowning achievement
Him Self . . .
                    By Cripes, we can share it
for one day's wonder in the Stop Press, local.
Was he brute or victim, this assassin?
Or were they simply muddlers, no-hopers
who bred and scrapped together?—who eked out
a widowhood from life behind a veil of gums
in a crazy dump with a cracked iron roof
too remote to be even called infamous.
Now in the darkening puddles of their blood,
briefly limelit, they become neighbours.
Did you ever! He went berserk!
                                    Unto Everyman,
according to his worth, acclaim for his labours.

## One Foot in the Door

During the Depression my grandmother
was plagued in her daft heart
by processions of hawkers. Supporting
a wry neck on two fingers she nodded
compulsively to tales of a little woman
and kids unlimited; bought from them
bootlaces, talc and Pears Soap galore
out of the soft purse of her own reduced circumstances.
            Her stocks increased, unused. I store
the days and years like that, supporting
myself during the depressions
with two fingers on an Olivetti and pitiless poems.

They still put their foot in the door
to stop the gap in their spare time, with a satchel
of handbills, hand-outs, something for the glory box,
fabulous Clean-up-Kits, bottling sets, Life Assurance,
an out-dated catalogue of grievances.
You fill in the spaces
but nothing comes or works. I stare
at their good new shoes, couldn't
tell you the dishonest colour of their eyes,
not for the very life of me laid down on paper.
            My stockings go down
over the varicose into the shivering shoes.
I feel the soft purse of my lips
snap like the stiff neck I hold erect to keep
my face. They can keep their charity.

Only the grave is warm, Granny,
isn't it. Lend me your arm.

# DOROTHY HEWETT

## *Moon-Man*

Stranded on the moon,
a librium dreamer in a lunar landscape,
the tabloids were full of your blurred, blown-up face,
the neat curled head, the secret animal eyes,
immolated forever in the Sea of Tranquillity.

I keep getting messages from outer space,
'Meet me at Cape Canaveral, Houston, Tullamarine.'
A telegram came through at dawn to the Dead Heart Tracking
    Station.
I wait on winter mornings in hangars
dwarfed by grounded crates like giant moths
    furred with frost.

Moon-pictures—you dance clumsily on the screen,
phosphorescent, domed, dehumanized,
    floating above the dust,
your robot voice hollow as bells.

The crowds queue for the late edition,
scan headlines avidly, their necks permanently awry,
looking for a sign, a scapegoat, a priest, a king:
the circulation is rising.

They say you have been knighted in your absence,
but those who swear they know you best,
assert you are still too radical to accept the honour.

They have sent several missions,
but at lift-off three astronauts fried,
    strapped in their webbing.
Plane-spotters on penthouse roofs
have sighted more UFOs.

Sometimes I go out at night
    to stare at the galaxies.
Is that your shadow, weightless,
    magnified in light,
man's flesh enclosed in armour,
suffering eyes in perspex looking down,
sacred and murderous from your sanctuary?

## Sanctuary

*'Who's the old doll reading her poetry under the light?'*

The winter's coming on,
the air swarms with leaves.
Driven in,
they gather in our house.
Outside the massacre begins.
The unsheathed razor,
footprints marked in blood,
pills spilt from a pack:
I have known the terror.
I gather them in
to the light's ambience;
it bathes a faint small round.

The shelter falls apart,
the light wavers in water,
a round skull on a pole
I turn and turn,
a weathercock, a totem out of time
who cannot catch the moment.
I have visited the crematorium three times.

'She rose unsteadily from the night,
Took two of orange and one of white.'

Old women wet their beds, cry softly,
rummage in each other's lockers, scavenge for life,

but the young lie like stone,
shrouded to the chin in a white sheet,
tubes draining the sleeping pills from every aperture.

She sits on a balcony in a private nursing home
in a white dress, skinny as a bone,
her head on a stalk nods from side to side,
a green creeper engulfs her from the world outside,
her eyes stare, she is still, listening, queer,
remembering the young husband who gassed himself last year
in the park, before the commuters came;
fixed the exhaust, wound up the windows, insane
people kill themselves; she locked the doors
and ate and ate, had food delivered from stores
in bulk, until they found her at last
and propped her on a balcony, a girl with a past
and no future, sitting up here alone
in a see-through dress in a private nursing home.

'She looks like Whistler's Mother!'

They grappled him out of river: it was on TV.
His parents watched, gripping the edge of their chairs
his hair turned white, his skin gone soggy: 'It can't be him,'
they said. 'He used to run along the foreshore in jockey shorts,
shining and scrubbed like . . . Colgates.'
They'd been searching for him in the sandhills for days before,
falling over the homosexuals with their togs pulled down.
Someone had seen him running alone in the dunes.
It was cold that weekend, he kept his head well down,
and went on running when they called.
Somebody thought they heard him moving in the hills,
crying for sanctuary amongst the thorn and rocks.
The parson found him and led him into the nave.
Under the stained glass window he laid him down,
on his black chin the lozenges played, scarlet and blue.
While the parson phoned in the vestry he slipped away.
They called and called and got out the dogs,
but all the time he was lying dead in his boat-bay

with three anchor chains wrapped round his body, like Christ
hauled out of the river, glittering wet in the arc lamps,
                              a spearing marlin!
and somebody else was crashing about through the hills,
unwashed, sleepless, a revolver cool on his ribcage.

This nervous hollow city is built on sand,
looped with wires, circled with shaven trees.
The bleeding pigeons tumble outside the windows,
the children wring their necks.
The exchange is jammed with outward calls,
the TV screen, jagged with light,
crackles and goes out.

The boy on drugs, his bandages slipping,
argues and pleads all day with the parking meters.
The filthy children of Christ lie on mattresses in the sun,
the pavement scrawled with graffiti, in excrement and blood.

Bare-footed children driven out over the plain,
thorny the mallee and spinifex, thumbing a ride interstate,
do not call me again and reverse the charges.
Winter is coming on.
I have dialled three times.
The whole city is engaged in a kind of slaughter.

I am only an old doll reading her poems in the lamplight,
waiting for a fourth cremation.

### This Version of Love

I have seen her, wonderful!
A waterfall of hair, body like glass,
Wading through the goldfish pools in winter,
Her white shark-skin dress dark-wet above her thighs,
The very shape and effigy of love:
Or turbanned, earringed, lying on the lawn
Among the clover burrs, her bangles clacking,
                    reading Ern Malley.

Oh! her nipples under her black lace bras
And flimsy blouses, her gold hair pins
Strewn in the car upholstery.

In the bar of the O.B.H. the creme de menthe
Slopped in the green squid bottles on the shelf,
The rain beat in great waves, running down
                    the plate glass windows.
On V.E. day a Yank gob somersaulted through
A jagged icy cut-out in the air,
Crusted with drops of blood.
'Shall I marry?
          Who shall I marry?
          Shall I die now
Swallowing lysol one glittering afternoon
Before my breasts fall and my womb tilts?'
Salt and water, the stomach pump
Coils like an evil creeper, wraps her round,
Choking and arching in the public ward.
In the queues outside the abortionist's
The white statues of cupids tumble at her feet.

The police-woman stands righteous beside her bed.
'Next time you try it you won't get away with it.'
'Obliterate me, save me, I go down
Hanging by my hair into the great avenues
                  of dust and leaves.'

Fugitive as morning light she moves
In a thin rain out and across the river
                leaving no footprints.

## MAX WILLIAMS

### *The Empty House*

The old house felt unfriendly
offering no apologies for the undressed rooms
and the stained wallpaper
or for sharing this familiarity
with others who might come anytime.
This had never been my home.

'They moved,' the neighbour said. 'A month ago.'
And I repeated it to an overcoat
hanging behind the door.

That night I sheltered in the empty house
tucked into myself like an abandoned dog
not caring for the advances people made
wrapped in an overcoat smelling of tobacco and grown ups.
This was my fathers smell, blanket warm and coarse.
Next day I watched an old lady crying
and demolition workers putting back the sky.

## CHRIS WALLACE-CRABBE

### *Citizen*

The roofs of cars were crusted thick with frost
And ice was notable on every pool;
Blue children stalked in overcoats and gloves
Past the Immaculate Heart of Mary School.

And where he walked the traffic ran one way—
Toward the sacred ritual of work—
While hasty breakfasts rumbled in those cars
Whose flying mud had stopped him with a jerk.

On villa, cottage, sweet-shop, bungalow,
Schoolroom and Gentlemen's, the morning grinned
Facetiously. He quietly picked his way
Among the houses where the world had sinned.

Now schizoid barbers packed their shaving gear,
Uncomfortable lovers caught the train
And everyone rushed. It was at times like this
That decent violence beset his brain.

'Complacent city with your brazen bells
And morning song . . .' He called for words to cease
For citizens to know their proper hells
And anger to bloom green upon the trees.

### The Rebel General

A foreign room, slab faces, dusty panes;
Up to the rocking of this table he
Was driven by the laws of history,
Straight as a die.

Not quite. It wasn't the pulsing of ideals;
No cloudy notions of perfected man
Beguiled him into playing politics.
A host of garbled impulses set going
This fruity public voice,
This poker face above the Chairman's chair,
Even this crab-walk of a freckled hand
On scribbled oak. Consider it this way,
What could he weave around such loneliness
But some or other fanciful cocoon?
What could he do but play a game
Tricked out with dogma, jargon, ways and means,
Lulled in procedure like an embryo?
The granite stance in which he figures here—
While fierce amendments shatter on his brow
And coarse opinions abrade to sand
Beneath his eye—seems imperturbable,

Complete, without a private cranny known
Or niche where feathered sorrows could be nesting.
Not quite, not quite. That monolith plays false.
His fine responses move,
Dappled and latticed on a shifting ground
As wind and sun through multifarious scrub
Create their nervous world of counterpoint.

But, come now. He could never show you this;
Must rap and bark and frown and set his jaw,
Seeking to be what others, too, are not,
A public voice, a poker face, a rock.

South of the border, that way lies the past,
Shut in the dull manoeuvres of reaction:
Wheels turning, cogs grinding
And slow mills crushing the rebellious grain.
Behind stone hills, behind the peasant wheels,
The sun he courted bears its axle down
And the dead past holds sway
Like waters on the flood plain near his home.
Boyish, he saw the ripe fields blend and glow
Toward the rim of possibility
But now in middle age, in no-man's-town,
He sees an alien sunbeam struggle down
To leave its thumbprint on the table-top,
And sits content with that.

It is the middle ground that disappears;
The distant past retains its colour still,
Reduced, perhaps, fastidiously composed
To false lucidity:
The portly trees there shadow pasture land,
Dust rises at the herdsman's foot as if
To drift and blend with smoke from kitchen fires,
Boys from the creek-bank plod their fishless way,
Sheep draw in close and bluish shadows run
Drowning, with moth and gnat,
Posterity's chaotic battlefield;

But of the battle, of that sweaty rout,
The end of all their possibilities,
Gateway to exile and the years of drought,
Nothing remains but hollowness and blur.

A foreign room, slab faces, dusty panes
Hedge the custodian of failure now;
The granite stance in which he figures here
Proclaims him plainly general but elides
All mention of the army that he lost,
Those draggled knots that fled the river-bank
Five years ago.
The past is dead; he draws the future out
As time unveiled the profile which he bends
To revolution and the common good
Among these second-rate conspirators,
Who bicker till his gavel calls a halt.

### The Dirigible
for Graham Burns

On, on, on
Over the Europe of books
And a shallow turquoise sea
That leaches the edges
Of stone civilizations,
On, dipping low, sailed
A fat imperial airship
Buoyed on the stuff of dreams;
Larger than life and
Just about lighter than air,
Purring toward the Nile,
Desert and lion-woman,
It drove absurdly, like
A cloud conceived in the head
Unpredictably dumping
Large pianos and crates of wine
Into the sea below
Where fishermen set out from pumice isles.

# VIVIAN SMITH

*Fishermen, Drowned Beyond the West Coast*

Someone said dead men make islands in the sea
but there are no trees, no green islands
growing from these mouths and hollow eyes.
Under the areas of empty sea they lie,
fishermen drowned in a storm all miles from land.
There are no trees growing from their broken eyes,
no island gathered round their love and pain,
only a sudden emptiness, a sea of noise and silence
that hurts the ear's dead drum.

Wind and sea grow over and under the open storm,
the quick and pointless tyranny of nets that tied their hands,
and fish caged forever in the boat's square well;
drowned in their fumbling nets all miles from land
and their boat storm-rolled like a dead bird in the sea.

But I think they are separated now; the nets unravelled;
the heavy wood floats anywhere, water-logged and split,
alone in all the areas of sea. Only
the nets and fish and storm kept them together
as men—and they were not lonely.

There are no green islands for the coastless birds;
no trees branching from those eyes to hang a thought upon;
nothing, nothing that the hands can find:
only another island, quiet and simple, forming in another mind.

*Reflections*
To Gwen Harwood

Is this the self I thought I knew, within
this narrow world of helpless self-concern,
where in fatigue huge images begin
to grope at knowledge, thinking to discern

recognitions, motives slyly caught,
suspicions looming in a hostile sky.
Hell is other people, Sartre thought.
The threat of others, ill-will; all my I . . .

And knowing in myself this edge of spite,
afraid of chaos, and of order, too,
a sense of balance which is rarely right,
I think of one now whom I hardly knew

who dreamt of constant threats against her life,
slights to a vast, imagined reputation;
saw in each glance intentions of a knife
to slash at her with pointless imputation.

The ego has such dramas of its own
and sudden lapses back into the sheer
world of acceptance that it thought outgrown,
but needs its sickness as a dog needs fear

and fleas, to know a certain sense of life.
Her mirror-world delusions are my own.
To break the long reflections of her strife
she filled each pocket with a clean white stone

and drowned herself face downwards in a stream
so shallow that it hardly wet her hair.
I wonder if the nightmare turned to dream
and how far down descended her despair.

I only know one tendency is mine:
to walk with images that change and chill
the contours of reality's design
along the failing tightrope of the will.

### Summer Band Concert

Tired with its dogs and doves
the park's distracted tunes
sprawl across the littered green,
these slow and tedious afternoons.

And there a brassy serenade
and here two lovers come to rest.
Beneath a pampered laurel-tree
he leans his head against her breast.

And round and round the waltzes go:
smeared lollies in a bag;
the formal tunes and gardens merge:
the light exhausts, the music drags—

and sleep condemns the lovers' eyes
the gardens blind . . . He draws her near
and puts his arm beneath her back
and whispers darkness in her ear

### At an Exhibition of Historical Paintings, Hobart

The sadness in the human visage stares
out of these frames, out of these distant eyes;
the static bodies painted without love
that only lack of talent could disguise.

Those bland receding hills are too remote
where the quaint natives squat with awkward calm.
One carries a kangaroo like a worn toy,
his axe alert with emphasized alarm.

Those nearer woollen hills are now all streets;
even the water in the harbour's changed.
Much is alike and yet a slight precise
disparity seems intended and arranged—

as in that late pink terrace's façade.
How neat the houses look. How clean each brick.
One cannot say they look much older now,
but somehow more themselves, less accurate.

And see the pride in this expansive view:
churches, houses, farms, a prison tower;
a grand gesture like wide-open arms
showing the artist's trust, his clumsy power.

And this much later vision, grander still:
the main street sedate carriages unroll
towards the inappropriate, tentative mountain:
a flow of lines the artist can't control—

the foreground nearly breaks out of its frame
the streets end so abruptly in the water . . .
But how some themes return. A whaling ship.
The last natives. Here that silent slaughter

is really not prefigured or avoided.
One merely sees a profile, a full face,
a body sitting stiffly in a chair:
the soon-forgotten absence of a race . . .

Album pieces: bowls of brown glazed fruit . . .
I'm drawn back yet again to those few studies
of native women whose long floral dresses
made them first aware of their own bodies.

History has made artists of all these
painters who lack energy and feature.
But how some gazes cling. Around the hall
the pathos of the past, the human creature.

# BULUGURU

## Working Song[1]

Shavings, fall from the carved stick.
Scales, drop off my carved snake.

# R. A. SIMPSON

## Antarctica

After his talking destroyed her
He looked down at the rocks below ...
The sea filling a cave, the way it retreated.

Left on that summer cliff above the breakers
He lifted his head to glimpse far off
A miracle—Antarctica
(Or so it seemed)—
A white, a glass thread
Incredibly expanding.

And then he knew he knew himself, grew cold.

## Diver

Alone on the tower
I'm not confident.
The water is black
And distant.

[1] Translated from the Yaoro by E. A. Worms

I think of style
And raise my arms and aim,
Holding back the plunge.
It's mostly a game

That touches terror,
Then terror goes—
I view my fingers,
My toes.

'Defiance, love and revolt
Make the diver dive
And prove, through dying,
He's alive,'
A voice preaches in my head ...

And so I dive.

Water gulps me down,
Chilling me with its grip,
Then arms pine up and up
Like worship.

## Lake

I can't hold it, keep it.
It's full of mountains fluttering down,
And trees—or rather their other selves.

I can break it with a stone,
My foot; and I can almost see
Just what it's thinking. I'm certain it's thinking.

A fisherman unpacks himself gently
On a ledge, and soon his line
Is holding the lake exactly.

# RANDOLPH STOW

## The Singing Bones

*'Out where the dead men lie.'* Barcroft Boake

Out there, beyond the boundary fence, beyond
the scrub-dark flat horizon that the crows
returned from, evenings, days of rusty wind
raised from the bones a stiff lament, whose sound
netted my childhood round, and even here still blows.

My country's heart is ash in the market-place,
is aftermath of martyrdom. Out there
its sand-enshrined lay saints lie piece by piece,
Leichhardt by Gibson, stealing the wind's voice,
and Lawson's tramps, by choice made mummia and air.

No pilgrims leave, no holy-days are kept
for these who died of landscape. Who can find,
even, the camp-sites where the saints last slept?
*Out there* their place is, where the charts are gapped,
unreachable, unmapped, and mainly in the mind.

They were all poets, so the poets said,
who kept their end in mind in all they wrote
and hymned their bones, and joined them. Gordon died
happy, one surf-loud dawn, shot through the head,
and Boake astonished, dead, his stockwhip round his throat.

Time, time and time again, when the inland wind
beats over myall from the dunes, I hear
the singing bones, their glum Victorian strain.
A ritual manliness, embracing pain
to know; to taste terrain their heirs need not draw near.

## from *Thailand Railway*
### For Russ Braddon

*Your memories, not mine; a debt to acknowledge a debt.*

THE JUNGLE

The planet is ours: and the blue and the desert spaces
submit, at last, to aggrandize our legend;

only the jungle works in the way of man,
moulding or melting the world to its own being.

I do not know the jungle, though it enfolds me;
I do not know this colonist of my fibres,

but I liken it to a great mouthless stomach:
listen, the ceaseless churn, that fermenting gut.

The jungle sleeps by my side and cries in its sleep,
and I wake afraid, for I cannot tell the jungle

from cries of the tortured, cries of the fever-demented
—bird or baboon? or a friend, near the end of pain.

The smell of the jungle, its rot and its bitterness,
clings to my flesh: my flesh that by leaf and thorn

the jungle has torn to give passage to voyagers
that navigate my veins like a skein of rivers.

I do not know the jungle, though it enfolds me,
but I liken the jungle trees to the legs of giants,

rotten with running ulcers, trailing foul rags,
sheathed in a shrunken and wrinkled purplish skin.

And their cries for the peace of death it must be that wake me.
And I think in my sleep it must be that I call to them.

THE SLEEPERS

Let the wick burn low: and suddenly I remember
(with tears in the throat, with anger, with disbelief)
that we are young.

These skeletons ribbed and tanned like droughtstruck sheep,
these monkey-faces, hooding their hot sunk eyeballs
—these are young men.

Limbs that the surf washed, lips that the girls farewelled,
fumble, shape words. I know these unaltering, nightly
homecomings. Dawn

will be heartbreak, exile, atrocities of light
on a tangle of rags and angled bones: but now
is years ago.

Thank God for sleep no captor steals indefinitely,
for death that brings a gift, the final privacy,
time to oneself.

My neighbour moans in his sleep, and I stretch my arm,
and he sighs and quietens under my arm like a child,
gaunt cheek on hand.

When I smashed my mirror his face still showed my face.
Thank God for a feeble light, for our phantom youth,
for need and tenderness.

## Ruins of the City of Hay

The wind has scattered my city to the sheep.
Capeweed and lovely lupins choke the street
where the wind wanders in great gaunt chimneys of hay
and straws cry out like keyholes.

Our yellow Petra of the fields: alas!
I walk the ruins of forum and capitol,
through quiet squares, by the temples of tranquillity.

Wisps of the metropolis brush my hair.
I become invisible in tears.

This was no ratbags' Eden: these were true haystacks.
Golden, but functional, our mansions sprang from dreams
of architects in love (*O my meadow queen!*).
No need for fires to be lit on the yellow hearthstones;
our walls were warmer than flesh, more sure than igloos.
On winter nights we squatted naked as Esquimaux,
chanting our sagas of innocent chauvinism.

In the street no vehicle passed. No telephone,
doorbell or till was heard in the canyons of hay.
No stir, no sound, but the sickle and the loom,
and the comments of emus begging by kitchen doors
in the moonlike silence of morning.

Though the neighbour states (said Lao Tse) lie in sight of the city
and their cocks wake and their watchdogs warn the inhabitants
the men of the city of hay will never go there
all the days of their lives.

But the wind of the world descended on lovely Petra
and the spires of the towers and the statues and belfries fell.
The bones of my brothers broke in the breaking columns.
The bones of my sisters, clasping their broken children,
cracked on the hearthstones, under the rooftrees of hay.
I alone mourn in the temples, by broken altars
bowered in black nightshade and mauve salvation-jane.

And the cocks of the neighbour nations scratch in the straw.
And their dogs rejoice in the bones of all my brethren.

## Dust

'Enough,' she said. But the dust still rained about her;
over her living-room (hideous, autumnal)
dropping its small defiance.
                              The clock turned green.

She spurned her broom and took a train. The neighbours
have heard nothing.

Jungles, deserts, stars—the six days of creation—
came floating in, gold on a chute of light.
In May, grudging farmers admired the carpet
and foretold a rich year.

Miraculous August! What shelves of yellow capeweed,
what pouffes of everlastings. We worship nature
in my country.

Never such heath as flowered on the virgin slopes
of the terrible armchairs. Never convolvulus
brighter than that which choked the china dogs.
Bushwalkers' Clubs boiled their billies with humility
in chimneys where orchids and treesnakes
luxuriantly intertwined.

A photographer came from The *West Australian*, and ten
teenage reportresses. Teachers of botany
overflowed to the garden.

Indeed, trains were run from Yalgoo and Oodnadatta.
But the neighbours slept behind sealed doors, with feather
dusters beside their beds.


BRUCE DAWE

*Abandonment of Autos*

'The City Council is reported to be concerned about the number of old cars being
abandoned in city streets.' News item

Something about the idea
Appeals to me immensely—the driver
Pulling up in some busy street,

After manoeuvring dexterously
For a parking-spot, applying the hand-brake,
Stepping out and closing the car-door
For the last time with grave tenderness ...
In place of the customary
Abject submission to the cold appraisal
Of the merchant
For whom an old heap is only an inventory of parts
(Working and non-working) there is in this
Seemingly casual walking away from the parked car
(Who is to know that he will not return?)
A largeness of gesture, satisfaction of a
Sense of gallantry in circumstances where
Sharp-faced men are forever lifting the bonnet with a frown,
Disdainfully kicking the tyres,
Discovering a leak in the radiator and offering,
In consequence, next-to-nothing.
It is the urban Arab's Farewell To His Steed,
Down to the final affectionate pat
On the near mudguard before turning away
To shoulder a passage through the indifferent crowds,
Made free in the moment of loss, the one true test,
Only the licence-plate which he carries with him
Into the new life stating as clearly
As any letter of recommendation:
'Here is one who senses the fitness of things.'


### Perpetuum Immobile
(GROUP PHOTO OUTSIDE MYER'S)

That's me, second from the left,
taking cover behind a Late City Extra
—not the loafer with synchronized gaze
swivelling over each blonde running
the blockade of his dreams—but his fiercely-indifferent
compatriot, propping the wall up next to him, eyes bloodshot
in the glare of neons whose apocryphal
and automatic life we share,

me and my cobbers riding the horizontal
asphalt escalators of any city
you care to think of, enigmatic answers
to a sociologist's prayer.

Note our instinctive choice of back-ground:
a glassed-off, flood-lit world, a beach-scene where
hairless young Apollos, heads chock-full of
gentlemanly plaster thoughts assume
a breathless summer in the company of several
blank-faced Aphrodites whose smooth
poreless limbs may chip and flake away
but never age.                This square of immaculate
shingle beneath their bolted feet runs down
to brutal disillusion, a dead stop
at the plate-glass on all sides.
                          If it's the sea
you're looking for, its belligerent dimensions have
no place in dummied Edens—you will have to turn
to us, in which case don't be shocked
if the water's cool as steel and each wave, seeming
buoyant and friendly in the imagined sun,
reveals a well-honed and deliberate edge
to mutilate your awkward charity.


### Americanized

She loves him ... and what small child could deny
the beneficence of that motherhood beamed across
the laminex breakfast-table-top each day?

'Shoosh ... shoosh ...' her fat friendly features say
whenever a vague passing spasm of loss
troubles him in his high-chair, makes him cry.

She loves him ... but will not allow him out.
'The streets are full of nasty cars and *men*,'
she whispers, popping him on his plastic pot.

His eyes grow round, his bowels quietly knot;
he strains to be a good boy, not knowing then
it takes years of training to bring that about . . .

'Today,' she tells him, putting on her hat
(she's off to nurse an invalid called the World)
'Today, I'll let you play with Mummy's things.'

The toys that mark his short life—christening,
birthday, Christmas—into a corner hurled . . .
Mummy's things! What could compare with that?

Crammed in a carton on the nursery-floor
are the varied treasures Mummy's world contains
from Pepsi-Cola figurines to Spam

('I think young, think big, therefore I am')
chewing-gum, hot dogs, electronic brains
—what child of simple origins could want more?

The afternoon passes, evening comes and still
he plays alone, hearing the traffic surge
beyond the house and children scream and run

Along the street (it *must* be rather fun!)
The nursery is in darkness—on the verge
of terror he hears those formidable

Footsteps approaching, suddenly the thin
membrane of reason lets in fear at last
to beat with bats' wings through the velvet room . . .

The door-knob turns, he sees her figure loom,
he tries to run, her large hands hold him fast . . .
She loves him . . . and the frightening fact sinks in.

## The Not-so-good Earth

For a while there we had 25-inch Chinese peasant families
famishing in comfort on the 25-inch screen
and even Uncle Billy whose eyesight's going fast
by hunching up real close to the convex glass
could just about make them out—the riot scene
in the capital city for example
he saw that better than anything, using the contrast knob
to bring them up dark—all those screaming faces
and bodies going under the horses' hooves—he did a terrific job
on that bit, not so successful though
on the quieter parts where they're just starving away
digging for roots in the not-so-good earth
cooking up a mess of old clay
and coming out with all those Confucian analects
to everybody's considerable satisfaction
(if I remember rightly Grandmother dies
with naturally a suspenseful break in the action
for a full symphony orchestra plug for Craven A
neat as a whistle probably damn glad
to be quit of the whole gang with their marvellous patience.)
We never did find out how it finished up . . . Dad
at this stage tripped over the main lead in the dark
hauling the whole set down smack on its inscrutable face,
wiping out in a blue flash and curlicue of smoke
600 million Chinese without a trace . . .

## Homecoming

All day, day after day, they're bringing them home,
they're picking them up, those they can find, and bringing them home,
they're bringing them in, piled on the hulls of Grants, in trucks, in
        convoys,
they're zipping them up in green plastic bags,
they're tagging them now in Saigon, in the mortuary coolness
they're giving them names, they're rolling them out of
the deep-freeze lockers—on the tarmac at Tan Son Nhut
the noble jets are whining like hounds,

they are bringing them home
—curly-heads, kinky-hairs, crew-cuts, balding non-coms
—they're high, now, high and higher, over the land, the steaming
    *chow mein*,
their shadows are tracing the blue curve of the Pacific
with sorrowful quick fingers, heading south, heading east,
home, home, home—an.' the coasts swing upward, the old ridiculous
    curvatures
of earth, the knuckled hills, the mangrove-swamps, the desert
    emptiness . . .
in their sterile housing they tilt towards these like skiers
—taxiing in, on the long runways, the howl of their home-coming rises
surrounding them like their last moments (the mash, the splendour)
then fading at length as they move
on to small towns where dogs in the frozen sunset
raise muzzles in mute salute,
and on to cities in whose wide web of suburbs
telegrams tremble like leaves from a wintering tree
and the spider grief swings in his bitter geometry
—they're bringing them home, now, too late, too early.

## Drifters

One day soon he'll tell her it's time to start packing,
and the kids will yell 'Truly?' and get wildly excited for no reason,
and the brown kelpie pup will start dashing about, tripping everyone
    up,
and she'll go out to the vegetable-patch and pick all the green tomatoes
    from the vines,
and notice how the oldest girl is close to tears because she was happy
    here,
and how the youngest girl is beaming because she wasn't.
And the first thing she'll put on the trailer will be the bottling-set she
    never unpacked from Grovedale,
and when the loaded ute bumps down the drive past the
    blackberry-canes with their last shrivelled fruit,
she won't even ask why they're leaving this time, or where they're
    heading for
—she'll only remember how, when they came here,

she held out her hands bright with berries,
the first of the season, and said:
'Make a wish, Tom, make a wish.'


# BRUCE BEAVER

from *Letters to Live Poets*


### II

I shop in the streets of my hometown with
my family. We hope it won't
rain, and go without umbrellas
into the streets, the sad and narrow
streets of asphalt fouled by pets
and the oil-leaking automobiles.
We shop in the food market with hundreds
of others hungry as we, the files
of window-shopping populace.
They do this every day, the others;
not all buying. Mostly they come
where the touchable crowd gathers
to look and be looked at, assuring themselves
they exist beyond the household's magic
circle, among the loaded shelves;
*I eat therefore I am*, they'll tell
the world within that busy street.

I don't really shop, I just come along
for the exercise, holding the bag
helping to carry the food
back to the house among
the close-stacked flats and the pines.

I stand outside the shops and look at
some of the people looking at me.
We all seem two dimensional, flat
as wafer biscuits in a tin.

You know, ugliness isn't so bad—
an honest ugliness, I mean.
It makes a statement from and to
concerning appearances now and then.
Like beauty it appears to be, it *is*
a silent volubility.
It's the ordinariness of faces and figures
that overwhelms and blinds the seeing
eye—the way some tall, thin men
walk with backsides lacking in loose
trousers, a brown butt like a scab
on the underlip, the smoker's cough personified,
ash falls with every gesture. The young wives drab,
swelling with hormones until their eyes
grow smaller in their fat, blank faces.
(In the butcher's window a dead pig
suspended on wires seems familiar.)
Or the shrilly thin driving a wedge
of offspring. And the sadder cases
of older people—the crazy hats
some of the older women wear,
with faces underneath like wrecking jobs
or superannuated tigers: the flour-
white powder and the blood-red bow.
They know it. That doesn't mean they know
themselves. They'd be the first to deny
they have to believe it as a fact.
And some of the surfers—their wry
faces find it too hard a thing
to live up to their bodies. *En masse*
people are uglier than ugly, more or less.

Diogenes had a fixed idea
of his own discriminativeness.
But you've stood as I have, seeing
yourself summed up in a delicatessen
window, a disembodied being,
a Cheshire grinning cheese, or else
morbid, a pig's foot among the coprolitic pickles.

You've looked once and moved on. I stay,
see movement when I look about me,
colour everywhere. Why don't I
reflect some therapeutically?
You tell me.


V

Three images of dying stick in my mind like morbid transfers
of the other side of life. First, a cow on my uncle's farm
had broken a leg calving. My uncle held a shot gun to its poll
and fired both barrels. The dogs ran in to lick the blood welling from
the nostrils. We hauled the carcase behind a wooden sled to the burial
     ground,
a small island of dark trees centring a wide field.
On the way the top of the cow's head came loose and left a trail.
Heifers followed us and shrieked with eyes rolling at the blood.
We piled the heavy carcase high with old tyres and lit the pyre.
Sleeping and waking I saw the shattered head for many years to come.

The second incident occurred years later in a goods' yard.
Near to a storage shed I came across a group of cats surrounding
such a scrawny bag of fur and bone it wasn't a bit funny.
This cat had eaten poisoned corn or a rat poisoned.
At first I'd thought it starving and had brought bacon from the galley.
The other cats moved back from me while I offered it the bacon.
It stretched out a claw at the meat, hooking it towards its mouth
then died before it bit. I watched the twitch of life pass up its spine,
centre, then go out like a light snuffed. Its eyes had closed before
its life. Blinded. Starved with poison. The other cats began to move
away. I stood and looked and knew mortality like an old wound.

The third time clawed me in a room filled with smoke and proof
     readers.
The air clanged with advertisements read aloud like crazy psalms.
A man was dying at his desk. His heart was broken and the kiss
of life rejected. As he died his fellow workers chanted on
and he was left with a handkerchief over his face where he lay dead
in his chair in a room full of the loud chanting of the living.

No one pleaded for silence while he remained or when he was gone
    stayed
their tongue. I read on then, knowing not a minute's silence will
the rest of us get. When they rang his ninety year old mother all she
    asked for
were his keys. Tomorrow we'll talk of life and sundry other things.

x

    The sou'wester whips the day awake.
    The pines are tossing 'monkey tails'
    about the gardens and the streets.
    The air hums and rushes overhead
    and next-door the little girl
    is calling out to it.
    All week she has blown
    a two-note whistle and called the tune
    her own. The white and blue weather
    excites her. The wind blows
    back into her face the tune.
    She catches it and feels it blown
    about her hair and face.
    It buzzes like wild bees;
    it stings with specks of dust and sand.
    Yet over it and under it is the cool
    to warmer charm of the September breeze,
    spiked with salt and mellowed with
    the mild juice of new grass.

    The sheets crack and flap a semaphore
    among the red and blue and black of 'coloureds'.
    She sits cross-legged beneath
    the carousel of washing, fluting
    and singing two notes, two words:
    'I am, I am'. The mother
    admonishes. She is thin and sallow,
    without a man. Has her reasons
    all about her like an angry
    counterpoint. All winter
    she has yelled at the child who yells

back at herself 'I am, I am'.
But the devas of the air and sky
respond 'We are, we are' and lift her
over the yards and the thrumming pines,
past gargling crows and creaking gulls,
above the splintering enamel
of the blue and whitening bay
back to where she is with a man
out of the clouds. The 'he' who'll spank
her mother good and bring them all
toffee apples every day.

How she sings and makes the whistle
talk with her. When she goes
inside the house her hair will crackle
and float about. Her mother will lick
the corner of a handkerchief
and clean the corners of her eyes.
Then by herself again
she'll clean the whistle's gritty mouth
and listen to it humming to
itself.
         Do you hear them now?
Have I admitted something past
my manhood? Do we recollect
blowing up a sunny storm
all by ourselves once upon
a time in a backyard garden
near the sea?
Or is it that all women
learn to sing to themselves early
that some men, early or late,
may listen?


## XII

Three anti-depressants and one diuretic a day
seven and five times a week respectively
save me from the pit.

I pray while I'm taking them and in between doses
because, as Dylan Thomas says, *I have seen the gates of hell.*

Once I drew back in distaste from the metho drinker
and his bleary lady friend—you've seen them
weaving a way through non-existent traffic.
He, swollen faced, with a backside kicked in
by what the tougher call life. She,
the terrible veteran doll of Pantagruel's nursery.
Let them pass into the peaceful holocaust.

In Rushcutter's park they congregated over bottles.
Walking, we avoided them as mined ground,
fearful of their implosions bloodying the day.
Later I fell so far into self-sickness
I envied them. My thoughts
haunted their submerged wreckage like a squid.
At their groaning subsidence I retreated
into a pall of ink.
                  Whatever I tell you,
you have heard before.
                      I remembered Swift's
fascination with the insane. I whistled
*Childe Roland to the Dark Tower Came*
outside the grimy walls of Callan Park.
Inside—*il miglior fabbro*—the best of us all
chewing bloody knuckles, wept dry,
daft as a headless chicken circling in the dust.
Where are prayers said for him and the parkside horrors?
Some prayed for us, I know. I'm still here
partially, trying to live detachedly.
Is it only the exceptional ones, the broken battlers,
shred me into uselessness? Does it mean
I'd pick and choose in hell? Discriminative?
Like a dog in rut—no,
self-abasement's out. So is complacency.
I'm never likely to forget
the day I walked on hands and knees
like Blake's Nebuchadnezzar, scenting the pit.

So it's one day at a time spent checking
the menagerie of self; seeing
the two-headed man has half as much
of twice of everything; curbing the tiger;
sunning the snake; taking stock of
Monkey, Piggsy, Sandy's belt of skulls.


### XIX

I welcome the anonymity of the middle years, years of the spreading
girth and conversational prolixity, when the whole being loosens
the stays of the thirties and lengthens out into paragraphs of
    perceptiveness
where once had bristled the pointed phrase. And the other aspect, the
    merely boring
raconteur, the redundant conversationalist; the not young
not old, twice told tale teller; the paunched, bejowelled double-chinned
bumbler. These I welcome, also the watcher unperceived on corners
from verandahs of youth, voyeuristic, grateful beyond the tang of sour
grapes to be no longer privy to the ingrowing secret, the deathly
held breaths of years, the cold and burning self-trials. The quaintly
acquainted with the antique masques of childhood, the mummies and
    daddies,
the nurses and doctors, the pantomimic routines of getting the hang of
living and dying young. No, childhood's well and truly categorised
and pigeon-holed somewhere within that depot of lapsed tenders, the
    unconscious. It's the witnessing
of the adolescent saga that sometimes chills me to my still vulnerable
marrow, burns me down to the fire of being and sifts me into a vacuum
of loveless nine to five nightmares on wretched wages, the between
    grown
and ungrown, the lonely braggart loping like werewolf past the
unattainable beauties on the peeling posters, past the burning
girls that, plain as sisters, would, and onto the illimitable
utmost, absolute and factual plateau of the self's serfdom
to solitude, the sad king in the bone castle, the bitter end
of beginnings and the beginning of fiddling appetites and the myriad
arbitrations of early manhood (in my case, alas, a prolongation
of mad simulated adolescence). Only now with hypertensive

head and lazy bowels, with a heart as whole as a tin of dog's meat
may I pause between poems of letters to you, my alter egos, and
    pronounce
peace be occasionally with you all and, at no matter what cost, with me
    here,
no longer (I pray) completely at odds with self and world,
    accommodating
room by room like a shabby genteel boarding house, age.


### XXX

Today the self-destroying anger.
The inner violence so close to the
surface of the mind. The terrible
images of wilful destruction.
The blood beating behind clouding
eyes. It was the constant heat of the
day began it. The blood cooking
within, the pores streaming and the
rage to be otherwise than meat
moving; to tear away the caul
of fantasy; to see blind and
whole as Oedipus the blank of
self; to walk slowly, feeling
the air with outstretched hands, feet
scuffing pebbles in the mountain's
ruined sanctuary; to taste
life in air upon the ravaged
face and make of it the true
words of suffering and of love:
the real prayer that takes a life
to utter.
         And depart, nor leave
as the actual Empedocles
so much as a sandal upon a sulphurous
ledge but to come down and miracle!
see again; to feel and bear such
pressure on this level, the lapsing
sea shore and to move among

the self-victimized as no
veteran of the sanctuary
but as the garrulous old man
of the market place. Never too distant
to hear the plea behind the jovial
insult, the fear within the oath.
In middle life I look towards this
balanced being who may greet
across the shining sands of years
a child among the tide line's rubble
and the empty, ocean-hymning shells.


### XXXIV

Mid-day and a heat haze over all
backed by the blue-black hammer of a storm.
The ocean trundles barrels of waves
up and down the shore. The hushed
rumble lulls the hour. Afloat
on several cups of tea I query
moments of my last night's dreaming.
Why the interminable tram-car ride
to nowhere in particular? Why the
attempted sexual assault
on the famous, ageing red-haired TV actress
who up till now had seemed
the epitome of cool humour?
Why the fantasy of living
a never-ending novel, slipping
from printed page to dreamt
actuality and back?
I have written a poem a day
for several weeks now—maybe the id
has tired of this pressure-releasing stint.

Hearing from you a state away
sets off garrulity like a long
fuse. It's nipped by a noise
two backyards distant, the tin

trumpet of a baby's grief.
I see the steamy infant swaddled,
half emerged from the dream of a dream
of now. The clenched red miniature
fists. The incredibly minute finger
nails. The smell of bread and milk and
waste. Too much in the sun-stewed room.
The afternoon is a prickly blanket,
a bumble-footed, sticky-beaking giant fly.

A baby seemed the plus and minus
of our first meeting,
reminding our other friends of one of their
raisons d'être. It was a blessing
that you should come at the time of their
loss *with gift bearing hands*
of poems, family and good claret.
We had so little but ourselves
and various senses of exile
with which to reciprocate such life.

The noon is past
already and the infant's crying
has given way to the ubiquitous
signalling of birds. The great
fane of blue re-echoes the psalms of tides.
Over the clipped green of the yard
the vague cabbage moths flutter
in and out of the day like blanks
of the mind. Elsewhere destinies
erupting blood and semen, the drivelling
race-rotting dialectics of war.
Here the *affirming flame* of friendship.

I set the seal on a book of letters
never to be posted, ever
to the live poets of my knowing,
not all writers, yet all conscious
of the gift of the living word.

# FAY ZWICKY

## *Summer Pogrom*

Spade-bearded grandfather, squat Lenin
In the snows of Donna Buang,
Your bicycle a wiry crutch, nomadic homburg
Alien black, correct. Beneath, the curt defiant
Filamented eye. Does it count the dead
Between the Cossack horses' legs in Kovno?

Those dead who sleep in me, me dry
In a garden veiled with myrtle and oleander,
Desert snows that powder memory's track
Scoured by burning winds from eastern rocks,
Flushing the lobes of mind,
Fat white dormant flowrets.

Aggressive under dappled shade, girl in a glove;
Collins Street in autumn, mirage of
Clattering crowds: Why don't you speak English?
I don't understand, *I don't understand!*
Sei nicht so ein Dummerchen, nobody cares.
*Not for you the upreared hooves of Nikolai,*
Eat your icecream, Kleine, *may his soul rot,*
These are good days.

Flared candles; gift of children; love
Need fulfilled, a name it has to have—how else to feel?
A radiance in the garden, the Electrolux man chats,
Cosy spectre of the afternoon's decay.

My eye his eye, the snows of Kovno cover us;
Is that my son bloodied outside Isaac the Baker's door?

The tepid river's edge, reeds creak, rats' nests fold and quiver,
My feet sink in sand; the children splash and call, sleek
Little satyrs diamond-eyed reined to summer's roundabout,
Hiding from me. Must I excavate you,
Agents of my death? Hushed snows are deep,
The dead lie deep in me.

# DAVID MALOUF

*Early Discoveries*

I find him in the garden. Staked tomato-plants are what
he walks among, the apples of paradise. He is eighty
and stoops, white-haired in baggy serge and braces. His moustache,

once warrior-fierce for quarrels in the small town of Zahle,
where honour divides houses, empties squares, droops and is thin
from stroking. He has come too far from his century to care

for more than these, the simplest ones: Webb's Wonders, salad-
    harmless,
stripped by the birds. He pantomimes a dervish-dance
among them and the birds creak off; his place at evening filled

by a stick that flares and swipes at air, a pin-striped waistcoat stuffed
with straw. It cuffs and swivels, I'm scared of it. Such temper-tantrums
are unpredictable; blind buffeting of storms that rattle

venetians, hiss off pavements in the sun. Grandpa is milder,
but when he hefts us high his white hairs prickle and the smell
is foreign. Is it garlic or old age? They are continents

I have not happened on, there time will come. Meanwhile he mutters
his blessings, I watch him practice his odd rites, hatchet in hand
as he martyrs chickens in the woodblock's dark, an old man struggling

with wings, or shakes a sieve while bright grain showers in a heap
and blown chaff flies and glitters, falling to the other mouths.
He comes and goes with daylight. He is the lord of vegetables,

the scourge of birds and nuns, those shoo-black crows his sullen
    daughters
taunt him with. His black-sheep son feeds rabbits live to greyhounds
in a cage behind choko-vines. The girls too go to the bad

in a foreign land, consorting with Carmelites, on hot nights tossing
on their high beds in a riot of lace doilies, painted virgins,
unwed. They dwell in another land. As I do, his eldest

grandson, aged four, where I nose through dusty beanstalks searching
for brothers under nine-week cabbages. He finds me there
and I dig behind his shadow down the rows. This is his garden,

a valley in Lebanon; you can smell the cedars on his breath
and the blood of massacres, the crescent flashing from ravines
to slice through half a family. He rolls furred sage between

thumb and stained forefinger, sniffs the snowy hills: bees shifting
gold as they forage sunlight among stones, churchbells wading
in through pools of silence. He has never quite migrated;

the weather in his head still upside-down as out of season
snow falls from his eyes on Queensland's green, and January's
midwinter still. These swelling suns are miracles. Tomatoes

in invisible glass-houses sweat in the heat of his attention,
like islands Columbus happens on. And me, whom he also finds
squatting, egg-plant tall and puzzled by his dark hands parting

the leaves. Where am I? This is Brisbane, our back yard. We let him
garden here behind a lattice wall. This house is ours
and home. He comes like a stranger, warrior-mustachioed,

un-Englished. These days I find him at all turns. One morning early
in Chios, I raise the shutter, and his garden, re-discovered,
shines: cucumbers, spinach, trellised vines. The old man finds me

watching; smiles and nods. Later, fresh on the marble step
in yesterday's newspaper (words of a tongue I cannot read)
his offering: two heads of new spring cabbage. I look under

the leaves (an ancient joke), there's nothing there. Just a sprinkling
of black soil on the headlines of another war, shaken
from the roots. That night I eat them, boiled, with oil and vinegar.

## Asphodel

Under this real estate—squared street on street
of split-level houses
with carport, garden swing—a chain
of waterlily ponds, arm of a sea
that has long since receded,
still sleeps under the still sleep of this suburb, showing itself
in flashes after rain.

We used to spend whole days there, skylarking
on an inch of blood-red water
we harried black marsh-birds through weed-thick shallows, the moon
    rose
heavy beneath us;
it tugged at our heels.
Now kids swing between pines, small limbs at nightfall
shine in the trees.

And once I almost drowned, stepping from clear skies ankle deep
into aeons of mud. I gaped. The earth
rushed in, my body's herds in sudden panic, then with a clamour
the night: I saw my life
of now I-lay-me-down and milk and clean sheets out of reach
on the lily-pond's black surface
—and was dragged out by the hair.

Face down in the bladey grass and pummeled alive again I gagged
on unfamiliar breath, my belly's
mud gave up its frogspawn, lily-pods, swamp-water whelmed in
    cataclysms
and broke from my lungs. Having been filled
a moment with its strangeness, I discovered
a lifelong taste for earth; gills fluttered at my throat, plant fossils
creaked in my thumbs.

Now the pond too is drained. Petrol bowsers
mark the spot where twice I took my small life down to touch
the kingdom of fishbones

and came up again. Station wagons
cruise under the leaves, lawn-sprinklers turn, overhead
through bars of moon-washed cloud-wrack
the nightlights of planes.

A frog gulps on the path, earth-bubble-green. Deep water
speaks in its throat.
And revenant at dawn a pale light ghosts among wrought-iron garden
    chairs a shoal
of vanished lily-ponds. I walk
on their clear light again and will not sink
—not this time. The garden
glows. Earth holds firm under my heel.

### This Day, Under My Hand
#### for Jill and Lance Phillips

Well, it was never mine,
not really. My father bought it
in my name to save
the tax in '45:
streaked weatherboard; no view
to speak of; only the sandhills
of Moreton Island, hump-
backed and white like whales.

My sister will fill its rooms
with cedar and old brass,
her kids with sandprints of
their sneakers on its floors,
small arms spread to conjure
again from blue-green shadows
the old rock-cod they hooked
at dawn out on the reef.

Sandcrabs throw their claws
in a copper pot, hiss horseshoe
red, their agonies
sealed off under a lid.

At nine the scrabble-board—
small word interlocking
down and across to fill
an evening, square by square.

Storm-lanterns. Tigermoths
at the wire-screen door. Slow fan
of the light at Cowan Cowan.
The cold Pacific banging—
an open gate. Australia
hitched like a water-tank
to the back veranda, all night
tugging at our sleep. . .

A world away, and nothing
to do with me: shearwater
gulls, the sundrenched crevice
where lobsters crawl, sharp salt
stinging the flesh like bees,
working its slow way into
the cracks in iron, laying
its white crust on the skin.

Now let it go, my foothold
on a continent!—I sign
my name, it blooms elsewhere
as salt, gull's cry, bruised flesh
of the reef that gasps and thrashes
its life out in our hands.
From the dark bay hissing
like crabs, red tropic suns.


### Wolf-boy

Cradled and warm, fur-warm, in the she-wolf's lair;
sky howling grey, the sweet milk of the planets
to suck; wolf-brothers tumbling—playful nips
of tooth and claw . . . On all fours going, safe
in the she-wolf's tracks, and closer to the earth.

How could he guess that days of separation
would come, when he on two feet must stand taller
and naked in the air? Feeling the itch
for warm fur on his skin. In his mouth raw words
to hurl at the grey-bitch sky that turned from him.

Walking in separation: in the forest
sweating before an iron-dark trap whose teeth
snapped at a foreleg; blood-spoors on the grass.
From his attic bed, hearing wolf-packs howl
at the edge of town—their low growls in his throat.

The boots, the books, the chairs! a firelit trestle
where cream goes round, frothing in wooden bowls.
The girls' bare arms disturb him. Wolf-skulls nailed
to planks, grey wolf-skins underfoot, the terrible
blue of their entrails in the gun-shot blast.

Sulking and blonde. Ashamed of his footsteps printing
the snow, cold water splashed from an iron basin
that stings and burns his chest, soft stroke of hands
in a game of blind-man's buff. Ashamed to feel
the strange goose-pimpling of his hairless flesh.

At night, past the last hut slouching, barred helm-tower
with its skew black cross, familiar faces clenched
on their own, their human pain. Caught in the red
-eyed blaze of the wolf's slow agony—its shadow
on all fours, shaggy, limping at his heel.


*Snow*


A stirring as among
cattle that lift their heads
through darkness to the scent
of water, horses snuffing

at thunder in the grass;
and nothing today will keep them
quiet or still
in the pinewood desks, or summon

their eyes to reflect
figures and cold facts
from the blackboard; they brim
with light, a window-square

where trees writhe, sky glows greenish
bronze and staggers white
like surf. Their senses catch it
from far off, something moves

towards them, edging closer
even than lead pencils,
or cats, chalk or the salty
creases in clothes—

an excitement whose crystals
fall through their veins, the open
spaces of the skull,
wavering towards them

(animal eyes, the nostrils
flared) like the feathers
of angels, sky-flakes
blessing the dull cobbles

and slant black roofs, bare playground,
pond. On their hands the taste
of stars, their foreign coldness,
colour of distances,

and all that is further off
than flesh. Falling light
strikes upward from earth. Its brightness
creaks under our shoes.

### An die Musik

We might have known it always: music
is the landscape we move through in our dreams, and in the Garden
it was music we shared
with the beasts. Even plants
unbend, are enchanted. A voice wading
*adagio* through air, high, clear, wordless, opens perspectives
in the deepest silence; clovers
hum; the jungle's layered
sound-mix seeks horizons, arranging itself as avenues.

What else does it make,
this *concert champetre*, if a not a space we might re-enter
in innocence, pure steps
of sound on which the creatures
descend at almost dusk to recognize, as in a pool,
their names (not *cat*, not *Moggy*), and passion-flowers
incline their busy flywheels to the sun, spinning a line
of melody that modulates from yellow
to green as in mirror fugues and counter-clockwise through the year.

So then, play your beanfield
Vivaldi's *Gloria* and see the thin pods swell, miraculous and many
as the mouths of Hosannah. Watch them
explode across a stave, the angel syllables,
zip-fresh, sky-packed, and flutter
*prestissimi* on strings in hemidemisemiquavers.
Let the countryside be filled
with a din, a chime, an agricultural boom, real orchestras
(the Boston Pops) in real market gardens.

Imagine as *Ein Heldenleben* blooms
in a paddock, the slow inner lives of pumpkins, big stones
cracking, a moon-washed field
astir like a symphony as Bruckner coaxes the zucchini.
The green things of the earth
discover a fifth season to push through to, all
grace notes, as their vegetable souls
aspire to 'the condition'. A new species
taps at the boundaries. Beethoven's Tenth is what it breathes.

# THOMAS W. SHAPCOTT

from *Piano Pieces*

SCHOENBERG OP. 11

'There is frost in the air
and a dark feeling about the edges of sight.
Why will the children still be noisy
and fight loudly in the cold street?
I look out the window at nothing to fear
and see all the city usual and busy.
In the quick dusk I hear a child shout
(laughter or terror?)
and am uneasy
so that I must turn away
and switch on all the lights.'

WEBERN

'Let me show you my love'
he cried
breaking a flower
from its green stem.

## Flying Fox

She tosses and rumples alone on the double bed:
when, damn him, when will his car cringe in
through their gate and clatter over the one loose stone
to announce his coming? Her life has become a code
of sound, a mesh of reassurances
and locks. She wills herself still and tight. No use,
each minute drums with the wrong silence, the wrong noise
on the rigid tendons of her own unease.

And still she waits, as tensely she listens, and hears
in the rank-growing neighbour pawpaw tree outside
a marauding flying-fox circle and flap and cling
scooping the ripe air, gripping with clawed wings
at its easy quarry, the fleshy neglected fruit,
and tear through its shallow skin, and feast on it.

### The Bicycle Rider

Just like that. When he brings the new bike home
his son is all legs with excitement. 'No, it's for me.'
'Go on, dad, ride it outside.' He knows how clumsy
he will be, first time. The boys race after him,
professionals in the district. 'Do a slewie.' They aim
for the park and circle it three times. He
is aching already—all this crazy industry
for the sake of a sagging gut and a remnant of dream!

If he had forgotten how you feel each bump and rise,
he is not a clerk, now, he *feels* as a boy feels; every street
is an alternative. 'Come this way, dad.' Sweet
indeed to become a novice in your son's eyes.
It is a race for home. How long can this go on?
The sweat creeps out on his forehead, it scatters in the sun.

### Near the School for Handicapped Children

His hat is rammed on
his shirt jerks at his body
his feet cannot hold in
   the sway   he cannot keep
              still.
When I see his face it is freckled
to remind me of nephews
his limbs remind me of how straight
is my own spine and that I take my fingers
 for granted.
He is waiting for the green light.
     My fingers clench
   I am hurt by my wholeness
   I cannot take my eyes from him
   I fear my daughter may be watching
He has been dressed carefully
   I'm here I'm here I'm here
his whole struggle rasps me like a whisper

and when the lights do change
   he skips across the road he
     skips he skips he dances and skips
      leaving us all behind like a skimming tambourine
       brittle with music.


### Sestina with Refrain

Why does he keep bruising against me my dead father why still
rub First War mud into his eyes   something won't die
something unspeakable   he survived 'got through' kept all
the parts to Soldier-On   'War Babies'   a tag stuck
to explain old-person nightmares   but not this other
disturbance   a voice faint and hoarse the call for water

and why me   so long after   War's so tired let it die
our century congeals with veterans all 'War Babies' all
with obsessive yarns (horrible: back off) poolrooms are stuck
with them *me mate's jaw shot clean through and something or other*
*gurgling there   a voice faint & hoarse the call for water*
what can you say   remember it's over dad   dead   lie still

*More* something insists *you have to listen damn you*   all
refuses at some moment   cities   Gods   belief's unstuck
men avoid your eyes   it's not you it's absences from each other
the absence voice faint and hoarse the call for water
there is no water   'War Baby'   not allowed to be still
to drown in that water   lips fester the nerves of the tongue die

no help to have seen in the Sack of Carthage a pike stuck
through the peasant wife's breasts or in Gaul another
staff through her mouth   a voice faint and hoarse the call for water
Vikings Saxons   into her hold her   hold her still
Bosch Anzac Marine stick the gun get it done   die
*Death* cry death to them enemy   into them into all

into   old man   dad   why drag me through the intestines of another
battleground of the voice faint and hoarse the call for water

not over not ever over not to be extinguished to be still
each witness remembering death goes into you to die
to haunt you haunting me    mocking my innocence all
my inheritance    out of your grip on me something has stuck

*Vietnam Corporal Cavil: A voice faint and hoarse the call for water*
*so we ripped off her clothes stabbed her breasts she wouldn't die still*
*we spreadeagled her shoved a trenching tool up she would not die*
*we shot her it was okay they were Gooks Commies that's all*
look dad these new veterans come home survivors stuck
into jobs and families    war babies    you know how they look past
    each other

wake at nights gulp the unspeakable threat    lie still
it is over lie still    there are others now to cry for all
the forgotten for the remembered voice faint and hoarse    the call for
    water.


### Autumn

We don't have much language for tragedy
we are not trained even for minor disaster
we are new here

> *a 38 yr old man removed his shoes and socks*
> *then climbed the rails of the Town Bridge.*
> *A passing cyclist saw him fall. Three hours*
> *later police recovered the body.*

I hear your silence Tommy Jennings
because you sat near my desk at school and because
I remember you reading cowboy comics in National Service
    and
seem to recall you always somewhere hanging around
this shabbybrick town    when did you fully realize
    there were no words left in your flesh?
    when    before jumping    did you look down and see?

I hear your silence
We don't have any gesture to exorcise failure
we are grossly inarticulate      even our bodies
seem to have atrophied      our arms are dolls
our tongues quite mechanical

> *Captain Oxley in his journal camping here noted*
> *how at dawn native women set up a ritual mourning*
> *for the dead      they carried woven bags of bones and relics ...*

still strangers here we are not trained for lament
the silence of a suicide affronts us      our own silence
is without echo we have no exchange with any past

This time of year the fragile light hurts
there is no silence in your silence Tommy
I can blow one note on a plucked reed      only bones
made into flutes will undeceive the dead      I hear you
Tommy Jennings      I deny the awful inarticulateness
of your silence      I deny that you found safety
outside language      I am not trained but know I must incise
for words      I cut fingerholes of a group memory
into the bones of an isolate numb man to deny his silence
because I know it was no discovery      Tommy Jennings
though you are cracked in the spine and drowned
I make a bone with you      a bone I must make
into magic      or a flute.


*The Litanies of Julia Pastrana (1832–1860)*

I

The Lord's name be praised
  for the health that keeps me performing my tasks each day without
    faltering
The Lord's name be praised
  for my very tidy figure and the good strength of my spine to keep
    me agile in dancing.

The Lord's name be hallowed
   for the sharpness of my eyes and the excellent juices of my
     digestion.
I am in debt to the Lord
   for all things even my present employment I who could have
     withered on the dustheap of the high village am enabled to travel
     to the curious and enquiring Capitals of Europe—
I am in debt to the Lord for all things
   even my present expectations
   for my Manager has made me a proposal of marriage. He loves me for
     my own sake.
I am indebted to the Lord of all things.
   My body covered with hair that made me cringe in the dark from
     the village stone-throwers has earned me true fortune and
     undreamt of advantages,
   my double row of teeth set in this bearded thick jaw that frightened
     even
   myself as a child looking in the well with its cruel reflections the
     Lord has
   made for me to be a wonder to the learned physicians of London,
   my wide thick nostrils that they called me ape-baby for in those
     terrible
   village days are no more strange in the Lord's eye than the
     immensely
   varied noses I see in the gaping audiences who are compelled to
     suffer without any rewards,
The Lord's name be hallowed and praised
   for I have been instructed to consider all my born qualities as
     accomplishments.

In my own tongue I sing a soft theme to the Lord,
In my own heart I dance with quietness—
   not so loud that the sightseers will hear me; yet when I have a
   new dress I remember its price and its prettiness, I hold myself
   straight and proud—the Lord knows there is beauty in the long
   black hair that covers my body. Let them see, let them stare. The
   Lord knows that. He gives me pride in that. They pay their pennies
   and I dance snappingly for their pennies and for the money my
     Manager

is keeping for me and for the Praise: the praise I say, of the good
   Lord
the brother of understanding
who was himself many days in the desert and was jeered at and has my
heart in his dear keeping.


## II

Why do I dream in my lungs
high air and the mountain tightness?
I will never return there.
I had brothers led the chase and the hunt
has me still panting, awake with strained
unweeping eyes from my mattress of goosefeathers.
I had a father.
How the heart winces across years
how the smallest flower is remembered
the first blows.
The Lord trembled for me in those years.
High air of Mexico, still claimant over me.
These European sea coast cities burden themselves
sometimes it is like a feeling of
being within intestines,
sometimes it is like
cells, not an open cage.
But to move constantly
(I move protected by blinds and veils)
is the Lord's way, who travelled
and was also homeless.


## III

'The Ugliest Woman in the World'
dances for your patronage
and your curiosity,
you curious ones
you with pink faces and puffy eyes and hands stuffed
   into tight cloth purchased with broken mountains
you with sour mouths hiding bone-yellow teeth that have chewed
   upon the produce of a quarry of blind children

you with delicate complexions powdered from the estates
   of pork barons and blood-slimy dealers in villages
you festering citizens of the bulbous pendulous cities
    you breathers of discharged curses, brothers of god
    yea even brothers

### IV

My red tinsel dress—will he tear roubles and banknotes into the Volga
managing my dowry—I told him I would adore I had such spirits in me
    he
was abashed then delighted he implored again—I tell you he implored,
    God,
and I had you, praise you, for the good things in my body—how he
    liked
me trim in red tinsel how he—is it now—my child will be—like you,
Lord, will be tall and fair and with a good strong spine to walk
    upright—
and without shadows and veils—is it always like this, the pain is
enlarging too widely—he will be with shiny black hair and black eyes
    they
can be my gift to him and the dance and strut of a proud man—God
    the way
my father had a strut in the plaza—it is coming yet? how many hours
    do you
have cloth to mop me, all the hair on my body drags as never before,
    all my
body over the matted hair is heavy down, sodden—it is to be, Lord,
    OPENING

### V

THE MUMMIFIED APE WOMAN AND THE MUMMY CHILD glassed,
strung on a perch like a parrot, the child. How grotesque! Look closer:
how terribly real, not like a waxwork at all but almost human. Lord!
Give thanks never to have
seen them
real
and alive
among
us.

# RODNEY HALL

*Mrs Macintosh*

Mrs Macintosh so simply
has reduced the world's dilemmas
to her fixed obsession, birdcage buying.
Now exhibits fill her rooms:
some are miniature pagodas,
and one a jail of cells.
The smallest, made from a lost
girl's hand, is bones enmeshed
in silver wire. The largest
looks an anarchy of cleverness
the total snub to cage-convention
a cloud so frail and knobbled
it dangles crazily askew, high
against the inconvenience of a wall.

These, her eccentricities,
are cherished catalogued
paraded for the delectation
of any visiting evangelist
salesman or charity collector.
Her cages, Mrs Macintosh
is careful to point out, are empty.
Birds revolt her—frighten
her wrinkled eye with theirs
and mock her ways with harsh high
female voices; or sing so sweetly
they could almost lure her back
to join the world. Unbearable.
No, she likes her symbolism:
cages free of birds, pure captivity
that's innocent of pain.

All day her hymns escape the house.

### Wedding Day at Nagasaki

In the flash of that explosion:
as if your face were silk
and one thread pulled,
the skin went crinkling
along a hairsbreadth
of perfection, this line
the boundaries of earth.

Two continents divide
the living beauty of my hopes.
But when the flesh is cool
we'll kiss again
and like strange birds
cry in the loaded air
*This is today! Today!*

### from *The Owner of My Face*

#### 1. AFTER A SULTRY MORNING

After a sultry morning—blazing walls and shadow holes—
we inhale cool langours of the patio

After the moist theatrics of vitality
rain slops across the street
drunks hitch unheard horses post to post to post
high-stepping tourists clear the old men sprawled among their dignities

a dozen pastel portraits blur toward completion
a togged-up thug turns artist
one foot is placed before the other
ancient markets must be painted up or battered down
this is how we take our pleasures

A drunk is dying to the same old shape
earth feels and roses scream
the cloud is architectural with laziness

You and I move charmed
where righteous men would vomit

Trees breathe warmth
some gaunt old singer has a young girl in his power
and he sings and he knows and
grateful fingers cage the neck of his guitar


2. LIPS AND NOSE

Lips and nose—these only
the broken moments of a face

and above beyond before them
                              —sky
the human dawning sky
inhuman blue or superhuman black

and broken off
            just floating
lips, nose

            and a pair of snapped off
left-hands holding
palm to palm in absolute repose

            and snapped off lotus
floating in the black the blue the dawning sky

and here a broken palmtree rich with dates
and still mature with light
                              flower, fruit
and the sun's hand curled with love in ours

these lips were polished to a jewel's depth
beyond simplicities of gender

They are lips and nose
what pedant asks whose hands were joined?

say humbly
and with all the praise of suffering entailed
*they are in repose*

### 3. SOME MAGNETISM IN THE SEA

Some magnetism in the sea
drags my bowels heart brain
body dangling from my head
skin smooth with knowledge of balloons
I do not care what happens to me now
Who would have chosen this?

I smiled at you I waved
there was nothing to disturb polite society
    but loose in the wrenched-open
    sea from air from sea
    some wild land beast took meat
I witness patterns but I don't care
what they mean.

from *Black Bagatelles*
(*Poems addressing Death*)

### 1. MY COFFIN IS A DECKCHAIR

My coffin is a deckchair
                empty sandals
half an avocado shell
             cup with tea leaves
and on the tepid bricks a steel watch slowing down

My coffin is the seconds as they used to be

What can I recall of childhood?
everything I used to think
             is as I think it now
who would suggest I've learnt the lessons of experience?
and what experience? I have nothing but my child-
            words to say

Get on with it: strike up the funeral jig
I can remember tomorrow as if it were only yesterday.


   2. THEY'RE DYING JUST THE SAME IN STATION HOMESTEADS
They're dying just the same in station homesteads
they're dying in Home Beautiful apartments
in among their lovely Danish furniture
on and across the furniture they're dying
spewing blood or stiffening dry and seeming never
to have been alive

in among the cushions, on the wondersprings
they're suffering the final anguish of bewilderment
(indeed the springs of wonder)
they're drowning in their scented baths
suffocating under mink
                never
were corpses made so comfortable

slashing wrists and rushing for the sink as blood
spurts hideous anarchic shapes among the carpet-roses
rushing out to save the Super Dreamland being ruined
but dying in the corridor (at least with purpose: Reach the
kitchen where it's easier to clean)

their working lives are spent on chocolate-coated poisons
on buying cancers for the stomach and the lungs
and nice fat cushions for the heart

bowing down before the TV idols they are dead
they're lopping off their
                    fingers pruning dwarf acacias
practising for death they're polishing the car
to look its best for when it hits the news

nothing now is out of place
—the children safely grown up, married, owners too
of things they cherish
things they simply could not live without

### 3. THE WORLD IS A MUSICIAN'S CLIFF HOUSE

The world is a musician's cliff house and a missionary's villa by the
    beach
        a piano softly hammers
        rhapsodies in place
                the introspective
        pianist has no need of anyone
        but his silent composer and silent self

        the instrument speaks
                oracular
        this flat wood box

        (the priest stores up his sum in memory
        our world's equation as an f sharp minor chord)

        it took a forest full of trees and animals
        for that piano to evolve
                and city states to fall
        for such a stable piece of music to be thought

The mad ocean fumes a skin of light across the windows of an airtight
    house

### 4. OCTOBER

    October: and the fires go out along the coast
    as this year's muttonbird migration streams
    its three-day wonder from the north

        birds fall but the flock won't fall
        None leads—they're led by those (as
        usual) closest to the common fear

Only a thousand years ago we had a word for it *Ourfather*
now with cameras to blind us
microphones to stop our mouths
the earth's crust is a book of folded leaves
the severed treetrunk nothing but a scroll
clouds a heap of knowledge

facts go fouling up the sea
definitions mummify the verbs we're left

> None leads but countless numbers follow
> all this will be different on return
> the long passion of the roostingplace
> will one day snap and we shall find
> we've flown around the world—we've
> killed ourselves because it's in us
> and because it's in us to come home
> —no more than that

I kiss and suck the huge black flank
                              night of mind or hope
this death of having nowhere left to go
the act without a history
                    meanwhile you
store your victims, stuff them down some crack
between the walls
plant them face packed back in river mud—
disperse their unburnt dust in cockroach bellies for a
month or two and call it purgatory

You're going to talk to me—that's what I'm leading to
your word the homefall of our meanings
your barcarolle across the lustrous absences of
                        things seen round the other way
your whispered treachery that meanings are indeed a
                    place and of the place (are
body-shaped) where each of us might fit our body perfectly

Death, is that you calling? Your wind-harp
sighing with the element of form?


### A Text for these Distracted Times

The children of dreams are in terror
and the children of dreams have nothing they dare say outside the
    dream

while those who have power and the generators of it
use up whole cities of electricity to burn off the brains of the helpless
to burn altogether their dreams of not being burnt

There are those with skill to plant orchards
who will not be permitted orchardspace
nor will those who have understanding of the land
be permitted land they might fulfil with understanding
                                                    just as
the cities shall outcast those who would live together in peace
and schools become solely concerned with obedience and what we sell
as from churchpulpits words first addressed to a desert people
from a desert people long dispersed are now addressed to us
                                                    or to
those among us with hopes there's still some other place than here
also to those of us about to set foot in fast cars even

even rockets ready for the moon are addressed as Arabia was by
        Palestine
or as those merchants spoke shuttling precious treasuries of words
between the Euphrates and the Nile

Flowers have broken through the stony ground
the desert flows green rivers in the wind
the factories of innocence are bottling blood
                    for when there might be not enough

we (links of this worldgrasping creature grasp at the world) know
what we know and all that we have known

The children of dreams are in terror with learning
the secrets of those who desire to know secrets and keep them

Our cannibals have put on white coats so we'll know them
the eaters of their kind are busy among tubes
the eaters of our kind busy themselves among tubes
and about them are the figures of their own inventing—
the rational day sits like a cataract on the dreaming eye

Yet we are the most beautiful world of the world

# JUDITH RODRIGUEZ

## *Eskimo Occasion*

I am in my Eskimo-hunting-song mood,
Aha!
The lawn is tundra    the car will not start
the sunlight is an avalanche    we are avalanche-struck at our breakfast
struck with sunlight through glass    me and my spoonfed daughters
out of this world in our kitchen.

I will sing the song of my daughter-hunting,
Oho!
The waves lay down    the ice grew strong
I sang the song    of dark water under ice
the song of winter fishing    the magic for seal rising
among the ancestor-masks.

I waited by water to dream new spirits,
Hoo!
The water spoke    the ice shouted
the sea opened    the sun made young shadows
they breathed my breathing    I took them from deep water
I brought them fur-warmed home.

I am dancing the years of the two great hunts,
Ya-hay!
It was I who waited    cold in the wind-break
I stamp like the bear    I call like the wind of the thaw
I leap like the sea spring-running. My sunstruck daughters splutter
and chuckle and bang their spoons:

Mummy is singing at breakfast and dancing!
So big!

## Rebeca in a Mirror

Our little tantrum, flushed and misery-hollow,
sits having it out
in a mirror; drawn stiff as it
till her joke of a body, from flat,
flaps with the spasms of crying.
The small eyes frighten
the small eyes clutching
out of such puffed intensity of rage.
She will not look at people about, or follow
a dangled toy. No-one can budge her huge
fury of refusal; being accustomed
to orchards of encouraging faces rolled in her lap,
cloud-bursts of ministering teats and spoons
and the pair of deft pin-wielding scavengers
that keep her clean,
she is appalled by her own lonely image.
And we, that she's into
this share of knowledge,
and is ridiculously
comic in her self-feeding anger,
her frantic
blindness by now to the refuge
of a dozen anchoring shoulders and outheld hands,
vassals,
her multitudes . . .

Yet who can be more alone, months walled
in her cot's white straw,
the family hushed
and hovering, afraid to touch
so small
a trigger of uproar;
or so much as flutter
one of her million or more
petulant rufflers spoiling for noise and action
around the nerve-end flares that signal ruction?
And think, she has not long come

through a year of twilight time in one gradual place
further and faster
than death, or the endless relays
of causeless disaster;
frail-cauled, a hero, past perils vaster than space
she has come—
and can never re-enter
the unasked bodily friendship
of her first home.


## At the Nature-Strip

In Lantana Street's mid-morning
an Italian grandmother is trying to happen.

The nature-strip's flat out parching.
All the hardy natives in sight have leaves on;

the garbos were through before the kids went,
the Council street-cleaner's rotary whiskers

slurped by at 6.30. All day begonias
are for nobody, till early each evening hoses them.

Mrs Whatwasitagain in black
is gazing cobbles out of half-melted bitumen,

also whitewash from her hillside village;
and nudging one-language housefronts into gossip

to boast of her Mimo, the smart one,
and of big Vito, tossing pizze downtown,

and Nino, in Bari, who'll be out soon.
Till a carload of shoulders cruising past

bare-faced and noisy as tourists
stalls under her arms-across watching,

worn shoe-heels planted,
head-scarf, and the front-on placid wrinkles;

they pick up in low—leave her standing—
half-focused—an exotic—too old, and simply

out of place. (Whose roots settle
for earth, old earth, with a blackboy endurance.)


## ANTIGONE KEFALA

### *Saturday Night*

Prophets at street corners, in neat grey suits.
Fixed eyes, unseeing, selling the old cures.
And everywhere the river,
midnight blue, flowing unheard above the silent trees
studded with magic signs.

Then we went up in our furs, in the rough foyer,
wooden horses under the stairs, 'to remind us
of our beginnings,' she said patting the little dog.
The walls covered in magician's tricks,
mirrors, and the paint dead.

When the play started we grew silent.
We watched them move under the plastic lights,
inner landscapes of dust and spare parts.
The ancient masks cast now in corrugated iron.

At the end we came out empty handed in the
narrow lanes, and down William Street,
through forests of broken walls and rubble,
so many pairs, holding hands, our gestures
no longer our own, multiplied to infinity
in windows. The world made of couples,
kissing, smiling at each other, stylized
movements following the eternal blueprint.

## LES A. MURRAY

### *An Absolutely Ordinary Rainbow*

The word goes round Repins,
the murmur goes round Lorenzinis,
at Tattersalls, men look up from sheets of numbers,
the Stock Exchange scribblers forget the chalk in their hands
and men with bread in their pockets leave the Greek Club:
There's a fellow crying in Martin Place. They can't stop him.

The traffic in George Street is banked up for half a mile
and drained of motion. The crowds are edgy with talk
and more crowds come hurrying. Many run in the back streets
which minutes ago were busy main streets, pointing:
There's a fellow weeping down there. No one can stop him.

The man we surround, the man no one approaches
simply weeps, and does not cover it, weeps
not like a child, not like the wind, like a man
and does not declaim it, nor beat his breast, nor even
sob very loudly—yet the dignity of his weeping

holds us back from his space, the hollow he makes about him
in the midday light, in his pentagram of sorrow,
and uniforms back in the crowd who tried to seize him
stare out at him, and feel, with amazement, their minds
longing for tears as children for a rainbow.

Some will say, in the years to come, a halo
or force stood around him. There is no such thing.
Some will say they were shocked and would have stopped him
but they will not have been there. The fiercest manhood,
the toughest reserve, the slickest wit amongst us

trembles with silence, and burns with unexpected
judgements of peace. Some in the concourse scream
who thought themselves happy. Only the smallest children
and such as look out of Paradise come near him
and sit at his feet, with dogs and dusty pigeons.

Ridiculous, says a man near me, and stops
his mouth with his hands, as if it uttered vomit—
and I see a woman, shining, stretch her hand
and shake as she receives the gift of weeping;
as many as follow her also receive it

and many weep for sheer acceptance, and more
refuse to weep for fear of all acceptance,
but the weeping man, like the earth, requires nothing,
the man who weeps ignores us, and cries out
of his writhen face and ordinary body

not words, but grief, not messages, but sorrow
hard as the earth, sheer, present as the sea—
and when he stops, he simply walks between us
mopping his face with the dignity of one
man who has wept, and now has finished weeping.

Evading believers, he hurries off down Pitt Street.


### Once in a Lifetime, Snow
#### for Chris and Mary Sharah

Winters at home brought wind,
black frost and raw
grey rain in barbed-wire fields,
but never more

until the day my uncle
rose at dawn
and stepped outside—to find
his paddocks gone,

his cattle to their hocks
in ghostly ground
and unaccustomed light
for miles around.

And he stopped short, and gazed
lit from below,
and half his wrinkles vanished
murmuring *Snow* . . .

A man of farm and fact
he stared to see
the facts of weather raised
to a mystery

white on the world he knew
and all he owned.
Snow? Here? he mused. I see.
High time I learned.

Now that the boys have got
the farm in hand
with all they know, and claim
to understand—

Here, guessing what he meant
had much to do
with that black earth dread old men
are given to,

he stooped to break the sheer
crust with delight
at finding the cold unknown
so deeply bright,

at feeling it take his prints
so softly deep,
as it if thought he knew
enough to sleep,

or else so little he
might seek to shift
its weight of wintry light
by a single drift,

perceiving which, he scuffed
his slippered feet
and scooped a handful up
to taste, and eat

in memory of the fact
that even he
might not have seen the end
of reality . . .

Then, turning, he tiptoed in
to a bedroom, smiled,
and wakened a murmuring child
and another child.


## The Names of the Humble

Fence beyond fence from breakfast
I climb through into my thought
and watch the slowing of herds into natural measures.

Nose down for hours, ingesting grass, they breathe grass,
trefoil, particles, out of the soft-focus earth
dampened by nose-damp. They have breathed great plateaux to dust.

But a cow's mouth circling on feed, the steady radius
shifting (dry sun) as she shifts
subsumes, say, two-thirds of mankind. Our cities, our circles.

They concede me a wide berth at first. I go on being harmless
and some graze closer, gradually. It is like watching
an emergence. Persons.

Where cattletracks mount
boustrophedon to the hills
I want to discern the names of all the humble.

*        *        *

A meaningful lack in the mother-tongue of factories:
how do you say *one* cattle? Cow, bull, steer
but nothing like *bos. Cattle* is *chattel*, is owned

by man the castrator,
body and innocence, cud and death-bellow and beef.
Bush people say *beast*, and no more fabulous creature

and indeed, from the moon to the alphabet, there aren't many.
Surely the most precious Phoenician cargo
was that trussed rough-breathing ox turned dawnward to lead

all Europe's journey.
                          *       *       *
Far back as I can glimpse with descendant sight
beyond roads or the stave-plough, there is a boy on cold upland,
gentle tapper of veins, a blood-porridge eater,
his ringlets new-dressed with dung, a spear in his fist,

it is thousands of moons to the cattle-raid of Cooley

but we could still find common knowledge, verb-roots
and noun-bark enough for an evening fire of sharing
cattle-wisdom,
though it is a great year yet
till Prithū will milk from the goddess (*O rich in cheer, come!*)
and down through his fingers into the rimmed vessel earth

grain and food-gardens.
We are entirely before
the seed-eater towns.
                          *       *       *
A sherry-eyed Jersey looks at me. Fragments of thoughts
that will not ripple together worry her head

it is sophistication trying to happen

there's been betrayal enough, and eons enough.
Or no more than focus, then,
trying to come up as far as her pupils.

Her calm gifts all central,
her forehead a spiked shield to wolves
she bobs in her hull-down affinities.

The knotted sway pole along which her big organs hang
(it will offer them ruthlessly downward when knob joints cave in)
rests unafraid in enzyme courtesies, though,

steadier than cognitions speckling brains.

Since I've sunk my presence into the law
that every beast shall be apportioned space
according to display, I unfurl a hand.

She dribbles, informing
her own weighted antique success
and stays to pump the simpler, infinite herbage.

        \*     \*     \*

Her Normandy bones
the nap of her Charolais colour

the ticks on her elder are such
muscatels of good blood.

If I envy her one thing
it is her ease with this epoch.
A wagtail switching left-right, left-right on her rump.

Where cattletracks climb
rice-terrace-wise to the hills
I want to speak the names of all the humble.

### Portrait of the Autist as a New World Driver

A car is also
a high-speed hermitage. Here
only the souls of policemen can get at you.
Who would put in a telephone,

that merciless foot-in-the-door
of realities, realties?

Delight of a stick-shift—
farms were abandoned for these pleasures. Second
to third in this Mazda is a stepped inflection
third back to first at the lights
a concessive
V of junction.

Under the overcoming
undiminishing sky you are scarcely supervised:
you can let out language
to exercise, to romp in the grass beyond Greek.
You can rejoice in tongues,
orotate parafundities.

They simplify
who say the Artist's a child
they miss the point closely: an artist
even if he has brothers, sisters, spouse
is an only child.

among the self-taught
the loners, chart-freaks, bush encyclopedists
there are protocols, too: we meet
gravely as stiff princes, and swap fact:
*did you know some bats can climb side on?*

mind you, Hitler was one of us.
He had a theory. We also count stern scholars
in whose disputes you almost hear the teenage
hobbyist still: *this then is no Persicum variant*
nor—alas, o fleeting time—a Messerschmitt variant.

These cabins are subversive.
On another road, another
driver may be saying *Suffering is bourgeois*
and in China, almost certainly

a truck-driver's shouting *Mao Tse-tung—who cares?*
*him and Confucius!*

Swapping cogs to pass a
mountainous rig and its prime mover, I
reflect that driving's a mastery the mastered
are holding on to.
It has gone down among the ancient crafts
to hide in our muscles.

Indeed, if you asked
where the New World is, I'd have to answer
he is in his car
he is booming down the highways
in that funnel of blue-green-gold, tree-flecked and streaming
light that a car is always breaking out of—

> we didn't come of
> the New World but we've owned it
> from a steady bang, ever more globes, flying outward
> strange tunings are between us
> of course we love our shells: they make the anthill
> bearable of course the price is blood.

### The Powerline Incarnation

When I ran to snatch the wires off our roof
hands bloomed teeth shouted I was almost seized
held back from this life
                O flumes O chariot reins
you cover me with lurids deck me with gaudies feed
my coronal   a scream sings in the air
above our dance   you slam it to me with farms
that you dark on and off, numb hideous strong friend
Tooma and Geehi freak and burr through me
rocks fire-trails damwalls mountain-ash trees slew
to darkness through me   I zap them underfoot
with the swords of my shoes

                          I am receiving mountains
piloting around me Crackenback    Anembo
the Fiery Walls    I make a hit in towns
I've never visited: smoke curls lightbulbs pop grey
discs hitch and slow    I plough the face of Mozart
and Johnny Cash    I bury and smooth their song
I crack it for copper links and fusebox spiders
I call my Friend from the circuitry of mixers
whipping cream for a birthday I distract the immortal
Inhuman from hospitals
                          to sustain my jazz
and here is Rigel in a glove of flesh
my starry hand discloses smoke, cold Angel.

Vehicles that run on death come howling into
our street with lights a thousandth of my blue
arms keep my wife from my beauty    from my species
the jewels in my tips
                          I would accept her in
blind white remarriage    cover her with wealth
to arrest the heart    we'd share Apache leaps
crying out *Disyzygy*!
                          shield her from me, humans
from this happiness I burn to share    this touch
sheet car    live ladder    wildfire garden shrub—
away off I hear the bombshell breakers thrown
diminishing me    a meaninglessness coming
over the circuits
                          the god's deserting me
but I have dived in the mainstream    jumped the graphs
I have transited the dreams of crew-cut boys named Buzz
and the hardening music
                          to the big bare place
where the strapped-down seekers, staining white clothes,
come to be shown the Zeitgeist    passion and death my skin
my heart all logic    I am starring there
and must soon flame out
                          having seen the present god
It who feels nothing    It who answers prayers.

# GEOFFREY LEHMANN

### *The Pigs*
for Chris Koch

My grey-eyed father kept pigs on his farm
In Tuscany. Like troubled bowels all night
They muttered in my childhood dreams, and grumbled
Slovenly in moonlight, sprawled in night-slush,
While chill winds dried the mud upon their hides.
I lay in the faint glow of oil-lamps,
In a musk-scented stillness,
And from the icy paddocks heard the pigs.

My thoughts were haunted by pig-greed, how pigs
Surge to their food-troughs, trample on each other,
And grunt and clamber swilling themselves full.
Often we emptied food on top of them,
So that they swam in muck. And then one day
When the wind splattered us with dust, my father
Heard a pig squealing, crushed beneath the press,
And we began to stone the pigs, and drew
Blood with our stones, but they just shook their buttocks,
And grunted, and still tore at cabbage leaves.

Passing a dozing boar one summer morning
My father pointed at two dead-pan eyes
Which rolled up quizzing me (and yet its head
And snout snoozed motionless, and flies
Fed and hopped undisturbed among the bristles).
Only a pig, my father now explained,
Could glance out of the corner of its eye.
I watch two bead-eyes turn and show
Their whites like death-flesh.

One dusk this huge old boar escaped and chased
Me through an olive-grove upon a hillside.
Dumpy, it thundered after me,
With murder in its eyes, like someone damned,

A glow of Hades perfuming the air.
That night my father took me in his arms
And told me that of all the animals
Only pigs knew of death
And knew we merely fattened them for slaughter.
Puddles of hatred against man, they wallowed
In greed, despair and viciousness,
Careless of clinging slops and vegetable scraps,
And the sows even eating their own young.
The knowledge of death made pigs into pigs.

Later that year this old boar ate
A peasant woman's baby and was burned
Alive one night by public ceremony.
My father stood there by my side,
His toga billowing in the rush of heat,
But in the flames my child-eyes saw
Not a pig, but myself,
Writhing with stump-legs and with envious eyes
Watching the men who calmly watched my death.

### Saving the Harvest

The darkened farmhouse is asleep
And we the sleepers burrow deep
With warm breath into the body's night,
Dumb in our soft quilts with no dreams,
Safe in the smell of timber beams,
Of cattle dung and milk and hay.

Stars burn cold fields with arctic light,
And hour by hour the mercury falls;
Night is a slowly tightening vice
Gripping the apple-trees with frost,
Menacing fragile blossoms with ice
So a whole harvest may be lost.
Numb in the night no animal calls
And tussocks shrivel in cold clay,

The blossoms will begin to die
Stiffened stars in the frozen night.

Wakened from far countries of sleep,
Groaning at three o'clock we creep
From bed, pull on our boots and light
Our hurricane lamps and tramp outside
Into the glacier of the air.
Through orchards of ice our ghost-breaths glide.
The cold has set off our warning bell,
Rattling beneath the frozen sky
So windows light up in the dark,
Dogs shake their chains and start to bark,
Rattling of death in sleepy ears,
The death of half a million flowers,
Blotched sour and withering in the freeze,
A year's work gone in a few hours.

Quickly we each light up a flare,
Run down the lines of apple-trees
And light the burners with a roar.
A hundred burners blast and pour
Heat at the sky, boiling with oil,
And apple-trees dance in their glare.
Ice cracks and thaws deep in the soil.

Slouching back to our rumpled beds
Gone cold, we scratch at listless dreams
And in our singed and frozen heads,
Tingling with hot and cold extremes,
See snow petals flicker with wild light,
And oil burners roaring in the night.

### Song for Past Midnight

The calico-pale paddocks through the window
Are glazed in stillness, two o'clock, the hour
Of dew and frost, stiff leaves, inert houses.

Moving amongst shadows of furniture
I drink a glass of water in the dark.
Deep in the night dark shapes of cows are feeding.

from *Ross's Poems*

MY FATHER'S A STILL DAY

My father's a still day
smoke rising vertically in the calm
from a distant horizon.
There are high cirrus clouds,
mare's tails, thin streaks of ice crystals
combed across the sky.

My sister's light air,
smoke drift, a faint breeze
you can feel on your face.
and leaves rustling under
a deep peach sky at sunset.

Mr Long is one of those small clouds
that sit on top of mountains,
a wry companion,
scud that rushes
across the sky in a storm,
laughing at the whole performance.

My mother is cumulus cloud,
brilliant white and puffy in fine weather,
billowing and changing shape with her mood,
while leaves and small twigs are in constant motion.

But then she starts raising dust and hen feathers,
the wattles around my house begin to sway,
and telegraph wires are whistling,
as mother becomes a gale.
Smoke venturing from my chimney
is shredded into nothing.

Our old white horse (that's me)
canters around the paddock, wondering
why the sky's become so black and blustery,
as branches are breaking off trees.

Then it's sunny again,
and Sally and Peter are playing on the hill
and find Loby the Truck in stones and dead grass.
Loby who was lost for years,
Loby, three inches of loved grey metal.

I've thought of all this,
on a summer night, silent
except for frogs which mean water,
smoking by myself on the veranda.
And the sky is lit by static lightning,
violet flashes. Jack.

### MUSIC IS UNEVENNESSES

Music is unevennesses
of pressure on the ear-drum.
Sight is the vibration
of rods in the eye.
My dog's called Joe.
Meaning to ask for Ock her son
I asked Mrs Wearne
'Where's Olly?' (Her dead husband)
'You tell me,' she said.
Waking in winter—
a big bush cat was sitting in the starlight
scratching at green parrots in a cardboard box.
And where was Olly?
You tell me.

### I WAS BORN AT A PLACE OF PINES

I was born at a place of pines
not far from a place of stones.
There's a town built at the place of stones.
That's where I meet people and go to weddings

and buy and sell,
but the place of pines is my permanent address.

At the place of stones there's a red brick church,
a bridge and willows by the river.
At the place of pines there are rusting cans
and fowls sitting in the dust
and a wagtail that sang all last night in my poplars.

At the place of stones there's a feed mill
and a broadcasting station.
They worry about neighbouring towns developing.
At the place of pines some of us go mad.
Ted Hutt who grew the fabulous tomato plant
shot his brains out in a tree.
My slow neighbour Nat, stickybeaking,
was told by the policeman to scoop them all up.
But there's not much development.

In the place of stones the houses stand in fenced allotments,
there's a high school and a golf-course,
and a mad woman tidying up scraps in the street,
screaming obscene abuse.
People in both places are much the same,
live under the same moon.

In the place of pines
my neighbours' properties are blowing away in the sky,
and there's a lot of dust flying past
I can't identify
from places hundreds of miles further west
(also overstocked).
This dust blows into the place of stones.

In the place of pines
there are damp patches on linoleum
where my dog Tom has licked up food-scraps,
and there are dead branches lying around
they'd collect for firewood in the place of stones.

The place of stones and place of pines
are both part of my mind.
Travelling between them
I stay sane.

### AUNTIE BRIDGE AND UNCLE PAT

Auntie Bridge and Uncle Pat—
the doors of certain bedrooms
will always be closed.
We speak by not speaking,
like my daughter's diary
hidden in the hollow of a tree
meant only for the wind to read,
and that's how I leave it.

There are certain mad people
whose madness consists of saying
whatever comes into their mind.

Some things I don't wish to know—
how a fine woman wasted herself
on a simpleton
and grew a garden of plants whose names
he mispronounced or didn't know—

Her roses and Dutchman's Pipe have vanished,
and a lifetime of frustration made tolerable
by not being acknowledged.

'What are you planting trees for at your age?'
I asked my aunt aged eighty.
'*Someone* has to plant them,' she said.

### SOME OF OUR KOORAWATHA SAINTS

Some of our Koorawatha saints shall be
amongst the whitest of the Central West,
our barber's two successive wives
for instance, both 'white angels,
and my grandfather

had the best handwriting
in the British Empire'.

When there's an inch of frost on the ground
there's a lot of Arthuritis in our district,
and old ones practising sainthood,
quickening with pain.
Our geology will show a heavenly host
of bony joint lesions
and decalcified spines,
but not many steel plates
from skiing accidents.

Our production of saints is so great
the cemetery authorities
are digging them all in deep for the time
they'll give the ground a second rake-over.

'You needn't make the hole for May too deep,'
I said to my friend the grave-digger,
'They'll never know the difference.'

And we dug the hole together
so May wouldn't be too far
from the aerations of spring.

Our local priest—
a millionaire in land—
dressed like a bishop in his ninety-year-old soutane
drove his ancient blue Ford
blowing clouds of smoke, shaking and jerking,
at the head of the procession,
putting on a burst of speed
to get up the final hill
('over the hill' as we call it).
'Our dearly beloved brother—um, sister,'
he said of May whom he'd known from boyhood—
in an overloud voice.
That's our style of funeral.

THERE ARE SOME LUSTY VOICES SINGING

There are some lusty voices singing
and hands clapping
of fine Aboriginal ladies
(in tune with the juke-box)
as I go past their saloon.

The walls are dirty turquoise,
the floorboards sodden with beer and cigarette butts.
The girls entertain black and white friends,
fall pregnant,
and die of poverty and alcohol.

It's degrading, you say (so do I).
but there's something I like
about the vehemence of their despair,
the way they throw their bodies at life
and don't care.
Black people on a winter night
will sit on boxes and kerosene tins
around a big fire
beneath overcast skies that don't move.

You can tell from the way they sing together
they've more compassion
than most Christian congregations.
Walking past I'm stirred by the voices
of girls in the turquoise saloon,
singing and clapping above the juke-box
with such despair and joy—
something we have lost.

# ANDREW TAYLOR

*The Invention of Fire*

Under every cathedral
there's a spring of pure emptiness
architects and priests search out these springs
wherever they find one a cathedral's built

without cathedrals emptiness would water the land
it would flow through the long wet lashes of grass
and under the massed white and yellow flowers
and under the faint red filmy leaves of spring
and over the sparkling stones and around the roots of trees

it would find out valleys and engrave them
with its own downward crashing capture of light
it would swell into rivers shaded and wept by willows
and join a sea forever empty of boats
forever empty of children playing on its shores
whom it aches to embrace and whose castles only
it could erase

inside each cathedral a fish floats
high in stone air and in a sky of glass
he is the sun's fish dreaming of that spring
and in his eye we swim to his dreamt heaven
around its shores little houses are built
and children clap at the incense of small fires

*Developing a Wife*

In the one cool room in the house
he held her face two inches under the water
rocking it ever so gently
ever so gently. Her smile
of two hours earlier came back to him
dimly at first through the water, then with more

boldness and more clarity.
The world is too much with us
on a hot day (he thought); better
this kind of drowning into a new degree,
a fraction of a second infinitely
protracted into purity. Her smile
free now of chemical and the perverse
alchemy of heat dust and destroying wind
free from the irritation, the tears
and the anger that had finally driven him
down to this moment,
was perfect, was
irreversible, a new reality.
Is it, he thought, that there is truth
here which she imperfectly embodies?
Or is it I that I'm developing here—
my dream, my vision of her,
my sleight of hand?
Perhaps, he thought, our marriage is like this?—
flimsy, unreal, but in its own way real:
a moment, a perfection glimpsed, then gone, gone
    utterly,
yet caught all the same, our axis, stationary,
the other side of drowning?
                            He bore
her smile out in the heat to her, as a gift.


GEOFF PAGE

*Country Nun*

In a cafe under a lazy fan
she talks with her brother,
the breath of cows upon him,
a line of sun and hat across his brow.
Wimpled above the steak and peas,

she drifts away / drifts back,
floating as she did
in cowfields of their childhood,
lingering on the few books in the living room,
always last to the pool.

From rough-sawn walls
beyond the memory of decision
she moves through knee-high pastures
to a convent gate
farewell.

Soon now
he will need to walk her back,
feeling her lift already
towards the pure insistence
of the bell.

## PETER KOCAN

### The Sleepers

Sprawled, like park derelicts, about
The lawn, their brains hardly register
The clash of cups from the pantry
Or the drone of a radio
Nibbling at the institutional calm.

The wrack of their broken minds
Is eased by the morning sun. Terrors
Melt on upturned eyelids as the
Earth heats to a slow doze. Peace,
Peace settles on them like strewn petals.

And nearby, beyond the wire,
Visitors stroll in Sunday clothes
And with rehearsed expressions;

And mortified, somehow, by the crunch
Of their feet on the dirt road.


### Bill

It is said there are those who can never be sane,
Who walk always between lost horizons
As outlaws; like the stones and stars,
Like you, Bill, Sex Beast of the newspapers,
Carrying bitter seed to nowhere.

In the season of our bursting rose bush
You share our captivity and exult
Unashamed in the lewd power
That throbs in your body, thrusts in your brain.

Aeons of your black pedigree hum
Beneath your skin like adrenalin,
Bringing an utter certainty
That you are the one. From you flows this
    passionate Spring,

You, bearer of a starry sperm.
You, with thighs of the lion and the grin
Of the prize boar. Tramp your cage!
Let your very bloodbeat drag
The lush world to the bars!


## ROBERT ADAMSON

### Action Would Kill It / A Gamble

When I couldn't he always discussed things.
His talk drew us together;
the government's new war, the best french brandies
and breaking the laws. And it seemed

a strange thing for us to be doing;
the surf right up the beach, wetting our
feet each wave.

On that isolated part of the Coast, counting over
the youngest politicians.
Huge shoulders of granite grew higher
as we walked on, cutting us from perspectives.
He swung his arms and kicked
lumps of quartz hard with bare feet, until I asked
him to stop it . . .

He didn't care about himself at all, and the sea
just licked his blood away.
The seemingly endless beach held us firm;
we walked and walked all day
until it was dark. The wind dropped off and the surf
flattened out, as silence grew round
us in the darkness.

We moved on, close together almost touching;
he wouldn't have noticed, our
walk covered time rather than distance.
When the beach ended,
we would have to split up. And as he spoke
clearly and without emotion
about the need for action, about killing people,
I wanted him.


### Things Going Out of My Life

The things that are going out of my life remain
in its wake a few yards

behind following me asking to be retrieved like
cigarette packets bobbing
at the stern of a boat leaving
with the tide

And it seldom occurs to me that they are not in
the water but could be falling
from my life

as it rises up from earth
or tumbling haphazardly downhill after me
These things leaving

often ask to be identified even though they know
it would be impossible

When I wake up mornings alone it is more disturbing
when I imagine it could be
the living things
that are going out of my life


### Sonnet to be Written from Prison

We will take it seriously as we open our morning paper.
Someone's broken loose, another child's been
wounded by a pen-knife. A small fire down the bottom
of a suburban garden smells of flesh. Dark circles under
the mother's eyes appear on television; she's seen
her baby at the morgue. Our country moves closer to the world:
a negro's book is on the shelves. The criminal's become
mythologized; though yesterday he curled
over and didn't make the news. So the myth continues, growing
fat and dangerous on a thousand impractical intuitions.
The bodies of old sharks hang on the butcher's hooks.
In broad day somewhere a prisoner is escaping.
The geriatrics are suddenly floating in their institutions.
The myth is torn apart and stashed away in books.


### Sail Away

Our day was composed of resemblances, take
the heavy cloud bank as a mountain, as it lifted
itself up from behind the headland: how

its appearance altered to disintegrating
fluxive streaks as we spoke. We were sitting quietly
by the river as the colours changed.

And as we spoke—however gingerly—we knew
the black bird in our voice, and watched it flying
there, high above the water, until our

conversation resembled its elusive song.
Though it was the bird who sang amidst the rolls
of thunder, and, as we listened, its notes

rose and fell around us on the ridiculous earth:
so that all we really saw was in the sky
of that electric evening. Maybe it was summer,

and it was summer's shifting colours,
through which our black bird tumbled, as if evening
was not an imagined time: so in the orange

atmosphere the black bird darted from my voice
to yours, and we almost held each other by the hand.
A breeze ran along the surface, as if it was

a breeze, and the surface of the river
kicked against it, as if there was a tide coming in.
The black bird sang as if it had a song.


### The Ribbon-Fish

They are the flesh we feed upon come from the depths
out beyond the Continental Shelf.

Their skins bright with silver-blue of our origins,
fins waving and curling
and throwing the spectrum.

Hauled out from the fires their eyes reflect,
into the salt-vats, the freezers
and the smoke-houses.

The colour of their skin
mingles with the blood of their predators,

the fibre, the oils and the acids broken down
sustenance for organs we love with.

We return again to the realm of our needs.
Our bodies are constantly drawn towards the slaughter.

Scraping the dry blood from our limbs
we tear off flesh.

Calling for new expression as we approach silence.
Our words are bright
with countless lives, our language

craves its animal body again.
How far we go just to feel something these days.

We see ourselves in what we say, are inarticulate.

Our spirits devour the life taken from oceanic chemistry,
life that finds new forms in thoughts of you.

The thoughts mingle with half-formed emotions

and your invading currents push through into the heart of me.

I see you in what I say, you govern the equilibrations.
There is nothing within us to decay.

We exist in eternity, our souls are waiting.

I have drawn blood for this sanctity, have driven out words
and armies of the workers in language.

I have betrayed the last compatriot,
and have silenced those who denied me silence—
I have freed myself from constraining instincts and affections.

You are all that is true in the things I say
and what you believe I have done.

I have boasted for you and am done with boasting.

We have crossed the ocean and our paths are wakes of blood.

### My House

My mother lives in a house
where nobody has ever died

she surrounds herself
and her family with light

each time I go home
I feels she is washing
and ironing the clothes of death

these clothes for work
and for going out
to the Club on Sunday
and for Jenny to take her baby
to the doctor in

death comes on the television
and mum laughs

saying there's death again
I must get those jeans taken up

# PETER SKRZYNECKI

### Feliks Skrzynecki

My gentle father
Kept pace only with the Joneses
Of his own mind's making—
Loved his garden like an only child,
Spent years walking its perimeter
From sunrise to sleep.
Alert, brisk and silent,
He swept its paths
Ten times around the world.

Hands darkened
From cement, fingers with cracks
Like the sods he broke,
I often wondered how he existed
On five or six hours' sleep each night—
Why his arms didn't fall off
From the soil he turned
And tobacco he rolled.

His Polish friends
Always shook hands too violently,
I thought ... *Feliks Skrzynecki,*
That formal address
I never got used to.
Talking, they reminisced
About farms where paddocks flowered
With corn and wheat,
Horses they bred, pigs
They were skilled in slaughtering.
Five years of forced labour in Germany
Did not dull the softness of his blue eyes.

I never once heard
Him complain of work, the weather
Or pain. When twice

They dug cancer out of his foot,
His comment was: 'but I'm alive'.

Growing older, I
Remember words he taught me,
Remnants of a language
I inherited unknowingly—
The curse that damned
A crew-cut, grey-haired
Department clerk
Who asked me in dancing-bear grunts:
'Did your father ever attempt to learn English?'

On the back steps of his house,
Bordered by golden cypress,
Lawns—geraniums younger
Than both parents,
My father sits out the evening
With his dog, smoking,
Watching stars and street lights come on,
Happy as I have never been.

At thirteen,
Stumbling over tenses in Caesar's *Gallic War*,
I forgot my first Polish word.
He repeated it so I never forgot.
After that, like a dumb prophet,
Watched me pegging my tents
Further and further south of Hadrian's Wall.

### Cattle

With their boxing-glove muzzles
They will stand in your path, heads lowered,
Or run stumbling through bracken
And creeks for no reason,
The grass alive with their fear.

Their bodies heavy
With milk and beef—awkward
As felled timber, they live
Herded by dogs and whips,
By our curses and impatience.

In downpours and mists
They stand like mute sentinels—immobile
With solemn, wide-open eyes,
Staring through hills and fences.

At night they bellow
Across paddocks and gullies,
Wake us from sleep and reassure us
Of our dreams and homestead.

Branded with fire
They have plodded through
Grass, mud and water for centuries——
Leaving, across continents,
A cleft print

That man will decipher
As an omen of his final hunger.


ROBERT GRAY

*5 poems*

A waterbird goes up
out of dead grass, with that slow flight—
its wings, the water lapping.


Some children's voices,
a piano, in the hollow School of Arts.
In the alley, rain floating.

A drop hung,
indoors, from the tap's blunt
beak. A bird sings.


Freewheeling on a bike—
the butterflies of sunlight
all over me.


A daytime movie,
and coming outside again, it's dark.
I choose the opposite direction.


## ROGER McDONALD

*Components*

Here are
blue teapot,
aluminium air.

A yellow desk,
straw matting,
wheaten lines of dusk.

A mango tree,
light climbing down
from day.

And distant thunder
walking into glass.

Here are
three components
equally clear.

The sound
of a millet broom
on stony ground.

A child's fist
pounding on boards
without rest.

A woman's voice
warping the afternoon
with its one choice.


## Two Summers in Moravia

That soldier with a machinegun bolted
to his motorcycle, I was going to say
ambled down to the pond to take
what geese he wanted; but he didn't.

This was whole days before the horizon trembled.

In the farmyard all the soldier did
was ask for eggs and milk.
He and the daughter (mother sweeping)
stood silent, the sky rounded
like a blue dish.

This was a day
when little happened,
though inch by inch everything changed.
A load of hay narrowly crossed the bridge,
the boy caught a fish underneath in shade,
and ducks quarreled in the reeds.
Surrounded by wheat, everyone heard the wind
whisper, at evening, as though grain already threshed
was poured from hand to hand.

This was a day possible to locate, years later,
on a similar occasion; geese alive,
the sky uncracked like a new dish,
even the wheat hissing with rumour.
I was going to say unchanged
completely, but somewhere behind
the soldier had tugged his cap,
kicked the motor to harsh life
and swayed off,
the nose of the machinegun tilted up.


*Bachelor Farmer*

At half-past five—the earth cooling,
the sweat of his shirt
soaked up in red dirt—
he tunnels his arm through the weight
of a bag of wheat, slowly withdraws it,
and sees how the yellow grains
shiver, as though magnetized away
from his skin, each one alone and trembling.

Walking beside the fence, in another paddock,
he discovers a grain
caught in the hairs of his wrist;
he bends down, allows it to fall,
and with the careful toe of his boot
presses it into the ground.

All night sprawled on the verandah of his hut,
he wakes to the call of the pallid cuckoo,
its blunted scale
low on the heads of unharvested wheat—

not rising towards him, not falling away,
but close by, unchanging, incomplete.

### Flights

At Eagle Farm I stand at the passenger gate
watching a Fokker Friendship with huge brown windows
fly slowly at eye level, its passengers staring
through aquarium glass, cool and untroubled,
as though the next moment they will not be burning
as they are, farther off,
behind the service hangar, in flickering silence.

I am there to look at the bodies, capsules of white,
each one already sewn up in stiff canvas.
Cows nibble the charcoal grass, women serve tea
from urns in a sports pavilion.

Another time, late afternoon,
I stand on the beach at Bribie Island
watching a DC3 dance on the underside of a cloud.
I think of the miniature controls, men struggling
as knobs and pedals grow smaller, shrinking
as the plane recedes to a dot, spitting down,
reappearing to curve like a globule of water,
slipping to join a wave.

And then the time comes for my own journey.
Someone forgets to close the door.
The hostess is left behind, she teeters
alone, and waves wildly.
Slicks of oil on the tarmac
glint as the wings pass over, moving sideways—
we are airborne.

Climbing, the only sound is the loose door banging
at the rear of the fuselage, and wind sliding
from rivets and moistured metal—
an irregular drumbeat, an incapable whistle.

The other passengers lean forward
as though searching.

I lean with them, the plane
tips over.
Aimed at a point on the ground
it releases its weight like an eagle;
the door slaps closed.
                    I dream we are falling upwards,
I dream on the plane I have climbed to safety,
though nothing I touch can save me.

### The Hollow Thesaurus

Names for everything I touch
were hatched in bibles, in poems cupped by madmen
on rocky hills, by marks on sheets of stone,
by humped and sticky lines in printed books.
Lexicographers burned their stringy eyeballs black
for the sake of my knowing. Instinctive generations
hammered their victories, threaded a chain,
and lowered their strung-up wisdom in a twist
of molecules. But with me in mind
their time was wasted.

When the bloodred, pewter, sickle, sick or meloned moon
swells from nowhere,
the chatter of vast informative print
spills varied as milk. Nothing prepares me
even for common arrivals like this.

Look. The moon comes up. Behind certain trees are bats
that wrench skyward like black sticks.
Light falls thinly on grass, from moon and open door.
This has not happened before.

# RAE DESMOND JONES

## *Age*

### 1

sometimes to think about age
& the possibilities of it & what it usually
does mean,

not the idealism of the young
which must so often be the desperation
of the inheritors, a fear of being robbed—

perhaps age could be the time
of resentment

not crabbed resentment but a passion
fusing the hesitant acceptance of separateness
with the other enemy

the quiet opposite, certain of dissolution
& although familiar never seen always rattling
underneath the dry leaves behind you &
is never there

no matter how quick you turn—

when your power is most feeble
your strength should be greater & social
justice may become the greater injustice

the bland impersonal welfare state
offering the created need for things ah
the bourgeois

such nobility more insidious & clever
than the fascist boot

the asthma of the not quite comfortable room
& the television screen streaking
& the smile of the new social worker

who just knows that you want to talk &
the tom piper meals on wheels all impinging
on one's right to dissolution

& one's right to be angry
about it, as though if you are to die you
should do it timidly & tidily & be

aware of your lack of sense
of social responsibility: the collective
denial of the embarrassment & benefit

of old age, the distillation of self into
the concentrated chemistry

of all the disinherited &
the suffering & stupidity of the oppressed
beyond the cynical tolerance of the oppressor.


2

i saw an old man this morning with all he owned
in a string bag & the sun was clear
& sharp

& he sat down near the water on a bench
with his neck tucked in like a pigeon &
small beads of mucus

rimmed the lower lids of his eyes
the discomfort of being without a comb & pushing
his hair back over his ear

with his fingers & his other hand holding
a cold square pie just above his lap

looking the harsh god of light
in the face & the light spread over
the edges of the world where men worked in
the daytime in concrete boxes

stuck like pegs into the horizon
& he looked out on the sky & the boats dipping
noses down in the swell & the spray fanned

up & fell as the deep hidden tides beat
against the rock


# RHYLL McMASTER

### *Profiles of My Father*

I

The night we went to see the Brisbane River
break its banks
my mother from her kitchen corner
stood on one foot and wailed, 'Oh Bill,
It's *dangerous*.'
'Darl,' my father reasoned,
'Don't be Uncle Willy,'

And took me right down to the edge
at South Brisbane, near the Gasworks,
the Austin's small insignia winking
in the rain.

A policeman helped a man load
a mattress on his truck.
At a white railing we saw the brown water
boil off into the dark.
It rolled midstream higher than its banks
and people cheered when a cat on a crate,
and a white fridge whizzed past.

II

Every summer morning at five-thirty in the dark
I rummaged for my swimming bag
among musty gym shoes and Mum's hats from 1940
in the brown hall cupboard.

And Dad and I purred down through the sweet, fresh morning
still cool, but getting rosy
at Paul's Ice Cream factory,
and turned left at the Gasworks for South Brisbane Baths.

The day I was knocked off my kickboard
by an aspiring Olympian aged ten
it was cool and quiet and green down on the bottom.
Above in the swaying ceiling limbs like pink logs,
and knifing arms churned past.
I looked at a crack in the cream wall
as I descended and thought of nothing.

When all of a sudden
Dad's legs, covered in silver bubbles,
his khaki shorts and feet in thongs
plunged into view like a new aquatic animal.

I was happy driving home;
Dad in a borrowed shirt with red poinsettias
and the Coach's light blue, shot-silk togs.


*Tanks*

Travelling,
where darkness hauls the world
back underground,
we pass a solid water tank;
squatting on wooden stumps
its corrugations gleam the dull combusting silver
of elephant hide.

Summer nights breed tanks
and a belief that the moon
was made from a tank smashed into sky passage,
empty and dank, corroded by lichens.

In hollows behind outhouses
or back of a wall of pepper trees, tanks
are sleeping, stirring.
They expand, become nervous and rough
and, grinning with iron dimples
begin to move out to the edge of town
to wait for the lorry to Places Unknown.

## A Round Song

World,
world you are wonderful—
cruel, clean, slow-lying;
you slide through me leaving butter rings.

I am not kind enough, nor are you free
but enter me with slipped laughter.
Intent, I listen:
Something screams in small cat-whispers.
I lean into you;
We smear each other in shiny images.

Open your mouth and birds will pour free,
hesitating rung above rung;
Brief and sharp,
how easy to deceive me.

But still I listen
full of such union,
and hear the round-rolling:
World you are good for me.

# JOHN TRANTER

## *The Death Circus*

the death circus moves in.
all you're worth is in it
the man with the plastic face
opens up his graves for you to see

the lady with the soft legs
opens up in the night
all the moon
long, the bitter light
chews at our faces.   you will not like
the happy flame circus in the roaring dark

we were taking a ride
way out south, somewhere you have never been
into a country of cold beauty
the salamander circus
followed like a hungry dog


## *Two Sonnets* from *Crying in Early Infancy*

It's bad luck with a coughing baby
and it's just as rough inside the pleasure resort
so don't bother with the Mandrax any more.
You'll get to sleep, and find a business there
that you'll just have to get used to once again.
These palaces you build, or auditoriums,
someone forgot to put the windows in and
all night long you're troubled by a noise outside

so that every day at daybreak you find yourself
asking the keeper 'Was that me? Was that
me and my trouble again?' And he answers variously
according to your face, 'It was a flock of birds,

sir, of red plumage,' or he guesses 'That, oh,
that was you again sir, pleading to be let in.'

\* \* \*

The spy bears his bald intent like a manic
rattle through the street. A bitter rain
stains the cobblestones. A clock stops; elsewhere
winter tightens up its creaking grip.
Why does the soldier pace the empty field?
Whose war is this, so grey and easily spent?
Slow cars patrol the autoway, children
stare at you cruelly from behind an iron gate

and a brutish gathering begins, somewhere
on the plains far in the hinterland.
The black clock has been still for a hundred years,
and no peasant bears the luck to win
in this poor lottery. Dull green trucks roll out
and the countryside is well advised to be empty.


PADDY BIRAN

*Paddy Biran's Song*[1]


*Ngaa* . . . now then
mist which lies across the country
a bulldozer nosing into Guymay-nginbi
dynamite which exploded
the place becoming cleared
mist which lies across the country
a bulldozer nosing into Guymay-nginbi
dynamite which exploded


[1] Translated from the Girramay by R. M. W. Dixon

*Ahh . . .*
my father's father's country
I had to sing about it
mist which lies across the country
the place becoming cleared
a bulldozer nosing into Guymay-nginbi
dynamite which exploded
Ahh . . . mist which lies over the country

mist which lies over the country
dynamite which exploded
the place becoming cleared
I had to sing about
my father's father's country
dynamite which exploded
a bulldozer nosing into Guymay-nginbi
mist which lies across the country
dynamite which exploded


# MICHAEL DRANSFIELD

## *Bum's Rush*

Becoming an eskimo isn't hard once you must.
You start by going far away, perhaps another land mass,
into the jungle of cold air and make a room a cave a hole
in the surface with your axe. Furnish it simply like devils island
carve a ledge for effigies and another to sleep on.
Land of the midnight sun it keeps you awake turns ice walls blue there
ice walls the effigies a bled white silhouette are blue
wrapt in a fur you try not to remember but its easier just to let go
and be re-tried re-convicted re-crucified after a few years you even
forget to bleed. Blue all year like a duke's veins
like her eyes might have been once
when she had eyes. Freezing to death is the cleanest place on earth.

And identity you need not concern yourself with names you are the
    last of your species.
The worst pain is the morphine blue crevasse and real eskimos
never mind that. Their hallucinations are red-etched norse demons
they etch those on stone make fifty prints and sell them at cape dorset.
In the early winter mornings
sometimes you will hear the snow winds blowing in on you
soon then you will become impatient as lost souls do
you will think you hear someone calling
when it comes to that all you need do is
take a last look at the effigy collection
say farewell to friends you may have made among the graven images
then walk as a human lemming would
out across the bay to where the ice is thinnest and let yourself vanish.


### Pas de Deux for Lovers

Morning ought not
to be complex.
The sun is a seed
cast at dawn into the long
furrow of history.

To wake
and go
would be so simple.

Yet

how the
first light
makes gold her hair

upon my arm.
How then
shall I leave,
and where away to go. Day
is so deep already with involvement.

## Loft
### for Hilary

sometime in the night i stir, rain
has been falling and darker than
evening is the sound of overspilling
water from the roof. two pairs of
jeans move slightly with a breeze
from the window. traffic. in the button
hole of my coat the yellow of a daisy.
thunder. lightning is a bruise of pale
havoc around my eye's coast, and my arm, or
hers, draws in under a blanket from
the first morning of winter


## Portrait of the Artist as an Old Man

In my father's house are many cobwebs.
I prefer not to live there—the ghosts
disturb me. I sleep in a loft
over the coach-house, and each morning cross
through a rearguard of hedges to wander in the house.
It looks as though it grew out of the ground
among its oaks and pines, under the great
ark of Moreton Bay figs.
My study is the largest room upstairs;
there, on wet days, I write
archaic poems at a cedar table.
Only portraits and spiders inhabit the hall
Of Courland Penders ... however,
I check the place each day for new arrivals.
Once, in the summerhouse, I found a pair
of diamond sparrows nesting on a sofa
among warped racquets and abandoned things.
Nobody visits Courland Penders; the town
is miles downriver, and few know me there.
Once there were houses nearby. They are gone

wherever houses go when they
fall down or burn down or are taken away on lorries.
It is peaceful enough. Birdsong flutes from the trees
seeking me among memories and clocks.
When night or winter comes, I light a fire
and watch the flames
rise and fall like waves. I regret nothing.

### Rainpoem

three days of rain: indoors
the mind runs over some
eternal mysteries
polishing them lightly: outdoors
noticing how
even the hugest man seems frail,
gentle, trying to keep dry
a loaf of new bread

### That Which We Call a Rose

Black greyed into white a nightmare of bicycling
over childhood roads harried peaceless
tomorrow came a mirage packed in hypodermic
the city we lived in then was not of your making
it was built by sculptors in the narcotic rooms of Stanley Street
we solved time an error in judgment
it was stolen by the bosses and marketed as the eight hour day

Waking under a bridge in Canberra to chill scrawl
seeing the designs we had painted on its concrete like gnawed fresco
Venice with princes feasting while Cimabue sank deeper into cobweb
as the huns approached in skin boats
back in the world Rick and George on the morgue-lists of morning
one dead of hunger the other of overdose their ideals precluded them
from the Great Society they are with the angels now

I dremt of satori a sudden crystal wherein civilization was seen
more truly than with cameras but it was your world not ours
yours is a glut of silent martyrs money and carbon monoxide
I dremt of next week perhaps then we would eat again sleep in a house
    again
perhaps we would wake to find humanity where at present
freedom is obsolete and honour a heresy. Innocently
I dremt that madness passes like a dream

> Writ out of ashes, out of twenty years of ashes
> For George Alexandrov and for Rick

## Epiderm

Canopy of nerve ends
marvellous tent
airship skying in crowds and blankets
pillowslip of serialised flesh
it wraps us rather neatly in our senses
but will not insulate against externals
does nothing to protect
merely notifies the brain
of conversation with a stimulus
I like to touch your skin
to feel your body against mine
two islets in an atoll of each other
spending all night in new discovery
of what the winds of passion have washed up
and what a jaded tide will find for us
to play with when this game begins to pall

## Geography

### III

in the forest, in unexplored
valleys of the sky, are chapels of pure
vision. there even the desolation of space cannot
sorrow you or imprison. i dream of the lucidity of the vacuum,
orders of saints consisting of parts of a rainbow,
identities of wild things / of
what the stars are saying to each other, up there
above the concrete and minimal existences, above
idols and wars and caring. tomorrow
we shall go there, you and your music and the
wind and i, leaving from very strange
stations of the cross, leaving from
high windows and from release,
from clearings
in the forest, the uncharted
uplands of the spirit

### VI

sky ceases. there is only
air, its taste of rain, its rain colour.
the grass and road through rain air
are more green, more grey. and the wind
in trees among hills, halts
and is shadow, or a still
coldness. air. the horses are restless, they
walk about, and a colt
runs down the field, its mane
describing autumn. i shall become
no more than movement, or stillness, or an idea of being.
there is no-one here: horses are landscape's creatures,
not mine: so, clouds, and the wind. it is a
possibility. now rain cleans the air, and falls,
and falls, and will be falling.

# MARTIN JOHNSTON

*Uncertain Sonnets*
for Julie

### (AIRPORT)

Her arms are gravelled at the undertow
of air flung across air as the monster flows
escaping air. A labyrinth, she knows,
is where all genial lies and no dreams go.
The shaggy dreambeast watches the golden leap
(a dream of Icarus caught in a dream) and still,
staring and weeping on a Cretan hill,
sucks at a dried-out marrowbone of sleep.
'Bloody well fly!'
                          The styles of our defining
are words in sleep, and when the words are said
we lie in the conch of night, entwining
our double-crossing limbs on the double bed.
Toppling unbalanced in the wind I hear
your words lost in the labyrinth of my ear.


### (VERNAL EQUINOX)

Polychromatic springtime's gay cadenza
fades, and the colour harpsichord is still,
then tinkles in the dark a chord of chill
deep green of Marvell, brittle green of Spenser.
The trees are green and silver in the rain,
in trees' bright traceries emerald peacocks roost,
in mirror-silver mail knights prance and joust
and motleys sing the summer in again.
This is the no-man's-land of time. The fingers
rustle across the keys. The scudding face
of the moon fades ... but the tourney lingers
under long tides, in coral where jewelfish race
among lutes and visors, and the dumb sharks sail.
The surface flashes like a coat of mail.

(DIRECTIONS FOR DREAMFISHING)
First you must blow a bottle round your sleep
in concave bottle-greens of drifting seas
around dreams' hot vermilions, where unease
will abrogate its fishing rights to deep
seas where your Dreamfish, bred and interbred
to swim upnight with what you most desire,
slides through the streaming cellstrands in your head
stippled with swirling wet St Elmo's fire
and surfacing flutters on the midnight wind,
as fish can't, as you know. The night is green
with loss. In fading dictionaries you find
'the sea-green beryl, or aquamarine.'
You wake in billingsgate, haggling for a drab
dead slice of Dreamfish on a beryl slab.


### Quantum

The art photographer alone
for whom a bottom is a pear
a breast a peach or God knows what
can praise the queer disjunction of each part
blunder on blunder to the gush we hail.
Does my thigh love your breast,
your back my belly, eye love neck, nape navel?
The mind grows soggy gasping down
the sweat of each improbable convulsion.
How am I to control a thousand touches,
how check the orgasm of the nose,
the fetid climax of the toes?
How, for God's sake, suppress a revolution
when barricades themselves grow fluid?
I do not love for my part, but observe
a glut of tiny lovings; feel myself
a weak old king, misled by ministers,
vaguely aware of sordid little deals
on all the borders (*are* the crooked guards
trafficking with the Vandals?)

Where in the vast perversion of each cell
am I to find room for my meagre coming?
The empire's funds have all been dissipated
I'll have to sell the candlesticks
the barbarians have gone all incorruptible
no wonder the old king
sometimes
nods his head . . .

                (it is a well-known fact
                that the penis
                is an invertebrate)

All of which explains my elation
when sometimes poor Justinian
in spite of upstart generals and adventurers,
dissensions, earthquakes, Ostrogoths and gout,
reforms the laws, or builds an aqueduct.


# CHARLES BUCKMASTER

*Vanzetti*

I don't
pity this man, I love him
—Vanzetti—

After the verdict is passed,
standing in the dock, speaking
in broken, halting English
—thanking the court after politely condemning it

. . . writing letters from the death cell to Dante—
no bitterness,
still
so full of hope; and love.

There were hardly the words
to express to the court
*the gratitude he felt*, for all
it had done

(yet, somehow, he found them
for he
was their embodiment

love.)

Forty-three years
and nothing has changed—
the same old bone-carts
still rattle down
the very same streets

carrying, perhaps, the very same martyrs, on each
journey

—their words, their bodies,
naturally perishable:
Yet that purpose survives—

and is
love



JENNIFER MAIDEN

*Climbing*

This shadow at my shoulder doesn't shed
The substantial night.
The rope twists all breath
From the mountain
As simple as a bed

Far above life in heavy wind you might
Fall beyond the common cliff of death.
With all my side and ear adhered to stone
There seems a place like hell to draw the dead
    Down so soft a body wouldn't wither
But hear the desperate lute lament ahead
    To lull the dog across a bloodless river


### Dew

Dawn is, in essence, sinister as fire.
A fume of birdcries
                in the foaming shadows.
The black and omnipresent burning dew.
A leaf as stiff as jade, inhabited
By curt quarrels of light. The novice sun
As cold as an old woman's righteous mouth.
And soil, itself astir
With sightless unquenched grief to walk alive.


### Slides

'There the Parthenon, & there
          the cloud's edge withers.
There the Thames smokes
      the fountains prance
in reining wind & there
like a baked alaska
the opera house still curves
its blanched & clipped
magniloquence & sugars
the deadpan of an azure
        plate of sky'
At night we wander
      like late tourists
        through our own blood
        shining torches
at rats & swallows burrowed warm
        in antique porticos.

# JOHN FORBES

## *TV*

dont bother telling me about the programs
describe what your set is like the casing the
curved screen its strip of white stillness like
beach sand at pools where the animals come
down to drink and a native hunter hides his
muscles, poised with a fire sharpened spear
until the sudden whirr of an anthropologist's
hidden camera sends gazelles leaping off in
their delicate slow motion caught on film
despite the impulsive killing of unlucky Doctor
Mathews whose body was found three months later
the film and camera intact save for a faint,
green mould on its hand-made leather casing


## *Four Heads & How to Do Them*

### THE CLASSICAL HEAD

Nature in her wisdom has formed the human head
so it stands at the very top of the body.

The head—or let us say the face—divides into 3,
the seats of wisdom, beauty & goodness respectively.

The eyebrows form a circle around the eyes, as
the semicircles of the ears are the size of the

open mouth & the mouth is one eye length from
the nose, itself the length of the lip & at the top

the nose is as wide as one eye. From the nose
to the ear is the length of the middle finger

and the chin is $2\frac{1}{2}$ times as thick as the finger.
The open hand in turn is as large as the face.

A man is ten faces tall & assuming one leaves out
the head the genitals mark his centre exactly.


### THE ROMANTIC HEAD

The Romantic head begins with the hands cupped
under the chin the little fingers resting on the nose
& the thumbs curling up the jaw line towards the ears.

The lips are ripe but pressed together as the eyes
are closed or narrowed, gazing in the direction of
the little fingers. The face as a whole exists to gesture.

The nose while beautiful is like the neck, ignored,
being merely a prop for the brow that is usually
well developed & creased in thought—consider the lines

'the wrinkled sea beneath him crawls' locating the centre
of the Romantic head above the hairline & between the ears;
so the artist must see shapes the normal eye is blind to.

This is achieved at the top of the cranium where the skull
opens to the air, zooms & merges with its own aurora.
Here the whole diurnal round passes through. In this way

the dissolution the quivering chin & supported jaw seemed
to fear, as the head longed for, takes place. The head, at
last one with the world, dissolves. The artist changes genre.


### THE SYMBOLIST HEAD

No longer begins with even a mention of anatomy,
the approach in fact leaves one with the whole glittering
universe from which only the head has been removed.
One attempts, in the teeth of an obvious fallacy, to find
the shape, colour, smell, to know the 'feel' of the head
without knowing the head at all. And the quarry is elusive!
If the stomach disappears, butterflies are liberated & while
the head teems with ideas who has ever seen one? Equally,
the sound of a head stroked with sponge rubber or the sound
of a head kicked along the street on Anzac Day could be
the sound of a million other things kicked or stroked.

The head leaves no prints in the air & the shape of an
absence baffles even metaphysics. But the body connects
to the head like a visible idea & so has its uses, for
what feeling is aroused by *The Winged Victory of Samothrace*
but piercing regret for the lost head? And beyond the body,
a landscape is not just our yearning to be a pane of glass
but a web of clues to its centre, the head. And here, like one day
finding a lone wig in the vast rubbish dump devoted to shoes,
the Symbolist head appears, a painting filled with love
for itself, an emotion useless as mirrors without a head.
This art verges on the sentimental. It's called 'Pillow Talk'

THE CONCEPTUAL HEAD

1) The breeze moves
   the branches as sleep moves the old man's head:
   neither move the poem.

2) The opening image becomes
   'poetic' only if visualized

3)                     but even so
   the head can't really be
                     seen,
                     heard,
                     touched
                     or smelt—
   the Objective Head would be raving nostalgia.

4) Yet the head is not a word
   & the word means 'head'
   only inside the head or its gesture,
             the mouth.
             So the poem can't escape,
                trapped inside its subject
   & longing to be a piece of flesh & blood
   as
        Ten Pounds of Ugly Fat
             versus
        The Immortal Taperecorder
   forever.

5) While anatomy is only a map, sketched
        from an engaging rumour,
  metaphor is the dream
  of its shape—
          from 'head in the stars'
          to 'head of lettuce'

  Between the two
  the poem of the head is endless.

6) Now the world of the head opens
  like the journals of old travellers
        & all your past emotions
  seem tiny, crude simulacra of its beauty.
  & you are totally free

7)        Greater than all Magellans
  you commence an adventure more huge & intricate
  than the complete idea of Mt Everest.

  And this academy can teach you no more.
          The voyage will branch out,
  seem boring & faraway from the head,
  but nothing can delay you
  for nothing is lost to the head.

8) Goodbye,
        send me postcards
        and colourful native stamps
                Good luck!

—— THE POETS ——

## ROBERT ADAMSON

Robert Adamson was born at Sydney in 1944 and grew up between Neutral Bay and Mooney Mooney on the Hawkesbury River. This beautiful river is the central, stable element in his flux of poetic styles and personae. Perhaps because, after he left school at thirteen, he spent so many years in reform school and gaols he seems to suffer in his poetry from a lack of belief in himself as a particular person. The benefit of this has been a restless energy, a reaching out and appropriation of whatever he needed at a given time. Having paraded in various masks, often with impressive panache, his own lines from 'The Final Solstice' speak of deeper feelings:

We dream of the day when there will be no disguises
of the day we can slide into our
personal waters among these fish we like to believe in

A stimulating presence in the literary community, Adamson has for many years been editor of *New Poetry* magazine and Prism books. His latest publishing ventures are Big Smoke Books and the firm of Adamson and Rankin.

Poems: pp. 355—360.

## ARANDA SONG

The first song was collected and translated in 1933 by the only white man ever known to have been brought up speaking an Aboriginal language as one of his native tongues. Aranda land in the Northern Territory and South Australia includes the areas around Alice Springs and Ayers Rock.

The people listening to the Ankotarinya song being sung and acted would have known the myth in detail already, so the song does not always make clear the plot. A summary is provided here adapted from the myth as told by T. G. H. Strehlow. Ankotarinya, a man who looked and behaved like fire, lived at Ankota asleep in the bosom of the earth. When he woke he saw the *tnatantjas* (totem poles) waving against the sky, *tnatantjas* belonging to other men and women. He began to breathe heavily, to sniff around into the four winds: a cold breeze blowing from the north . . . a cold breeze blowing from the south . . . a cold breeze blowing from the east . . . but there! a warm breeze coming from the west. He drew the warm scent in eagerly and followed it. Soon he disappeared under the ground and emerged at Irbunngurerea about seventy miles to the west. He found footprints, he continued on their trail like a dog, 'From this camp they have gone away yesterday only'. Then he saw the thin spiral of smoke from a deserted campfire: 'They have left here only today.' In his hunger he was eager to devour them. Then he found burning embers. He crouched down till he saw them sitting helpless, gazing away into the distance. He came upon them, crouching flat in the long grass. In their midst their great *tnatantja* rose to the sky. In a moment he was upon them, like a whirlwind raking them together, gnashing them up and swallowing them down. Sated, he slept. There he was found by other men from the west who hurled a *tjurunga* at the sleeping form, hitting the monster in the nape of the neck, breaking its head off. The head rolled away, and the swallowed men were all disgorged, spilled out like water. At once they climbed on the rocky hills again, swinging their bull-roarers and decorating their heads with green twigs and wallaby tails. The living head of Ankotarinya then rolled back underground home to where it came from at Ankota.

The powerful fire imagery speaks for itself.

The second song, published in 1962, also translated by the late T. G. H. Strehlow, is from an Eastern Aranda myth which describes how a local kangaroo totemic ancestor returned from his last hunt one evening and then turned to stone—a rock or mountain still there.

Poems: pp. 38–40.

## DOROTHY AUCHTERLONIE

Dorothy Auchterlonie was born in Sunderland, Durham, UK, within sight and sound of the North Sea. 'Nobody swam much in the North Sea, it was too cold, but I once remember going for a swim on a summer day and being notorious for a long time afterwards.' When twelve she was brought to Australia (her mother was born in Rockhampton, Queensland). At Sydney University she studied under the philosopher John Anderson and the orientalist A. L. Sadler who 'opened windows for me'. She worked as a teacher and a journalist for the ABC news service. She left the ABC to marry the critic H. M. Green. After a stint as headmistress of the Presbyterian Girls' College in Warwick, Queensland, Dorothy Auchterlonie became the first woman lecturer appointed to the staff of the new Monash University in Melbourne— and later taught at the Australian National University and the Royal Military College, Duntroon. She was also trained as a singer and for some years sang alto solos in the *Messiah* and other oratorios with such celebrated artists as William Herbert and Stanley Clarkson. 'Inside,' she says, 'I have had a great hunger to be a singer always, to be an expressive artist.' Our finest critic, her massive and energetic study of the novels of Henry Handel Richardson, *Ulysses Bound* (1974) builds an argument philosophically complex and at the same time moving in its portrait of an intense, awkward person. It remains a landmark in Australian literary history.

Poems: pp. 221–222.


## BALGU SONG

This *djabi* is in the Balgu language of the Pilbara district in north-west Western Australia. It belongs to Donald Norman and was sung by a man (now dead) who had it from the composer and who added his own guitar accompaniment. This version was translated by Clancy McKenna in 1978.

Poem: p. 142.

## 'WILLIAM BAYLEBRIDGE'

Most of William Baylebridge's books were privately printed at the author's expense and privately distributed. The earlier ones were published under his real name William Blocksidge. He continually revised and reprinted poems, but unfortunately in these revisions never shed the mannered archaic diction he inherited from John Keats, nor the rhythms and forms that leant so heavily on Shakespeare. Many of his poems contain single lines or images of real power and even, on occasion, metaphysical insight; but seldom do the poems work as a whole.

He was born in Brisbane on 12 December 1883. His father was a real estate agent. He himself was wealthy enough to support his writing habit on independent means. He died in Sydney on 7 May 1942.

Poem: p. 97.

## BRUCE BEAVER

Bruce Beaver was born in Sydney on 14 February 1928. He attended Manly Public School and Sydney Boys' High School. He had many jobs, mainly of the semi-skilled kind and then went to New Zealand at the age of thirty; including a six months' stay on Norfolk Island, he was away four years. In his first three books of poems he refined a personal style of rather rambling lines and circuitous syntax. Then, with *Letters to Live Poets* (1969) he achieved a breakthrough into an even greater assurance. Enjoyable as the other books were, this was the one that put him right at the centre of what was new and mattered. The several books which have followed this, confirm his stature.

Bruce Beaver is married and lives in Manly, New South Wales.

Poems: pp. 295–304.

## PADDY BIRAN

Paddy Biran died recently. He had lived in North Queensland in the Tully district. In 1963 he recorded this song in the Girramay language for Professor R. M. W. Dixon of the Australian National University, who comments: 'The Queensland government had just given to King Ranch, an American pastoral company, the lease on a large tract of Girramaygan territory, and they were clearing the country with bulldozers and dynamite, destroying many traditional sites and causing great concern to the survivors of the tribe ... It belongs to the Ja-ngala style—used for songs of strong emotional message.' This is a new translation made specially for the present anthology.

Poem: pp. 375–376.

## JOHN BLIGHT

'Goethe comes closest for me,' John Blight says, 'in his definition of poetry—a criticism of life. If you are looking for a theme in my poetry, take heed of Goethe's definition. I like to examine closely this quality of matter—life. It is simple then to become intense and excited about it—to become poetical.'

John Blight is an example of the problems a poet can face when the reputations industry takes over a literature. He was quickly tagged and filed as a specialist in sea sonnets, a miniaturist with a knotty style. For example, Douglas Stewart has written of him, 'John Blight's contribution to Australian poetry is no doubt minor ...' and though he goes on to make some accurate observations about the poems themselves, this opening remark sets a tone which is, to say the least, unfortunate—especially coming as recently as 1975. One is tempted to think that had Blight claimed his hundreds of sea sonnets to be a single massive poem (in other words, played their game and stuck a label on what he was doing) the critics might have given him a different rating.

It is noteworthy that once the post-Lindsayite Charm School no longer dominated journal and book publishing, Blight blossomed into his present style, freer, more risky, and more than ever idiosyncratic. The point is that these are true poems with their own wonderful logic of form and argument. They seem to me unlike anybody else's poetry that I have read, and to defy comparative evaluation.

John Blight was born in Unley, South Australia, on 30 July 1913. He has worked as a clerk, orchardist, public servant, and secretary to a sawmilling company. The greater part of his life has been spent in Queensland, where he still lives.

Poems: pp. 215–220.

## BARCROFT BOAKE

Barcroft Boake was born in Sydney on 26 March 1866 and committed suicide there on 2 May 1892. At the age of nine he was taken to live in Noumea for several years and acquired a good working knowledge of French. He completed his schooling in Sydney and was apprenticed to a land surveyor but failed to take his licence. He travelled outback and took work as a boundary-rider. During this time he was introduced to the new balladry. Mr A. L. Raymond remembered, 'Boake was brimming over with Adam Lindsay Gordon; and I have no hesitation in saying that Gordon was the father of his poetry.' Though a healthy and active young man, Barcroft Boake soon fell prey to paralysing fits of depression during which he seldom spoke or looked his family in the face. His principal activity during these times of debility was smoking. The noted editor and critic A. G. Stephens wrote in his memoir: 'The pipe was never out of his mouth ... He was killed by three things in particular: his sensitive brain, his weak heart, and tobacco.'

A fortnight after hearing that 'my best girl is going to be married', he went missing. In his father's account: 'The place Bartie chose was on the shore of Long Bay, one of the arms of Middle Harbour. His body was found, suspended by the lash of his stockwhip from the limb of a tree, by a man engaged in clearing the bush for a proposed sewer. So secluded was the spot that he might otherwise have hung there for months.'

His only book, *Where the Dead Men Lie and other poems* (1897), was published posthumously.

Poems: pp. 46–49.

## BRALGU SONG

In this Arnhem Land song, Djalbarmiwi's narrator blames her husband Banggalawi for the death of their daughter. She is already jealous of her younger co-wife Jandin. This song comes from Yirrkalla, north-east Arnhem Land, in the Northern Territory; Djalbarmiwi is the woman who sang it.

Poem: p. 209.

## CHRISTOPHER BRENNAN

Christopher Brennan was, for half a century, looked up to as Australia's major poet and the first to write as a citizen of the world. Neither claim is much heard now and, fine as his best poems are, he didn't write many of them. His significance in literary historic terms is of great importance, but one which this anthology does not attempt to represent. Certainly he was remarkable for the unique position he claimed and the courage to set out disdaining the common reader, attempting poetry for the elite. This is especially so considering the misery of much of his life. Brennan makes a tragic figure with a touch of grandeur: a distinguished scholar sufficiently unorthodox to be jealously excluded from university positions for years, slighted by lesser men, an advocate for the importance of passion who was unable to relate this to people in his own life, miserable in his marriage, and when finally appointed Associate Professor of German and Comparative Literature at Sydney University, he was dismissed following publication of his wife's action for divorce and on the grounds of drunkenness.

Christopher Brennan's parents had migrated, independently, from Ireland. He was born on 1 November 1870. He died on 5 October 1932. Most of his poetry was written by the time he was thirty-three, but late in life when he fell in love with Violet (Vie) Bird, the few things he wrote for her are moving in their directness—such as the last poem included here—and their freedom from literary pretensions.

Poems: pp. 90–93.

## R. F. BRISSENDEN

Robert F. Brissenden was born in Wentworthville, New South Wales, in 1928 and was educated at Cowra High School and the universities of Sydney and Leeds. He has published *Virtue in Distress*, a critical study of the eighteenth-century novel, is joint editor of a series, *Studies in the Eighteenth Century*, and is Reader in English at the Australian National University. He has made frequent visits overseas: one of his Indonesian poems is included here, 'Walking down Jalan Thamrin'. Dr Brissenden is married and lives in Canberra with his wife and children.

His latest book is *The Whale in Darkness* (1980), from which both these poems are taken.

Poems: pp. 261–262.

## VINCENT BUCKLEY

Vincent Buckley was born in a Victorian country town on 8 July 1925. His parents were Irish. His childhood and education were Irish-Australian and his deep interest in Irish matters and his Roman Catholic faith have remained with him to the present day. He is one of the few poets whose influence as a critic has been widely felt. His *Essays in Poetry, Mainly Australian* (1957) was an important definition of where Australian poetry stood at that time. And as poetry editor of The *Bulletin* during the brief period 1961–63 he helped the rise of a whole new school of poetry reacting against the Stewart-Slessor establishment of the day. Since 1967 he has been a Professor of English at Melbourne Univeristy.

Both in his poetry and his criticism he is concerned at our growing disorientation from the psychic and mythic roots of European civiliza-tion. He is much involved with the values of religion, politics and the arts. His published works include *Arcady and Other Places: Poems* (1966), *Golden Builders* (1975) and *Poetry and the Sacred* (1968).

Poems: pp. 257–260.

## CHARLES BUCKMASTER

Charles Buckmaster, like his friend Michael Dransfield, died young. He was closely associated with the sub-culture of the 1960s, the exploration of drug-induced experiences, and the repudiation of bourgeois values. He was born in Lilydale, Victoria, in 1951 and died in 1972. He was closely involved with the poetry readings at the La Mama Theatre workshop in Melbourne which began in 1966 and which became very influential on the directions of new poetry in that city. His major publication was *The Lost Forest* (1971).

Poem: pp. 384–385.


## BULUGURU

The translator of Buluguru's song, E. A. Worms, explains: 'When old Buluguru leaves his camp he first places a carved snake in the brush. It will watch the camp and drive away any invader. Should the latter, under the impression that he is facing a real snake, put himself in an attitude of defence and try to kill it, the snake will quickly change into a stick again. It is 38 cm long.

'I found Buluguru busily carving a sinuous snake and accompanying his work with a song asking the shavings to come off more quickly, repeating the same few words again and again.'

This song, from the east Kimberleys in Western Australia, was translated from the Yaoro language and first published in 1957.

Poem: p. 283.


## DAVID CAMPBELL

David Campbell was born on a sheep station out of Adelong, New South Wales. Brought up on this isolated property, his childhood provided a rich store of material which he used throughout his writing life. 'My father was very good with people but with children I think he felt that my mother got on well enough with us and he was busy, so he rather disregarded us ... I remember the first time we were brought into the sittingroom to say goodnight to my father—we had a very good nurse called Leah—Leah took us in and we shook hands with him for the first time.' David Campbell went to boarding school and afterwards to Cambridge. 'At school we all scoffed at poetry and thought sport was everything,' he says. But at university a fellow Australian encouraged him to read contemporary poetry; 'At that stage I owe more to John Manifold than I can say' ... and he developed a keen taste for Elizabethan lyrics as well. Later in life he hoped he had brought the Elizabethan and the 'Banjo' Paterson traditions together.

He played international rugby with the England team and served with distinction in the Second World War. He published books of poems and short stories, including *Selected Poems 1942–1968*, and *Deaths and Pretty Cousins* (1975). He died in 1979.

Poems: pp. 210–214.


## ZORA CROSS

Zora Cross was born in Brisbane in 1890 and educated at Ipswich Girls' Grammar School. After working for three years as a teacher, she took up a career as an actress and went on the stage. Later she gave this up in favour of journalism. She married David McKee Wright, one-time literary editor of The *Bulletin* and author of some of the most whimsical, coy, faery poesy in all world literature. She, by contrast, wrote constantly of personal relationships. There are books of sonnets on love and motherhood. Her main collections were *Songs of Love and Life* (1917) and *The Lilt of Life* (1918).

Poems: p. 98.

## VICTOR DALEY

Victor Daley was born in Ireland on 5 September 1858. When he was three his father died, and he recalled that 'we were always poor and improvident'. Daley's final year at school was in England and then he worked for three years as a railway clerk. He migrated to Adelaide to join relatives here. He landed at Sydney in 1878 and began working his way south, losing all his money at the Melbourne Cup on the way. Then he turned north again to the gold diggings in the Queanbeyan district of New South Wales, but ended up as a journalist on the newspaper there. Later he settled in Sydney and wrote under the pen-name Creeve Roe. He presented himself as rumbustious and theatrical, making a profession of his Irishness, but some who knew him thought him quiet and unromantic. Henry Lawson, in his memorial tribute 'To Victor Daley' contrasted his public reputation ('The blustering false Bohemian/That you have never been') with the private man:

> You spoke not of the fair and 'fast',
>> But of the pure and true—
> 'Sweet ugly women of the past'
>> Who stood so well by you.

When health failed him, Victor Daley tried several rest cures, including a South Pacific cruise and convalescence in the country. The latter he eventually gave up with the comment 'I am tired of Nature. We don't understand each other . . . Back in the city at least I shall be able to be ill in a more congenial environment.' He died of tuberculosis on 29 December 1905.

Poems: pp. 81–83.

## JACK DAVIS

Both Jack Davis' mother and his father were taken as children from their (different) tribes in the far north-west of Western Australia and reared by white people. He looks back on his own childhood as a happy time. While white people were suffering from the Depression, 'we would stay out in the bush sometimes up to periods of three to four months. We caught kangaroos, we caught possums out of season, we sold the skins ... Those were really wonderful times when I look back because we had so much freedom.'

For many years now Jack Davis has been engaged in social welfare for Aborigines in Perth, and active in national campaigns for Aboriginal rights.

Poem: p. 153.

# BRUCE DAWE

When Bruce Dawe's first book *No Fixed Address* appeared in 1962 it introduced a brilliant new voice, which was to become very influential in the next decade. Despite the fact that certain academic critics poured scorn of what they took to be a lack of formal structure in the poems, poets were highly enthusiastic. His poems address themselves to great public issues through private intuitions, and they do so with wit and inventiveness. Occasionally he succeeds with poems of quieter tone, achieving in 'Drifters' a touch of nobility.

Bruce Dawe was born in Geelong, Victoria, on 15 February 1930. He left Northcote High School when he was sixteen and worked variously as farm-hand, mill-hand, copy-boy, gardener and postman. Later he joined the RAAF. And the having taken a degree, he took his present teaching job at the Darling Downs College of Advanced Education in Toowoomba, Queensland. He is much sought-after to take part in poetry readings, having a laconic delivery justly popular with audiences.

He is married and has four children.

Unfortunately a contractual agreement between Bruce Dawe and his publisher prevents us from reprinting more of his poems than those included here.

Poems: pp. 289–295.

## C. J. DENNIS

Clarence James Dennis was Australia's most popular writer of comic verse. In the period between the outbreak of the First World War and the end of the Second, his characters and their humour helped clarify for huge numbers of people what it was to be Australian. *The Songs of a Sentimental Bloke* (1915) and *The Moods of Ginger Mick* (1916) between them sold over 100,000 copies in their first editions. They have been through many editions since then and are still available. Dennis' verse is sprightly, cheeky and inventive, nearly all of it printed in dialect which, though common enough at the time, can now seem a barrier almost too irritating to bother fighting past to find out what the poems are saying.

He was the son of a retired sea captain who kept a hotel. Born on 7 September 1876 in Auburn, South Australia, he was educated at a Christian Brothers' college. Discharged from his first job for finding Rider Haggard's novels more interesting than his office work, he joined the staff of the *Critic*. Afterwards he travelled outback supporting himself with various labouring jobs. Though married, Dennis had no children. He died on 21 June 1938.

Poem: pp. 78–81.

## ROSEMARY DOBSON

Rosemary (de Brissac) Dobson was born on 18 June 1920 in Sydney, granddaughter of the Victorian poet Austin Dobson. A great many of her poems are about European paintings, to which she brings a sensitive eye. At their best they illuminate some fragment of the human experience, as neatly framed as the pictures themselves. The texture of the poems is also finely wrought. And though a whole book of them can seem constricted, like a gallery full of miniatures, individually their contemplative mode skilfully examines the effects of a work of art (both painting and poem). 'Being Called For' is an example of how, occasionally, she is free from the protected world of art and speaks movingly and subtlely of great issues. Her books include *Child with a*

*Cockatoo and Other Poems* (1948), *Collected Poems* (1973) and *Over the Frontier* (1978).

Poems: pp. 190–193.


## MICHAEL DRANSFIELD

Michael Dransfield, born on 12 September 1948, died on Good Friday 1973. He was so gifted that by the age of nineteen he was already writing mature poems which, in the conservative context of much Australian literature, announced a colourful, exotic presence. He wrote prolifically and during his short lifetime published three collections, *Streets of the Long Voyage* (1970), *The Inspector of Tides* (1972), *Drug Poems* (1972) and three more have appeared posthumously. His success was immediate and he became something of a cult-hero among the young for his courage in declaring his involvement with illegal drug-taking and his insight into this experience. He had a passion for ritual and the trappings of aristocracy. He spent a short while in a monastery and toyed with the idea of becoming a monk; he pored over books of heraldry and claimed ancient lineage for his family, both on his mother's and his father's side.

After several stultifying jobs in the Public Service and as a cadet journalist at Casino, New South Wales, he lived a peripatetic life, supporting himself largely by an astute process of falling in love with small rural properties, buying them for a song and later selling them at a profit. This was never entered upon as a business, but it was successful enough. The last months of his life were dogged with injury and illness, yet during this time he produced an enormous body of work.

Poems: pp. 376–381.

## GEOFFREY DUTTON

Geoffrey Dutton was born on Anlaby, the family sheep station, Kapunda, South Australia on 2 August 1922. He is a well-known publisher, having been a founder-editor of *Angry Penguins* in the 1940s and *Australian Letters* in the 1950s–60s, both in close association with Max Harris. He then edited an Australian series for Penguin Books, and afterwards founded Sun Books. He is at present literary editor of The *Bulletin*. Like others of his generation, he points out that when he was brought up 'we had all the English tradition to digest. I never had any Australian literature at school, never had any Australian history, not one bit of either.' He is one of those who has set out consciously to help forge a new tradition in recent times. Apart from his editorial and publishing career, he has written many books of a great variety of kinds, including novels, poetry and biography.

Geoffrey Dutton lives in Adelaide and has long been a central figure in organizing Writers' Week at the Adelaide Arts Festival.

Poems: pp. 226–227.

## EDWARD DYSON

Edward Dyson was born at Morrisons near Ballarat, Victoria, in March 1865. The family led a roving life around the gold diggings. At twelve he began work as assistant to a travelling draper, after which he was a whim-boy in a gold mine. Later he worked as a journalist. At nineteen he was writing verse. He published many books of fiction, short stories and poems, a great deal of it comic, a great deal nostalgic for the gold rush days he remembered from his youth. Even when he succumbed to the sentimentality so dear to the age, his poetry was saved by sharp detail and lurking good-humour in *Rhymes from the Mines* (1896).

He died after a long illness on 22 August 1931.

Poems: pp. 73–77.

## 'E'

Mary E. Fullerton published taut crystalline poems under the pen-name 'E' for forty years until her death in England in 1946. She was born in Glenmaggie, Victoria, in 1868 and educated at the local state school. Of her four collections of verse, the last was *The Wonder and the Apple* (1946). And, as well as six books of fiction, she was the author of a description of outback life *The Australian Bush* (1928) which became popular in England.

Poems: pp. 87–89.

## YITYANGU ('NEW') EJONG

This song from north-west Western Australia by the late Yityangu Ejong appears in Frank Wordick's forthcoming book *The Yindjibarndi Language*.

Poem: p. 196.

## ANNE ELDER

During the Second World War, when ballet in Australia was the Borovansky Company and very little else, Anne Elder was one of the soloists. She was born in Auckland, New Zealand and came to Australia at the age of three. She wrote poetry for most of her life but didn't begin seeking publication until the mid 1960s. Then came a sudden stream of these nervy, quirkily humorous, dark and startling poems. In terms of how they address the reader they are, perhaps, reminiscent of the English poet Stevie Smith, but in most other respects they are wholly indiosyncratic. She herself said, 'I detest obscure, phantasist poetry, so I have aimed at lucidity without being mundane.'

Anne Elder died in 1976. She had published two books *For the Record* (1972) and *Crazy Woman* (1976).

Poems: pp. 265–269.

## R. D. FITZGERALD

Robert D, FitzGerald describes himself as a 'land surveyor and versifier'. Born on 22 February 1902 in Hunter's Hill, Sydney (where he still lives), his mother was sister to John le Gay Brereton, a well-known literary figure early this century. On leaving Sydney Grammar School in 1922 he was articled to a firm of surveyors. He qualified in 1925 and was fortunate enough to get a job as a Native Lands Commission surveyor in Fiji. His wife—they married just before he sailed—joined him there some months later. 'The first home I ever took her to was a tent.' They stayed in Fiji till 1936.

Throughout his poetry there is an impressive force: the individual standing up and confronting the world as he finds it, and drawing strength from this and the understanding it gives him. FitzGerald is an affirmative writer, serious and thoughtful. His voice is seldom smooth or sonorous, it's too personal for that. Only in his most recent verse has there been any bad-temper in his tone—and this is reserved for modernist poets. He makes quite clear he doesn't like what he doesn't understand. But in other ways he has kept very much alive to the concerns of society, and during the shameful days of our involvement in the undeclared war on Vietnam, he alone among his generation of poets spoke out publicly and consistently against it. In all his books there is both imaginative and moral force. Robert FitzGerald's collected *Forty Years' Poems* has been followed by one other collection *Product* (1978). There is a sense in which all his most successful poems build models of experience out of compiled images and then make these interact to produce ideas, even philosophy of a basic kind.

Poems: pp. 131–140.

## JOHN FORBES

John Forbes writes with an elegant intellectualism. He has published two small collections, *Tropical Skiing* (1976) and *On the Beach* (1977). In common with many of his generation, he is interested in the poem as a fact and an event. His poems frequently examine themselves as they go along—rather the way in one poem here he directs attention to the television set as well as what it is showing. John Forbes was born in Melbourne in 1950 and currently he lives in Sydney, collecting prizes and writing about the American poet Frank O'Hara.

Poems: pp. 387–390.

# WILLIAM FORSTER

The Premier of New South Wales in 1859, William Forster led an active political and literary life. He was elected to the New South Wales Legislative Assembly when it was first constituted. Though a Tory he opposed the system of nominating (rather than electing) members of the Legislative Council and supported a massive program of railway construction. At various times he held the seats of Queanbeyan, East Sydney and Gundagai. Once described as 'disagreeable in opposition, insufferable as a supporter, and fatal as a colleague', he was the kind of old-style conservative who trenchantly opposed graft and manipulation whether in his own party or any other. As an author, he was chiefly known in his time for a satire on Governor George Gipps, *The Devil and the Governor*. But he published several other plays. His poems appeared either in periodicals or as an adjunct to his dramas, printed at the back of the book. Both *The Weirwolf* [sic] (1876) and *The Brothers* (1877) included verse. He was offered the position of Leader of the Opposition in 1880 but declined.

William Forster was born in Madras, India, in 1818 and was brought to Australia when eleven. He died in Sydney on 30 October 1882.

Poems: pp. 22–25.

# LEON GELLERT

One-time editor of *Art in Australia* and then *Home* magazine, literary editor of The *Sydney Morning Herald*, Leon Gellert's writing career was principally concerned with journals. But he also published several books, notably the First World War poems in *Songs of a Campaign* (1917). He served in the AIF and was at the landing at Gallipoli. He was born at Walkerville, Adelaide, in 1892 and died on 22 August 1977.

Poems: p. 99.

## MARY GILMORE

Mary Gilmore was an idealist. While she was still Miss Mary Jean Cameron, schoolteacher, she joined William Lane's New Australia movement. They applied for a grant of land to set up an alternative society free of money and based on equality of labour and return. In Australia they were unsuccessful, but on applying to Paraguay they were granted 10,000 hectares. About 200 people set sail on 16 July 1893. So this utopia of racially exclusive socialists was set up and there Mary Cameron married William Alexander Gilmore. The venture died of altruism, agricultural incompetence and creeping tyranny in 1899. Mary Gilmore then went to Argentina and later taught English in Patagonia.

She returned to Australia in 1902 and conducted the women's pages of The *Worker* for thirty-three years. She was a foundation member of the Fellowship of Australian Writers in 1928; and patron at the time of her death. She wrote a great many books of verse, much of which is trite, self-righteous and clumsy. But in each of her books there are a few superb pieces, strong, direct and resonant. At her best she is amazingly free from dated mannerisms, she speaks of mankind's needs and aspirations with a dignity that transcends nationalism.

Born near Goulburn, New South Wales, on 16 August 1865 Mary Gilmore, eventually Dame Mary Gilmore, died in Sydney at the age of ninety-seven on 3 December 1962.

Poems: pp. 84–87.

## ADAM LINDSAY GORDON

'He who flashed upon us suddenly ... Who sang the first great songs these lands can claim to be their own ...' wrote Henry Kendall in his memorial poem to Adam Lindsay Gordon. He started writing fairly late, being thirty-one when his first poem was published, but there had been plenty to fill his life. Born at Fayal in the Azores on 19 October 1833, he went to school in Cheltenham, UK, and then attended the Military Academy. But he behaved wildly and recklessly, excelling only at boxing and horse riding, and was withdrawn from the academy.

He lived an enjoyable, racy life till 1853 when he was sent by his distraught father to start a new life in Adelaide. This didn't work out either and he became a trooper in the mounted police, then a horse-breaker. A superb rider, he competed on his own horses in many races. Since he was half-blind and could scarcely see beyond the horse's ears the experience of riding at breakneck speed through the bush must have been an extraordinary sensation calling for a particular kind of courage. Throughout his life he seemed incapable of taking the safe course or managing his affairs. He was an unsuccessful member of the South Australian House of Assembly and resigned. When, in 1867, he went into business, renting livery stables at Ballarat, he soon reduced the firm to ruin through sheer hard work and no acumen. In 1868 he had a serious riding accident and the following month his only child, Annie, died at eleven months. In 1870 he had another bad fall, riding in a steeplechase at Flemington. From this he never really recovered, suffering acute depression. On 23 June that same year his last book of poems, *Bush Ballads and Galloping Rhymes*, was published. But the following day, when told what he owed for the printing, he went off into the scrub near his home at Brighton, Victoria, and shot himself.

Poems: pp. 30–38.

## ROBERT GRAY

Robert Gray has been deeply influenced by Asian ideas and art. His poetry often assumes forms such as haiku, and a Buddhist view of life.

He has forged a successful blend of these with the landscape of his childhood, the Coff's Harbour district on the north coast of New South Wales. He has worked at various jobs, mainly as an advertising copywriter. He was born in February 1945.

Poems: pp. 363–364.

## RODNEY HALL

When the Bucklands of Kangaroo Valley, New South Wales, were ruined by the 1923 fires, they set sail for England to try their luck in that land of opportunity, taking their daughters with them. One, already a young woman, married Percy Edgar Hall. Their second son, Rodney, was born in Solihull, Warwickshire, on 18 November 1935. His father died six months later. During bombing raids in the Second World War, the family would creep into a tunnel formed by the back of the sofa pushed against the piano keyboard; there, protected in case the ceiling fell in, they pored over faded family photographs to keep their minds off the bombs, peering at them by dim torchlight. The pictures were of their grandparents standing beside anthills as high as a house, holding earthworms two metres long, shooting giant snakes under ferns the size of trees. And there they'd talk over their plans for returning home. 'I knew exactly what Australia would be like,' he says, 'with monstrous plants and animals, no houses, and everybody would carry a rifle like my grandfather. It was never explained to me that the giant anthills weren't made by giant ants.' His experience of school at Brisbane Boys' College came as a shock, only relieved when he left on his sixteenth birthday to go to work.

Most of his adult life he has lived as a writer, actor and musician, just occasionally lapsing into respectable employment. He married Bet MacPhail in 1962 and they have three daughters. He has published two novels and many other books, including *Selected Poems* (1975) and *Black Bagatelles* (1978). For eleven years he was poetry editor of The *Australian*.

Poems: pp. 322–329.

## LESBIA HARFORD

Lesbia Harford was born in Brighton, Victoria, on 9 April 1891 and graduated in Arts and Law from Melbourne University. She was very concerned with social issues and justice. After a stint as a social worker, she elected to join the workforce of the underprivileged herself, and despite ill-health went to work in a clothing factory. Also she agitated for women's rights.

She died on 5 July 1927. Her only book of poems was collected after her death and edited by Nettie Palmer.

Poems: p. 120.

## CHARLES HARPUR

Charles Harpur was born on 23 January 1813 at Windsor, New South Wales, the son of ex-convicts. He was educated at the Government School, Parramatta, where his father was a teacher. He published his first poem in 1837 while he was working as a postal clerk. In 1859 he was appointed Gold Commissioner for the Araluen field and later took up farming further down near the coast. His importance to Australian literature has frequently been stressed, mainly because he took the responsibilities of a poet very seriously, dedicating himself to clarifying the ideal through inspired language. Only occasionally did he achieve this inspired language, however. Even so, his descriptions of the bush are the earliest examples of any poet attempting genuine Australianness of detail with the English language. He published several books of verse in his lifetime, plus a play *The Bushrangers* which was the first play written by an Australian-born author to be printed in this country. Harpur died of tuberculosis on 8 June 1868, after several years of severe hardship, surviving floods and family tragedy.

Of his own poetry, he wrote: 'It has never been a mere art with me— a tuneful medium of forced thoughts and affected passion; but always the vehicle of earnest purpose. Nay, rather might I say, that it has always been the audible expression of the inmost impulses of my moral being—the very breath of my spiritual life.'

'Marvellous Martin' is a satire on Sir James Martin (1820–86).

Poems: pp. 26–30.

## GWEN HARWOOD

Walter Lehmann, Miriam Stone, Francis Geyer, T. F. Kline and Gwen Harwood inhabit the same flesh, living on the coast outside Hobart and hearing from Bruny Island across the channel the faint keening of a murdered native race. Gwen Harwood began publishing under these pen-names to escape the ignominy of easy acceptance once her reputation had been made. And this is what most impresses, reading her total output to date, how she scorns short-cuts. The poems, the experiences, the ideas must be the most demanding or nothing. And everything from the harsh truths of suburbia to the luminous wisdom of Wittgenstein must be caught in language as clear and complex as nursery rhymes. Gwen Harwood has the trained musician's grasp of form; her poems weave themes like sonatas. She avoids free verse, perhaps because it is not a provable skill. One of her most persistent themes is learning: from the Professor Eisenbart poems in which he struggles for the humility to learn from pupils, amorous or academic, to Kröte the musician with his talent crippled by the necessity to teach for a living, the blind woman learning what others see, the contemporary composer teaching us new sounds, and to the poet herself learning from her father, from experience and from pain. Her savage resignation to suburbia, her concern for the meanings of art and the moral seriousness of ideas call to mind Patrick White.

Gwen Harwood was born in Brisbane, Queensland, on 8 June 1920. Her first book, *Poems*, was not published till she was forty-three. She acknowledges Vincent Buckley's help in making the selection. She has since published *Poems: Volume Two* (1968) and *New and Selected Poems* (1974).

Poems: pp. 243–257.

## DOROTHY HEWETT

Dorothy Hewett was born in Perth in 1923 and brought up on a remote farm, being educated by correspondence. At nineteen she joined the Communist Party but, as she puts it, 'as a bohemian anarchist I felt I wasn't virtuous enough to be a communist!' She married but later ran away to Sydney with another man and worked in factories. She remarried and had more children. After the invasion of Czechoslovakia she left the Communist Party. 'I'm not apolitical, I suppose I'm Left but Left in a very individualistic way.' She is now married to Merv Lilley, her third husband. They have two daughters.

She is well-known as a playwright having forged a dramatic style as unique as her poems. She has also appeared as an actress in several films. She reads her own work with memorable vitality and style.

Poems: pp. 270–274.

## A. D. HOPE

When *The Wandering Islands* appeared in 1955, the Sydney Charm School of poetry suffered a blow from which it never fully recovered. A. D. Hope was forty-eight when this, his first book, was published. Already well-known for occasional poems in magazines and anthologies, also as a ruthless critic, nothing quite prepared the insular poetic establishment for the impact of *The Wandering Islands*. In formal, metrical verse Hope spoke with rivetting clarity of sex and guilt, sensuality and religion. It was unheard of. It was also unfashionable, influenced by W. H. Auden rather than T. S. Eliot (or at the other extreme Robert Frost). Despite the nobility and decorum of his best lines, the poetry did carry an uncomfortably insistent literariness too. This further irritated his contemporaries in that it emphasized a very particular avoidance of specifically Australian themes and speech rhythms. His poetry still has these characteristics, twenty-five years later. It is as if Hope's work belongs more to the English-writing tradition than to the present English-speaking world. Inclined to be mandarin, it makes a point of standing against innovation, just as Australia itself has remained (till very recent years) largely outside the social and intellectual environment of modernism and most of what has followed. It could possibly be seen as the poetry of a man isolated from his sources. But whether or not this is so, it has wit and magnificent presence. There is great force in the combination of such savage insights and the staid measured pace of the verse.

Alec Derwent Hope was born in Cooma, New South Wales, on 21 July 1907. He was for many years Professor of English at the Australian National Unviersity. Since his *Collected Poems* (1972) he has continued to issue a steady stream of books of poems and critical comment.

Poems: pp. 162–176.


## REX INGAMELLS

Rex (Reginald Charles) Ingamells was born in 1913 at Orroroo, South Australia, and educated at Port Lincoln High School and Prince Alfred College. He obtained his BA at Adelaide University. In 1938 he founded the Jindyworobak Club with the intention of voicing environmental values, by learning from the Aborigines and by an intense and clear-eyed vision of Australia, free from the values and traditions of Europe. Australian imagery, he argued, should be derived from Australia not loaded down with imported innuendo. Unfortunately his command of technique was not strong enough for him to put this vigorous pro-gramme into effect. For a start his verse-forms were far more deeply rooted in English traditions than some of his predecessors such as Furnley Maurice. And although he must be credited with energy for establishing the *Jindyworobak Anthology*, which was published annually for some fifteen years (minus a couple of the war years), very few of the poems chosen for these books showed more than superficial concern for the declared aims of the club. Rex Ingamells' most daring publication was the huge, didactic verse-history *The Great South Land* (1951), a poem of over 300 pages which made a unique attempt to view this history also from the Aboriginal point of view, as in the extract here. He died in a car crash in 1955.

Poems: pp. 153–155.

## MARTIN JOHNSTON

Martin Johnston is perhaps the most European of all Australian-born poets. He was brought up in England and the island of Hydra in the Aegean. He speaks perfect Greek. His English speech is also remarkable for its precision—undoubtedly a factor in the skilful management of sound in his poems. He is an antiquarian by nature and has a profound knowledge and love of ancient things. While still at high school in Greece he produced some precociously sophisticated translations of *Kleftika* (bandit) songs. *Ithaka* (1973) is a collection of contemporary Greek verse in his translations. He has also published two books of his own poems, *Shadowmass* (1971) and *The Sea-Cucumber* (1978). Born in 1947 in Sydney, his parents were the distinguished writers George Johnston and Charmian Clift.

Poems: pp. 382–384.

## RAE DESMOND JONES

Rae Desmond Jones has worked at a variety of manual jobs, also for Telecom and the Commonwealth Employment Service. He has published three collections of poems, the most recent being *Shakti* (1977). He has also written a collection of short stories, *Walking the Line* (1980), desolating in their view of society today. His books may at first appear to be filled with violence and hatred, but the violence and hatred are frequently shown to be protective shells for considerable tenderness and vulnerability.

Rae Desmond Jones was born in Broken Hill, New South Wales, in 1941. He left school (where he was, in his own words, 'a totally useless pupil and a highly successful juvenile delinquent') at fourteen.

Poem: pp. 369–371.

## NANCY KEESING

Nancy Keesing was born in Syndey in 1923. Her first book was published by the Lyre-bird Writers Co-operative in 1951. She has since published many books of various kinds including the large and influential collection *Australian Bush Ballads* which she edited together with Douglas Stewart. Nancy Keesing was, for some years, chairman of the Literature Board of the Australia Council.

Poem: pp. 263–264.

## ANTIGONE KEFALA

Antigóne Kefalâ was born in Rumania of Greek parents. In 1951 the family moved to New Zealand; she began attending university there in 1955, then came to Australia in 1969. Most of the time since then she has worked on the staff of the Australia Council, making a valuable contribution to arts administration, especially among ethnic artists and community groups. She has published several collections of poems and a book of novellas. 'It is very difficult,' she says, 'to write in a language not your own. . . . How to judge it, how to measure it, how to utilize it, its weight, its structure, its colouring, and also the fact that you bring to it an approach which is very un-English . . . In poetry today there is so much understatement, which is very difficult to get used to for a person coming from another tradition.'

Poem: p. 333.

## HENRY KENDALL

Henry Kendall and his twin brother were born in Kirmington, New South Wales, on 18 April 1839. The family was poor and their father died when the boys were twelve. At sixteen, Kendall went to sea as a cabin boy with his uncle, whaling down towards the Antarctic. He found the life too harsh for him. When he returned several years later to Sydney, he worked as a shop-assistant until taken up by the solicitor James Lionel Michael who was becoming well-known as a writer of verse. When Michael moved his practice to Grafton, he took the young Kendall with him as a clerk and treated him with great kindness. On his return to Sydney he worked as a civil servant and began to figure in literary circles of the day, being friends with Marcus Clarke and Adam Lindsay Gordon. He was taken up by Henry Parkes who later became Premier of New South Wales and an architect of Federation. However, he was frequently in financial difficulties and ill-health. He died on 1 August 1882. He wrote some pompous occasional verse, such as the *Cantata Written Expressly for the Opening Ceremony of the Sydney International Exhibition*, but his true poetry is far removed from this and has best been described by the critic A. G. Stephens as 'singing pictures'.

Poems: pp. 40–46.

## PETER KOCAN

On 26 June 1966 a nineteen-year-old factory worker took a sawn-off .22 rifle to the window of a car outside the Mosman Town Hall and shot the man inside, the Federal Opposition Leader of the day, Arthur Calwell. Calwell survived and adopted a generous attitude to the young man. '*Dear Peter, Your letter of apology for the distress you caused me two years ago at Mosman touches me deeply ...*' he wrote in 1968 to Kocan who was in Morisset psychiatric hospital, where he spent ten years. At this time, Peter Kocan began writing. He says, 'The thing I appreciate about poetry is its very democratic nature. It's one of the only fields where the work of the convict is of the same value as the work of the king.' He acknowledges the influence of the English poet Wilfred Owen, especially for his integrity. Peter Kocan's own poetry has a powerful sense of integrity. He has published a courageously frank autobiography, as well as several collections of poems.

Poems: pp. 354–355.

## HENRY LAWSON

Perhaps no poet since the invasion in 1788 has had so profound an effect on shaping our national character as Henry Lawson. It is an influence almost wholly rejected nowadays, but right through the early years of this century up till the time of the Depression Lawson's vision of people and society struck a powerful response. He was born in a tent on the gold-diggings near Grenfell, New South Wales, on 17 June 1867. His mother was a journalist and a leading feminist of the time. When The *Bulletin* printed his first poems in October 1887, the editor added the comment, 'In publishing the subjoined verses we take pleasure in stating that the writer is a boy of 17 years, a young Australian, who has as yet had an imperfect education and is earning his living under some difficulties as a housepainter, a youth whose poetic genius here speaks eloquently for itself.' Lawson was twenty, not seventeen, but such a launching was a wonderful encouragement.

He was a shy, modest personality, afflicted by near-deafness since the age of nine, but he had a tremendous capacity to make friends. Besides his verses, he wrote many fine short stories which won him fame throughout the country. Though most of his best work was written by the time he was forty, he lived to be fifty-five, a good few of these later years spent in the misery of alcoholism and illness. He died in Sydney on 22 September 1922 and was honoured with a State Funeral.

One of the poems included here, 'Up the Country', was part of a verse debate he cooked up with Paterson, in which they attacked one another's (respectively) pessimistic and optimistic views of life in the bush.

Poems: pp. 50–61.

## GEOFFREY LEHMANN

Geoffrey Lehmann was born 28 June 1940 at Crown Street Hospital, Sydney. His young childhood was spent in the oldest house on McMahon's Point right on the harbour. 'The chief obsession of my childhood,' he says, 'was pirate books; big technicolor galleons and people digging up treasure.' And still, in his *Ross's Poems* (1978) there is a sense of discovering precious fragments—only this time of folk wisdom. These poems are based on the reminiscences of his father-in-law, Ross McInerney. Precisely because Lehmann does treat them as precious he is able to achieve a most demanding test of craft, creating a poetic environment in which they can live: it is impossible to say where Ross ends and Lehmann begins. Whatever else Ross' poems have, they avoid the ponderous declaration, so dear to some of his contemporaries, of elevating the countryman to literature. 'Literature,' he says, 'makes me feel slightly uncomfortable. Life makes me feel very comfortable. And this is why I liked being a solicitor, handling people's mortgages and conveyances and births and deaths and marriages, it's very much of an earth rhythm, rather like being a farmer in the city.'

Poems: pp. 343–351.


## LIAGARANG

This song, as sung by Liagarang is from the Wuradilagu Songs (a *jiridja* moiety cycle) made up of a series of clan songs. Liagarang, a Northern Territory man of the Dharlwangu clan of north-east Arnhem Land, sings traditional Yirrkalla songs.

Poem: p. 210.


## MILTON LOCKYER

This song in the Yindjibarndi language is taken from *Taruru*, a collection assembled by von Brandenstein and Thomas, specially translated for the present anthology by Frank Wordick.

Poem: p. 196.

## FREDERICK T. MACARTNEY

Frederick Thomas Macartney worked as a clerk of courts and a sheriff in the Northern Territory till he resigned at forty-six and moved back to Melbourne where he had come from. Soon he was well-known as a travelling lecturer on Australian literature at a time when this was not thought to be a respectable subject for serious consideration. He was also a prolific book reviewer. His major critical work was the extension, enlargement and up-dating of Professor E. Morris Miller's invaluable reference book *Australian Literature* (1956). Macartney's poetry is unexpectedly modern in its sensibility, its celebration of sun, surf and nakedness. His first book appeared in 1912. He was born in Melbourne on 27 September 1887 and died there just three weeks short of his ninety-third birthday on 2 September 1980. During his lifetime he wrote and edited many books, and illustrated several collections of his poems with his own lino-cuts.

Poems: pp. 140–142.

## KENNETH MACKENZIE

Kenneth Mackenzie was unique in his generation for the power and range of his poems about love and marriage. Seldom strained, their intensity is achieved by subtle effects and a direct appeal to the reader's own experience. Kenneth Mackenzie was born in Perth in 1913 and spent his childhood at Pinjarra, Western Australia. He studied Arts and Law at university and then earned his living as a journalist and an agricultural worker. While in the army he was at the prison garrison in Cowra when the mass escape of Japanese occurred, which he wrote about in his novel *Dead Men Rising* (1951). Awarded a succession of Commonwealth Literary Fund fellowships, he wrote four novels as Seaforth Mackenzie and two books of poetry. *Collected Poems* was published in 1972 after his death. Curiously, having written a poem about drowning, 'Heat', early in his career, he himself was drowned in Tallong Creek near Goulburn, New South Wales, in January 1955.

Poems: pp. 155–162.

## JENNIFER MAIDEN

Jennifer Maiden was born in Penrith, New South Wales, on 7 April 1949. She still lives there. Her father, a physiotherapist, was blind. But despite the warmth of her memories, she recollects: 'I was a most unsuccessful child. I couldn't wait not to be one.'

  Her poems explore constant moral pressures, personal and social, often related to war. They carry deep allusions of suffering and doom. At the other extreme, she can be sharply satirical.

Poems: pp. 385–386.

## 'ERN MALLEY'

The question of Ern Malley's existence has resulted in much controversy since the hoax first reached the newspaper headlines and the law courts. He was invented by James McAuley and Harold Stewart. They wanted to demonstrate that the avant-garde magazines lacked editorial standards, and wouldn't recognize nonsense when it was put in front of them. They had an enjoyable time concocting poem-like objects and an author to fit, the redoubtable primitive, Ern. They sent the poems to Max Harris and John Reed at *Angry Penguins*, a Melbourne magazine, and they accepted them with pleasure. The hoax was a tremendous success; except that it then went off the rails and involved a court case over the alleged obscenity of some of the poems. On top of which, there has been discussion ever since, suggesting that Ern Malley may have been real in that he released in his creators poetic springs they didn't touch in their sober literary careers. Ern Malley's only book was *The Darkening Ecliptic* published in 1944. Subsequently there have been six further editions.

Poem: p. 190.

## DAVID MALOUF

David Malouf was born in Brisbane in 1934. His mother's family came from England and his father's from Lebanon. He grew up in Brisbane which, during the Second World War, was thought of as a potential frontier town with American servicemen garrisoned there. After graduating from Queensland University he went overseas. 'I went to central Europe and saw baroque architecture for the first time, and it seemed to me that a whole sensibility I was in tune with was dramatised there, in the shape of the building, in the kind of decoration, and even in the kind of baroque music the organ was playing while you were walking round.'

He has been back and forth numerous times since, but now he lives mainly in Tuscany. His books include *Bicycle* (1970) and *First Things Last* (1980). He has also written several novels.

Poems: pp. 306–313.

## JOHN MANIFOLD

Poet, musician, soldier and scholar—John Manifold is about as near as we come to the all-round Renaissance man. He can fence, he can ride ('we rode pretty much before we could walk'), quote Latin verses by the yard and sing a bawdy song to his own guitar accompaniment. If only he could be persuaded to build a couple of palaces, the likeness would be complete. Born into a wealthy family of graziers, he became a communist at Cambridge University and has remained a member ever since. To some degree his literary life has been dogged by a doctrinaire desire to address the common people. Accordingly he has written many entertainment ballads recalling the style of the 1890s, which he performs with panache at the drop of a hat. More significantly he carried out pioneer work in collecting the tunes of traditional bush ballads: in many cases the words were already well-known from A. B. Paterson's *The Old Bush Songs* (1905) but, typical of the literary community, hardly anyone had the musical ability to save the tunes before they died out. Many of these songs were collected later as *The*

*Penguin Australian Song Book* (1964), edited by John Manifold. he has also written a book on the use of music in the Elizabethan/Jacobean theatre. His published poems include *Selected Verse* (1947) in American and English editions, and *Collected Verse* (1978). Born in Melbourne on 21 April 1915, he now lives at Wynnum near Brisbane.

Poems: pp. 176–184.

## RAY MATHEW

Ray Mathew had to endure a brilliant early success. Like Randolph Stow, who was similarly afflicted, he seems to have found difficulty writing beyond this. His poems are fresh, especially the love poetry, and perky. He has published three books of poems, the first, *With Cypress Pine* appeared in 1951. It is many years since the last collection was issued. Ray Mathew was born in Sydney in 1929 and now lives in England.

Poems: pp. 228–230.

## 'FURNLEY MAURICE'

Henry William Wilmot was secretary of the first socialist group to be formed in Victoria. His son Frank, at the age of sixteen, was already contributing verse to the *Tocsin*, a Melbourne Labor weekly. When he was twenty-one, Frank Wilmot started a small monthly, the *Microbe*, a 'journalette' as he called it, the purpose of which was to attack A. G. Stephens. He believed Stephens, literary editor of The *Bulletin*, unfairly discriminated against him in rejecting his manuscripts—feelings familiar to many young writers before and since. For the purpose of the attack he adopted a pen-name, Furnley Maurice, which he used for the rest of his life, though occasionally signing poems with disguised initials. His first book of real importance *Unconditioned Songs* (1913) bore no author's name at all.

Most of his adult life he worked as a bookseller in Melbourne, first at the giant Cole's Book Arcade then, when the business failed in 1929, opening his own bookshop-library. After this he managed Melbourne University Press.

Furnley Maurice is chiefly remembered for his vivacious poems about contemporary Melbourne, his use of free rhythms and his willingness to treat poetry not only as work but as play too. He liked the effect of montage, freely using the living vernacular of the streets. He was a cheerful nationalist, ever involved in political, moral and social issues, and optimistic about Australia as a venture being carried out by sensible, considerate (but often faintly ridiculous) people. If his poetry frequently seems undisciplined and garrulous, one should take into account that for quite a few years the editor he submitted his manuscripts to was David McKee Wright, a proven merchant of pretentions. And Maurice, after all, was out to ridicule cautiousness, and to break through English constraint to a genuine Australian utterance. Frank Wilmot was born in Melbourne on 6 April 1881, where he died suddenly and unexpectedly on 22 February 1942.

Poems: pp. 107–119.


## JAMES McAULEY

James McAuley was born in Lakemba, New South Wales, on 12 October 1917. During the Second World War he served with the AIF. Afterwards he became founder-editor of *Quadrant*. During the 1940s he had vigorously opposed the notion put up by the Jindyworobak Club that we should have some kind of nationalist programme, that poems should be full of coolibahs and wombats, or that we should show ourselves ignorant of European culture or dulled to it. A firm believer in poetry as pattern-making and metrical in form, he despised free verse as shoddy. He also had definite views about the laws of metrics and upon his arrival in Poona in 1970 he announced to the delight of his distinguished Indian hosts, 'I am here to stamp out the spondee!'

He became converted to Roman Catholicism around 1950 and from then on throughout the Cold War was an articulate anti-Communist. In 1951 he was appointed Professor of English at the University of Tasmania, a chair which he held till his death in October 1976.

Poems: pp. 184–190.

## HUGH McCRAE

Hugh McCrae was noted as a regular contributor to The *Bulletin* for many years. He had also made a living as an actor taking small parts and even touring in the USA. He was one of the main followers of Norman Lindsay and energetically entered the game of peopling the bush with satyrs and nymphs. A great many of these poems read very datedly today, but their redeeming feature is wit. Even at his most whimsical and precious he is attractively high-spirited and good-humoured. It is interesting that of all moribund archaisms to choose for poems, he should have selected the mythical pastoral figures so common in eighteenth-century verse—the century in which colonization began—as if the industrial nineteenth century had never existed.

Hugh McCrae, who was born in 1876, died in February 1958. His books included *Satyrs and Sunlight: Silvarum Libri*, decorations by Norman Lindsay (1909), *Colombine* (1920) and *Idyllia* (1922) both illustrated by Norman Lindsay, *Forests of Pan* (1944) and *Voice of the Forests* (1945).

Poems: pp. 121–122.

## ROGER McDONALD

Born on 23 June 1941 in Young, New South Wales, Roger McDonald was educated at Sydney University, worked as a schoolteacher, a radio producer for the ABC and as a publisher's editor at the University of Queensland Press. In this last job he was the architect of UQP's impressive poetry publishing programme for a decade from 1969.

He writes a great deal about the 1914–18 war (including the novel *1915*) but always in the mode of first-hand observation. The use of exact detail to carry emotional implications and to pivot from past to present has allowed him to make one image illuminate two periods of time—this technique is clearly shown in his 'Two Summers in Moravia'. Similarly, he telescopes the process of language itself, writing about his medium as a means of demonstrating it. Roger McDonald lives in Canberra with his wife (Rhyll McMaster) and their two daughters—keeping bees and learning to fly light aircraft.

Poems: pp. 364–368.

## RHYLL McMASTER

Rhyll McMaster's poems and short stories convey a strong individual personality. Her hard-edged portraits of objects and people (herself included) show them in hauntingly odd light. The poems are frequently built of laconic understatement or jaunty familiarities. Rhyll McMaster has published one book to date, *The Brineshrimp* (1972). She was born in Brisbane in 1947.

Poems: pp. 371–373.

## LES A. MURRAY

Les Murray was born in Bunyah on the New South Wales north coast on 17 October 1938. He grew up on his father's dairy farm, attending various schools: Blackfriars Correspondence, Bulby Brush Public, Wyong High, Nabiac Central, Taree High and then to Sydney University. He has worked with the translation unit at the Australian National University. Accomplished in other languages, he has an adventurous way with English, and such poems as 'The Powerline Incarnation' show this vividly. He has published a volume of criticism, and is co-editor of *Poetry Australia*. A convert to Roman Catholicism, he often writes of spiritual values. He admires 'the middle voice', poetry which can reach a wide audience with clarity and resonance. His principal subjects are drawn from the country, its landscapes, its people and their folklore. His books include *Selected Poems: The Vernacular Republic* (1976) and *Ethnic Radio* (1978). A gifted storyteller, Les Murray cuts quite a figure at literary gatherings.

Poems: pp. 334–342.

## SHAW NEILSON

John Shaw Neilson suffered a congenital eye disorder and throughout his life could read very little. He attended school for two periods, each of about fifteen months. His chief reading at home was the Bible, Robert Burns and Thomas Hood, the influence of all of which is clear in his poems. His father (a Scotsman who also wrote verse) encouraged his talent. He developed a style all his own partly because, while working at one or other of the manual labouring jobs he had, he memorized the lines as he thought of them, repeated them to himself (thus working in a way akin to the oral folk ballad) and wrote them down later. Or, when particularly troubled by his poor eyesight, dictated his poems to fellow labourers who wrote them down for him. His first audience, then, was often a shearer, a fruit-picker or a roadworker. Like Burns he could speak to these readers as well as the art-loving bourgeoisie, and this was a privilege.

Shaw Neilson's fragile poems, like 'The Orange Tree' resist academic analysis, perhaps because the wrong tradition is being applied to them. But there were other sides to his poetry—as the influence of Hood would suggest. He also wrote out of a keen sense of social justice, an admiration for stoicism and a repugnance for war and national chauvinism. Throughout most of his writing life he had a powerful and enthusiastic advocate in A. G. Stephens, Red Page editor of The *Bulletin* who once claimed in print that some of the poems were 'unsurpassed in the range of English lyrics'. He spoke of himself always as a rhymer. Concerning his most famous poem 'The Orange Tree' he explains in his moving autobiography that he got some of the ideas when weeding oranges at Merbein and 'There was also something which I tried to drag in, some enchantment or other. I have seen prints of Botticelli's wonderful picture *Spring*, it . . . fills me with emotion.' Born in Penola, South Australia, 22 February 1872, he died in Melbourne 12 May 1942.

Poems: pp. 100–106.

## BERNARD O'DOWD

Bernard O'Dowd was born in Beaufort, Victoria, on 11 April 1866. He was an admirer of the American poet Walt Whitman, with whom he had a friendly correspondence. His poems are full of energy, but they are marred for the most part by a hectoring determination to prove himself right politically and artistically, combined with nationalism at the level of propaganda. His first book of poems *Dawnward?* appeared in 1903 and his collected poems in 1941. In 1934 he refused a knighthood for services to literature. He was a librarian and later State Parliamentary Draughtsman. He died in Melbourne on 1 September 1953.

Poem: pp. 93–94.

## GEOFF PAGE

Born in Grafton, New South Wales, in 1940, Geoff Page was educated at The Armidale School and the University of New England. In the late 1960s he began to publish poetry which was immediately appreciated for its precision of detail and technical lightness of touch. His most recent book is *Cassandra Paddocks* (1980). He is a schoolteacher in Canberra and currently reviews poetry for newspapers and ABC radio.

Poem: pp. 353–354.

## A. B. ('BANJO') PATERSON

In this success story the author had the satisfaction of seeing his 'Waltzing Matilda' become the undisputed national song of Australia. The most accomplished and witty of the balladists, he wrote under the pen-name 'The Banjo'. He wore his intellectuality lightly and—at the opposite extreme to Christopher Brennan—relished the challenge of appealing simultaneously to the educated and the uneducated, people of the bush and the city. However, there is unmistakeably the touch of the grazier, the landowner, in his verse, as distinct from the bush worker. This is clear in the tone of 'Clancy of the Overflow' which begins with the balladist receiving a note 'written with a thumbnail dipped in tar ... "Clancy's gone to Queensland droving, and we don't know where he are."' So very different from Lawson's 'Will yer Write it Down for me?' which is in no way patronizing.

Paterson was born in Narrambla near Orange, New South Wales, on 17 February 1864, and educated at Sydney Grammar School. After qualifying as a solicitor he spent periods of his life as a war correspondent in South Africa, the Philippines and China and, during the Great War was a remount officer for the Light Horse (on one of these occasions meeting the finest of the English balladists, Kipling). He was also a newspaper editor and a grazier. He died in Sydney on 5 February 1941.

Poems: pp. 62–70.


## RODERIC QUINN

For most of his life, after he gave up being editor of the *North Sydney News*, Roderic Quinn made his living as a freelance writer, with a great many stories, poems and articles published in The *Bulletin* and elsewhere. He was born in Sydney in 1867 and died in 1949.

Poem: pp. 96–97.

## ELIZABETH RIDDELL

Elizabeth Riddell (Mrs Greatorex in private life) is one of Australia's most perceptive and independent journalists. It was work as a journalist that first brought her to this country at the age of eighteen. 'My people,' she says, 'were Welsh, English, Jewish, border Scottish, a mixture who settled in New Zealand after the Maori wars.' She was born in Napier, New Zealand, in 1909.

While her career as a journalist has taken her to positions in New York, London and Paris, and has continued to the present, she stopped writing poetry when her husband died in 1964 and did not begin again until 1980. 'My life has been a writing life, but it has not been a literary life.' Her books, however, are still read and admired.

Poems: pp. 142–143.

## ROLAND ROBINSON

Roland Robinson was born on 14 June 1912 in Balbriggan, Ireland, of English parents. He came to Australia aged fourteen. After he left school he worked in the country in New South Wales and as a clerk in the Northern Territory then, towards the end of the war in 1944, he joined the Kirsova Ballet till 1947. He has since made his name as a poet of the bush and as a bookreviewer. He was associated for years with the Jindyworobak movement and very much committed to celebrating the beauty and richness of the bush in his poems—poems noted for their limpid style and firm rhythms. 'A poem,' he says, 'should have the texture and character of its subject. I detest abstract cerebral verse.' He was the driving force behind organizing the Lyre Bird Writers' co-operative publishing venture in the 1950s.

Poems: pp. 194–196.

## JUDITH RODRIGUEZ

Judith Rodriguez (Judith Green) was born in Perth in 1936. She has lectured in English at the Universities of Queensland and the West Indies and is now at La Trobe University. She married a Colombian whom she met in Jamaica. Widely travelled, she is a person of tremendous vitality and enthusiasm for experience. She has illustrated her own books of poems with lino-cuts, notably *Water Life* (1976) and *Mudcrab at Gambaro's* (1980). She is also an accomplished violinist. Judith Rodriguez is poetry editor of *Meanjin Quarterly*.

Poems: pp. 330–333.

## DAVID ROWBOTHAM

David Rowbotham was born in Toowoomba, Queensland, on 27 August 1924. For many years he has been a journalist and books editor-reviewer for the Brisbane *Courier-Mail*. He published his short stories and sketches in *Town and City* (1956) which contained some crisp prose and particularly sharp, amusing scenes of life on the Darling Downs. He has written many books of poems, of which he says, 'I have been concerned with being and words. I have not been engaged with furnishing values and fighting causes, only with seeing and speaking as myself in the issue called life.'

Poems: pp. 224–225.

## J. R. ROWLAND

At present Australian Ambassador in Paris, formerly in Moscow and elsewhere, John Rowland is a diplomat and only an occasional writer. His books offer cool, carefully constructed personal views of people and places. He was born in Armidale, New South Wales, on 10 February 1925.

Poems: pp. 220–221.

## THOMAS W. SHAPCOTT

Thomas William Shapcott was born in Ipswich, Queensland, on 21 March 1935. He and his twin brother are opposites in physical colouring and temperament; being a twin has haunted his poetry though he rarely writes about it directly, there is a recurrent fear of being incomplete, imperfect, together with a powerful urge to give, to be generous and to be loved. One of the most individual of Australian poets, gifted with a fine ear for rhythm, he has restlessly turned from one mode to another—even to the fringes of concrete poetry and to a full book of long perambulatory pieces in the American style of talking to himself, while walking round the streets of Brisbane. Apart from his *Selected Poems* (1978), perhaps his most notable books are *Shabbytown Calendar* (1975), from which 'Autumn' is taken, a ruthless vision of his origins, an exploration of his hometown far removed from the romancing of his earlier works, and a major anthology *Contemporary American and Australian Poetry* (1976).

He has been awarded a Churchill Fellowship and many other prizes and distinctions. At present he is the authors' representative on the Public Lending Right committee.

Poems: pp. 314–321.

## R. A. SIMPSON

Ronald Albert Simpson was born in Melbourne on 1 February 1929. Apart from brief trips away, he has lived in Melbourne all his life. At present he works for the Victorian Department of Education. As poetry editor of The *Bulletin*, 1963–65, he took over from Vincent Buckley. Since 1969 he has been poetry editor of The *Age*. The epitome of the friendly, unassuming citizen, he admits, 'I met my wife in 1952—I didn't tell her I wrote poetry until about 1954. I never really meant it to be an outgoing thing. I wanted to be a painter.' In fact he studied art at the Royal Melbourne Institute of Technology and drawing and painting with George Bell. Nevertheless it is by his poetry that he is known. Simpson's style is one of pared down language even when he is dealing with heavy social issues, which he quite often does. As an editor, he has been open to a great variety of new work and has encouraged many young authors.

Poems: pp. 283–284.

## PETER SKRZYNECKI

Praised by Kenneth Slessor for poems 'filled with brilliant and unusual imagery of the Australian landscape', Peter Skrzynecki does write about the kind of subjects that preoccupied poets of an older generation, though he brings to this a more autobiographical voice. Many of them are addressed, rather like letters, to specific people. He was born in 1945 and brought to Australia in 1949. His people are Polish-Ukrainian.

Poems: pp. 361–363.

## KENNETH SLESSOR

Kenneth Slessor's collected poems (published in 1944) show a steady, even curve as he clarifies what he wants to say and how to say it. The last third of his book is full of mature and brilliant poetry. He had found his voice, the poetry is timeless. And having achieved this, he then stopped and for the remaining thirty years of his life wrote no more poems. Once when asked by an unknown woman why this was, he replied with exemplary courtesy, 'I suppose I fully expressed the person I was and could never discover another personality in me. What else could I do but stop, or repeat myself?' The early poems are heavily influenced by Norman Lindsay's drawings and by the verses of Hugh McCrae—crammed full of whimsy and hollow jollities. They then move through a period of legendary romances to the historical romance of the 'Five Visions of Captain Cook', till quite suddenly, swept away by the language and music of T. S. Eliot, the imagery changes from the colourful to the illuminating, and the poetry begins to say something wholly memorable, wholly personal.

'Five Bells', his most ambitious poem, commemorates Joe Lynch, a friend who drowned in Sydney Harbour in the thirties.

Kenneth Slessor was born in Orange, New South Wales, on 27 March 1901. He attended the Church of England Grammar School in Sydney and in 1920 became a reporter for the Sydney *Sun*. In 1927 he joined the staff of *Smith's Weekly* and became editor and then editor-in-chief. He moved to The *Daily Telegraph* and reviewed books for that paper for many years, often with sarcasm and ungenerosity to new writers or poets working in styles unlike his own. In personality he was inclined to be reserved, aloof and polite. He died on 30 June 1971.

Poems: pp. 122–131.

## VIVIAN SMITH

A man of brilliant wit in person, Vivian Smith in his poetry is quiet and meditative. He was born in Hobart, Tasmania, on 3 June 1933, and later educated at the University of Tasmania. He has written numerous regional poems about his home State, often with an historical perspective. While his verse-forms are conservative, his themes are frequently searching, in quest of large significances and the reassurance of shapeliness in the universe. He has taught both French and English at universities, is married and lives in Sydney.

Poems: pp. 279–282.

## DOUGLAS STEWART

Douglas Stewart was literary editor of The *Bulletin* for twenty-one years from 1940 to 1961, then became literary advisor to the country's main poetry publisher Angus & Robertson, 1961–73. Meanwhile he was also a hardworking member of the government committee for assisting literature, the Commonwealth Literary Fund, during the seventeen years 1955–72. Almost every poet in this anthology between Slessor and Lehmann had to submit their poems to him, in one or other of his roles, to achieve publication.

Douglas Stewart's own poetry is less commanding in nature; indeed most of it is light, frequently witty, frequently tender, always accessible. He does have a tendency (in common with quite a few others, including James McAuley and Francis Webb) to cast about for hero figures to populate the landscape. His long poem on Rutherford demonstrates the basically weak position this puts the poet in—being somewhere between biographer and public relations promoter. But there is no question of his admirable narrative gift and his skill with the forms he chooses. Stewart has written a great deal about the land and its animals. These he focuses upon closely, showing for a moment rare tints of light, the beauty of sharp outlines, and something more— the civilized fascination with things for their own sake, rather than the use to which they can be put. Occasionally, as in 'The Silkworms', his focus has great depth of field and we are shown ourselves in the background, living out the image he has chosen for us. Douglas Stewart was born in Eltham, New Zealand, on 6 May 1913. He lives in Sydney.

Poems: pp. 144–152.

## RANDOLPH STOW

(Julian) Randolph Stow was born in Geraldton, Western Australia, on 28 November 1935. After graduating from the University of Western Australia he lived and worked in New Guinea (in the Trobriand Islands he learnt the language and compiled a dictionary), then he went to Britain to recover from a tropical disease and has been based there ever since. His poems, however, have been fundamentally concerned with relating to Australia. By the time he had turned twenty-one he had three books in print or on the way. The impact of his novels and poems was immediate and has lasted despite the fact that during the past twenty years he has produced comparatively little. He is at present exploring an historian's interest in the Europeans in the Indian Ocean, the various East India Companies. He explains: 'My family has a rather extraordinary record of having been British colonists since the reign of James I, in Virginia, Newfoundland, South Australia and South Africa.'

In his poems the craft is often concentrated on creating unity of tone. His books include *A Counterfeit Silence, Selected Poems* (1969).

Poems: pp. 285–289.

## ANDREW TAYLOR

Andrew Taylor was born in Warrnambool, Victoria, in 1940, the youngest of three children. When he left school he studied arts and law at Melbourne University where Vincent Buckley encouraged his early attempts at poetry. He then went to Florence to study; the influences of Italy and the Renaissance may still be traced in his poems. His books include *The Invention of Fire* (1976) and *The Crystal Absences, the Trout* (1978). He lives in Adelaide.

Poems: pp. 352–353.

## JOHN TRANTER

John Tranter was born on 29 April 1943 in Cooma, New South Wales. He grew up very much a solitary child during the years when his father was the teacher at a one-teacher school at Bredbo on the Monaro and later a farmer, then a cordial-manufacturer at Moruya on the south coast. 'As a child,' he says, 'my most distinct impression was that of loneliness, sitting on the verandah looking out at three million gumtrees.'

After he left university, he travelled to Europe and Asia and worked as Asian editor for the publisher Angus & Robertson in Singapore. When he returned to Australia he worked as a producer for ABC radio in Brisbane. In his poetry and criticism he is very much preoccupied with the polemics of modernity and deeply influenced by American poets such as Frank O'Hara and John Ashbery.

Poems: pp. 374–375.

## DIMITRIS TSALOUMAS

Dimitris Tsaloumas was born in 1921 on the Aegean island of Leros. In 1952 he migrated to Australia. At present he lives in Melbourne with his wife and four children and holds a senior teaching post with the Victorian Department of Education. Writing in Greek, he attempts to bring the past and present into equal focus and achieve poems in which the imagery is as immediate in terms of Australia and the Pacific as in terms of Greece and the Aegean.

Poem: pp. 222–223.

## URUMBULA SONG

This is an extract taken from the long Urumbula Song of the Simpson Desert, Central Australia. The *tnatantja* is a totem pole, described as being very tall and having a cross-arm, which is by its irresistible magic power the Milky Way. The song was collected and first published in this translation in 1962.

Poem: pp. 94–95.

## MARIA VALLI

Maria Valli has published four novels and several books of poems in Italian. In Brisbane, still writing in Italian, she set out to communicate her feelings to an Australian audience. Born in Bologna, her books have been highly praised in Italy. Alberto Moravia commended her 'sensitive and intimate style'. A collection of her Brisbane poems was published in 1972 with the Italian and English interleaved, *Poesie Australiane/Australian Poems*. She is married to a diplomat.

Poem: p. 194.

## CHRIS WALLACE-CRABBE

Chris Wallace-Crabbe was born in Richmond, Victoria, on 6 May 1934. He has had a successful academic career, being now a Professor of English at Melbourne University. His verse is notable for its clean dry texture and emphasis on reason and moderation. He says: 'I am resistant to fashionable notions of defeatism, alienation, impending destruction ... along with this I think I have a peculiar vanity. Somewhere deep down, I do believe that against all odds one can make, build, do—that the burden is finally and absolutely on one's own shoulders.'

Poems: pp. 275–278.

## KATH WALKER

Kath Walker was born on 3 November 1920. She grew up on Stradbroke Island, in Moreton Bay, Queensland, still able to experience a life in which the family hunted in the bush to supplement their food, and ate a part-Aboriginal diet. Her father was of the Noonuccle tribe, carpet snake totem. Her mother was an inland Aborigine. At thirteen she left school to work as a domestic for 2/6d a week. Then she joined the army, the AWAS, was married and had two sons, Denis and Vivian. In the 1950s she began writing poems. And with outstanding courage and eloquence she became a spokesman for her people who suffer untold humiliation in a country where discrimination is still written into the laws of some States.

When her book *We Are Going* appeared in 1964 it was the first ever to be published by an Aborigine and became an immediate success, running into many editions.

Poems: pp. 207–208.

# FRANCIS WEBB

Francis Webb was born in Adelaide on 8 February 1925 and educated by various Christian Brothers schools. He served with the RAAF in the Second World War. As a poet he launched straight into large sets of poems on historic themes with *A Drum for Ben Boyd* (1948) and *Leichhardt in Theatre* (1952), 'The Canticle' about St Francis of Assisi, and a curious verse drama for radio about Hitler, called *Birthday* (1953). Webb's powerful, dense poetry reaches its highest achievement in the later works 'Ward Two' (included here complete) and 'Around Costessy' a montage of people and events associated with a Norfolk village, which had a strong impact when first published in The *Bulletin* by Vincent Buckley. Many poets, such as Bruce Beaver and Robert Adamson acknowledge his influence on their work.

Francis Webb's last years were spent in a mental hospital, which he wrote about with piercing intensity. The pain and suffering explored in much of his poetry carries with it a Christian perspective of redemption through sacrifice. His *Collected Poems* appeared in 1969. He died at Callan Park Hospital on 22 November 1973.

Poems: pp. 230–243.

## WENBERI

Wenberi was a singer of the Woiworung tribe whose district was around Mount Macedon in Victoria, between Ballarat and Bendigo. The song was given to Berak who sang it to the translator, A. W. Howitt in 1887. Berak explained that Wenberi came of poetic stock: 'His father and his father's father had been the makers of song which made men sad or joyful when they heard them.' Howitt records that when the old man sang this song to him 'I was moved almost to tears by the melancholy which the words conveyed.' He goes on to explain, 'In the tribes with which I have acquaintance I find it a common belief that the songs, using that word in its widest meaning, as including all kinds of Aboriginal poetry, are obtained by the bards from the spirits of the deceased, usually their relatives, during sleep in dreams.'

Poem: p. 49.

## MAX WILLIAMS

Max Williams has written a brilliant, warm and harrowing auto-biography *Dingo! My Life on the Run* (1980) in which he tells how he ran wild in the streets of Redfern, Sydney, during his young childhood in the Depression, committing his first offence at the age of five and being sent to a boys' home. And from then on he spent most of his life in various punitive institutions and prisons, always desperate to escape, his main obsession being freedom and breaking out.

Since 1972 he has lived a quiet life in the country becoming a knowledgeable bushman, an expert gardener and a poet. He has published poems in various books, most notably his collection *The Poor Man's Bean* (1975). He has been granted a fellowship by the Literature Board of the Australia Council and has been active in local Australian Labor Party politics. He was born in Guildford, New South Wales.

Poem: p. 275.

# WONGURI-MANDJIGAI SONG

This song is from the Wonguri linguistic group of the Mandjigai tribe of north-eastern Arnhem Land, Northern Territory. The mythology of the tribe is here related to the Moon, his death and rebirth. The simple and mystical theme is of the moon waning through his phases to a thin bone resting on the horizon and then sinking to become a nautilus shell. And ever since, the ritual has been repeated, the moon shedding his bone, feeding on lily roots and rising again.

The translator, Professor Ronald Berndt, has written that 'the general translation is a poetic rendering of the song. And for the purpose of accuracy as well as beauty, the arrangement and formation of ideas have been kept as closely as possible to the original text. It should be mentioned, however, that, as in most translations, the euphony of the verse, the play of words, and the native subtlety of expression, have to some extent been lost. But we may, nevertheless, reach some understanding of the true worth of native poetry, expressed as it is through song, and learn to appreciate the Aborigine's deep relationship with the traditional past, and his essential harmony with his natural environment.' The songs are generally sung in camp accompanied by clapsticks, didgeridoo and dancing by the women. 'The songs,' Professor Berndt explains, 'are usually sung straight through to a particular rhythm, and then repeated any number of times; so that the whole cycle is rarely completed in the one evening. Reiteration of words has great appeal. This form of verbal literature seems to have no defined punctuation in the actual singing; sentences and phrases may run from one to the other without apparent break.' The song was collected in 1946–47.

One immediate problem with rendering the original into English involves the question of rhythm. Aboriginal song, though highly rhythmic, is not metrical (the rhythms do not fall into regular, repeated 'feet' of two or three stressed or unstressed syllables). Here, the translator, a distinguished anthropologist, has tackled the problem, boldly preferring a firmly European metre, sufficiently derived from the King James version of *The Book of Numbers* to convey a sense of ritual and sacredness adequate for the tone of this magnificent song.

Poem: pp. 13–19.

## JUDITH WRIGHT

Judith Wright was born on 31 May 1915 at Thalgarrah Station near Armidale, New South Wales, into a pastoral family who had been pioneer settlers of the New England district. Her mother died when she was ten. After boarding school and university she had various jobs and travelled to Europe, returning just before the outbreak of war in 1939. When her brothers enlisted, she returned home to the property to help with the work. 'At that time I began writing some poetry, largely because the country seemed to me very beautiful and very threatened.' This motive could, perhaps, be extended right through to her latest book, though the nature of the threat has changed. She has, for many years been a tireless worker for conservation organizations, fighting to protect the forests, the wildlife and the Great Barrier Reef from the onslaught of transnational companies and governments whose principal values are expediency and short-term cash.

Apart from her books of poetry, her rich output which has made her justly one of the most loved of Australian poets, she also published a family history in 1959, *The Generations of Men*. One of the most important influences on her work was her husband, J. P. McKinney, who was for many years writing a natural history of European thought, *The Structure of Modern Thought*. They lived with their daughter Meredith on Tamborine Mountain, Queensland, till Jack McKinney died in 1966.

Judith Wright suffers a serious hearing loss, but is still very active on committees and campaigns to conserve the environment, and frequently gives poetry readings. This poetry is remarkable for its tireless energy in seeking out new directions, a fresh immediacy of language and subject.

Poems: pp. 197–207.

## FAY ZWICKY

The Rosefield Trio, violin, cello and piano, were three sisters. The pianist, Fay Zwicky, had begun giving public concerts at six years of age. For seventeen years she was divided between a career as a concert performer and a career in literature. She married a Swiss zoologist while on a concert tour of Indonesia (1956–57). She now lives in Perth and teaches English literature at the University of Western Australia. She has written notably on Jewish themes, about her family and others.

Poem: p. 305.

# —— ACKNOWLEDGEMENTS ——

Acknowledgement is made to the following publishers for their permission to reprint poems:

Angus & Robertson for poems by Robert Adamson, Christopher Brennan, 'William Baylebridge', David Campbell, Rosemary Dobson, Edward Dyson, Anne Elder, R. D. FitzGerald, John Forbes, Mary Gilmore, Gwen Harwood, A. D. Hope, Nancy Keesing, Geoffrey Lehmann, Frederick T. Macartney, Kenneth Mackenzie, Ray Mathew, James McAuley, Hugh McCrae, Les A. Murray, Shaw Neilson, A. B. Paterson, Elizabeth Riddell, Roland Robinson, J. R. Rowland, Kenneth Slessor, Vivian Smith, Douglas Stewart, Randolph Stow, Chris Wallace-Crabbe, Francis Webb and Judith Wright.

Australian Letters for a poem by Geoffrey Dutton

Australian Consolidated Press for a poem by Roderic Quinn.

Australian National University Press for poems by Dorothy Auchterlonie and R. F. Brissenden.

Big Smoke Books for a poem by Robert Adamson.

Jacaranda Wiley for poems by Kath Walker.

Mr Max Harris for a poem by 'Ern Malley'.

Longman Cheshire for poems by Bruce Dawe.

Lothian Publishing Company for poems by Furnley Maurice and Bernard O'Dowd.

Lyre-Bird Writers for poems by Ray Mathew.

Makar Press for poems by Rae Desmond Jones, Antigone Kefala and John Tranter.

Melbourne University Press for poems by Vincent Buckley and Lesbia Harford.

New Poetry Magazine for poems by Charles Buckmaster, Dorothy Hewett and Max Williams.

South Head Press for poems by Bruce Beaver.

The Strehlow Research Foundation for songs translated from the Aranda by T. G. H. Strehlow.

# ACKNOWLEDGEMENTS

University of Queensland Press for poems by Michael Dransfield, Robert Gray, Rodney Hall, Martin Johnston, Peter Kocan, Jennifer Maiden, David Malouf, John Manifold, Roger McDonald, Rhyll McMaster, Geoff Page, Judith Rodriguez, David Rowbotham, Thomas W. Shapcott, R. A. Simpson, Peter Skrzynecki, Andrew Taylor and Maria Valli.

Where special permissions were required, the following have kindly agreed to let work be reproduced:

Catherine and Ronald Berndt, John Blight, Mrs David Campbell, Jack Davis, Geoffrey Dutton, John Manifold, Rhyll McMaster, Roland Robinson, Vivian Smith, Dimitris Tsaloumas, Fay Zwicky.

# —— ACKNOWLEDGEMENT ——
## OF SOURCES

**ANONYMOUS**

Jim Jones; Moreton Bay; The Streets of Forbes: *The Penguin Australian Song Book*, ed. John Manifold, Penguin 1964.

The Boss's Wife; Much Distressed: *Comic Australian Verse*, ed. G. Lehmann, Angus and Robertson, 1972.

**ROBERT ADAMSON**

Action Would Kill It/A Gamble; Things Going out of my Life; Sonnet to be Written from Prison; Sail Away; The Ribbon-Fish: *Selected Poems*, Angus and Robertson, 1977.

My House: *Where I Come From*, Big Smoke Books, 1979.

**DOROTHY AUCHTERLONIE**

Waiting for the Post; Meditation of a Mariner: *The Dolphin*, Australian National University Press, 1967.

**BALGU SONG**

Balgu Song: translated by Clancy McKenna, previously unpublished.

**'WILLIAM BAYLEBRIDGE'**

Love Redeemed CVII: *The Growth of Love, Collected Works of William Baylebridge*, Vol III, Angus and Robertson, 1963.

**BRUCE BEAVER**

Letters to Live Poets II, V, X, XII, XIX, XXX, XXXIV: *Letters to Live Poets*, South Head Press, 1969.

**PADDY BIRAN**

Paddy Biran's song: translated by R. M. W. Dixon, this version previously unpublished.

JOHN BLIGHT

The Gate's Open; Down from the Country; Cormorants; Death of a Whale; Pearl Perch: *Selected Poems*, Thomas Nelson, 1976.

Morgan; Evolution; The Letter: *Hart*, Thomas Nelson, 1975.

Tenant at Number 9: *Pageantry for a Lost Empire*, Thomas Nelson, 1977.

BARCROFT BOAKE

An Allegory; At Devlin's Siding; Where the Dead Men Lie: *Where the Dead Men Lie and Other Poems*, Angus and Robertson, 1897.

BRALGU SONG

Djalbarmiwi's Song: translated by Catherine H. Berndt in 'Expressions of Grief among Aboriginal Women', in *Oceania*, Vol. XX, No. 4, 1950.

CHRISTOPHER BRENNAN

The Wanderer; The Quest of Silence: *Poems*, G. B. Philip, 1913.

Because She Would Ask Me Why I Loved Her: *Selected Verse*, Angus and Robertson, 1973.

R. F. BRISSENDEN

Verandahs; Walking Down Jalan Thamrin: *The Whale in Darkness*, Australian National University Press, 1980.

VINCENT BUCKLEY

Good Friday and the Present Crucifixion; Return of a Popular Statesman; No New Thing; Parents: *Arcady and Other Places*, Melbourne University Press, 1966.

CHARLES BUCKMASTER

Vanzetti: *Australians Aware*, ed. Rodney Hall, Ure Smith, 1975.

BULUGURU

Working Song: translated by E. A. Worms in *Annali Lateranensi*, Vol. 21, 1957.

DAVID CAMPBELL

Ariel; Night Sowing; On Frosty Days; Pallid Cuckoo; The Australian Dream: *Selected Poems*, Angus and Robertson, 1973.

Fox: *Words with a Black Orpington*, Angus and Robertson, 1978.

Mr Hughes, Ulinda: *Deaths and Pretty Cousins*, Australian National University Press, 1975.

ZORA CROSS

Love Sonnet XLIX; Love Sonnet LIV: *Songs of Love and Life*, Tyrrell's, 1917.

VICTOR DALEY

Tall Hat: *Creeve Roe: Poetry by Victor Daley*, ed. Muir Holburn and Marjorie Pizer, Pinchgut Press, 1947.

Lachesis; When London Calls: *At Dawn and Dusk*, Angus and Robertson, 1898.

JACK DAVIS
Day Flight: *The First-Born*, Angus and Robertson, 1970.

BRUCE DAWE
Perpetuum Immobile: *No Fixed Address*, F. W. Cheshire, 1962.

Abandonment of Autos; Americanized: *A Need of Similar Name*, F. W. Cheshire, 1965.

The Not-so-good Earth; Drifters: *An Eye for a Tooth*, F. W. Cheshire, 1968.

Homecoming: *Beyond the Subdivisions*, Cheshire, 1969.

C. J. DENNIS
The Martyred Democrat: *Backblock Ballads and Other Verses*, E. W. Cole, 1913.

ROSEMARY DOBSON
In a Café; The Bystander; Child with a Cockatoo; Being Called For: *Selected Poems*, Angus and Robertson, 1973.

MICHAEL DRANSFIELD
Bum's Rush; Pas de Deux for Lovers; Portrait of the Artist as an Old Man; That Which We Call a Rose; Epiderm; *Streets of the Long Voyage*, University of Queensland Press, 1970.

Loft; Geography III; Geography VI: *The Inspector of Tides*, University of Queensland Press, 1972.

GEOFFREY DUTTON
The Stranded Whales: *A Body of Words*, Edwards and Shaw, 1977.

Time of Waiting: *Findings and Keepings*, Australian Letters, 1970.

EDWARD DYSON
The Old Whim Horse; A Friendly Game of Football: *Rhymes from the Mines*, Angus and Robertson, 1896.

'E'
Stupidity; Martyr; The Farmer; A Man's Sliding Mood; Ninety: *The Wonder and the Apple*, Angus and Robertson, 1946.

YITYANGU ('NEW') EJONG
Long Song: translated by Frank Wordick, previously unpublished.

ANNE ELDER
School Cadets; Carried Away; Farmer Goes Berserk; One Foot in the Door: *Crazy Woman and Other Poems*, Angus and Robertson, 1976.

R. D. FITZGERALD
Edge; The Face of the Waters; 1918–1941; Essay on Memory; Bog and Candle; Favour: *Forty Years' Poems*, Angus and Robertson, 1965.

JOHN FORBES
Four Heads and How to Do Them; TV: *Tropical Skiing*, Angus and Robertson, 1976.

WILLIAM FORSTER

The Devil and the Governor: signed with the pseudonym 'Sylvanus', in The *Atlas*, Vol. 1, No. 25, Saturday, 17 May 1845. Sonnet on the Crimean War; Love has Eyes; The Poor of London: *The Weirwolf: a Tragedy*, Williams and Norgate, 1876.

LEON GELLERT

House-Mates; Before Action: *Songs of a Campaign*, Angus and Robertson, 1917.

MARY GILMORE

Nationality, Fourteen Men: *Fourteen Men*, Angus and Robertson, 1954.

Eve-song; Heritage: *The Passionate Heart and Other Poems*, Angus and Robertson, 1918.

The Tenancy: *Battlefields*, Angus and Robertson, 1939.

The Myall in Prison: *Under the Wilgas*, Robertson and Mullens, 1932.

ADAM LINDSAY GORDON

A Dedication; Hippodromania; How We Beat the Favourite; The Sick Stockrider: *Bush Ballads and Galloping Rhymes*, Clarson, Massina, 1870.

ROBERT GRAY

27 Poems: *Creek Water Journal*, University of Queensland Press, 1974.

RODNEY HALL

Mrs Macintosh; Wedding Day at Nagasaki; After a Sultry Morning; Lips and Nose; Some Magnetism in the Sea: *Selected Poems*, University of Queensland Press, 1975.

My Coffin is a Deckchair; They're Dying Just the Same at Station Homesteads; The World is a Musician's Cliff House; October: *Black Bagatelles*, University of Queensland Press, 1978.

A Text for these Distracted Times: in *New Poetry Magazine*, Vol. 24, No. 4, 1976.

LESBIA HARFORD

Experience; Beauty and Terror: *Poetry*, Melbourne University Press, 1941.

CHARLES HARPUR

Bush Justice; Marvellous Martin; A Coast View; The Creek of the Four Graves: *Charles Harpur*, ed. Adrian Mitchell, Sun Books, 1973.

GWEN HARWOOD

The Second Life of Lazarus; At the Sea's Edge; In the Park; Prize-giving; Panther and Peacock: *Poems*, Angus and Robertson, 1963.

Suburban Sonnet; New Music: *Poems/Volume Two*, Angus and Robertson, 1968.

Night Thoughts: Baby & Demon; Father and Child; Carnal Knowledge: *Selected Poems*, Angus and Robertson, 1975.

**DOROTHY HEWETT**

Moon-Man; Sanctuary; This Version of Love: *Rapunzel in Suburbia*, Prism, 1975.

**A. D. HOPE**

Imperial Adam; The Martyrdom of St Teresa; On an Engraving by Casserius; The Double Looking Glass; Moschus Moschiferus: *Collected Poems 1930–1970*, Angus and Robertson, 1972.

**REX INGAMELLS**

The Great South Land: *The Great South Land*, Georgian House, 1951. Memory of Hills: *Memory of Hills*, F. W. Preece, 1940.

**MARTIN JOHNSTON**

Airport; Vernal Equinox; Directions for Dreamfishing; Quantum: *The Sea-cucumber*, University of Queensland Press, 1978.

**RAE DESMOND JONES**

Age: *Shakti*, Makar Press, 1977.

**NANCY KEESING**

Reverie of a Mum: *Showground Sketchbook*, Angus and Robertson, 1968.

**ANTIGONE KEFALA**

Saturday Night: *The Alien*, Makar Press, 1973.

**HENRY KENDALL**

The Last of His Tribe; Orara; Christmas Creek; *Leaves from Australian Forests*, George Robertson, 1869.

**PETER KOCAN**

The Sleepers; Bill: *The Other Side of the Fence*, University of Queensland Press, 1975.

**HENRY LAWSON**

Faces in the Street; The Teams; The Horseman on the Skyline; Up the Country; Ned's Delicate Way; Will Yer Write It Down for Me?: *Collected Verse*, ed. Colin Roderick, Angus and Robertson, 1968.

Ripperty! Kye! Ahoo!: *Poetical Works of Henry Lawson*, Angus and Robertson, 1925.

**GEOFFREY LEHMANN**

The Pigs: *The Ilex Tree*, Australian National University Press, 1965.

Song for Past Midnight: *Selected Poems*, Angus and Robertson, 1976.

Saving the Harvest: *A Voyage of Lions*, Angus and Robertson, 1968.

My Father's a Still Day, Music is Unevennesses; I was Born at a Place of Pines; Auntie Bridge and Uncle Pat; Some of our Koorawatha Saints; There are Some Lusty Voices Singing: *Ross's Poems*, Angus and Robertson, 1978.

LIAGARANG

Snails: translated by R. M. Berndt in 'The Wuradilgu Song Cycle of Northeastern Arnhem Land', in *The Anthropologist Looks at Myth*, (compiled by M. Jacobs, edited by J. Greenway), The University of Texas Press, 1966.

MILTON LOCKYER

Dark Mountains: translated by Frank Wordick, previously unpublished.

FREDERICK T. MACARTNEY

No Less than Prisoners; Early Summer Sea-Tryst: *Selected Poems*, Angus and Robertson, 1961.

KENNETH MACKENZIE

Heat: in The *Bulletin*, 1 February 1939.

Autumn Mushrooms; Two Trinities; God! How I Long for You; Caesura; New Arrival; Matron; Earth Buried: *The Poems of Kenneth MacKenzie*, Angus and Robertson, 1972.

JENNIFER MAIDEN

Climbing; Dew; Slides: *Tactics*, University of Queensland Press, 1974.

'ERN MALLEY'

Dürer: Innsbruck, 1495: *The Darkening Ecliptic*, Reed and Harris, 1944.

DAVID MALOUF

Early Discoveries; Asphodel: *Neighbours in a Thicket*, University of Queensland Press, 1974.

This Day, under my Hand; Wolf-boy; Snow: *Bicycle*, University of Queensland Press, 1970.

An die Musik: *First Things Last*, University of Queensland Press, 1980.

JOHN MANIFOLD

Garcia Lorca Murdered in Granada: *Nightmares & Sunhorses*, Overland, 1961.

Fife Tune; Making Contact; The Deserter; The Tomb of Lt John Learmonth, AIF; Fencing School: *Selected Verse*, Dennis Dobson, 1948.

L'embarquement pour Cythère; Makhno's Philosophers: *Collected Verse*, University of Queensland Press, 1978.

Assignation with a Somnambulist: previously unpublished.

RAY MATHEW

A Good Thing: *South of the Equator*, Angus and Robertson, 1961.

Lover's Meeting; Wynyard Sailor: *Song and Dance*, Lyre-Bird Writers, 1956.

'FURNLEY MAURICE'

The Supremer Sacrifice: *Poems by Furnley Maurice*, Thomas Lothian, 1944.

The Agricultural Show, Flemington, Victoria; On a Grey-haired Old Lady Knitting at an Orchestral Concert; Upon a Row of Old Boots and

'FURNLEY MAURICE' *contd*
Shoes in a Pawnbroker's Window: *Melbourne Odes*, Thomas Lothian, 1934.
The Team: *The Gully*, A. H. Spencer, 1925.

JAMES McAULEY
Jesus; A Letter to John Dryden; Merry-go-round; Pietà; In the Huon Valley; Because; Convalescence: *Collected Poems*, Angus and Robertson, 1971.

HUGH McCRAE
Song of the Rain; Winds: *The Best Poems of Hugh McCrae*, ed. R. G. Howarth, Angus and Robertson, 1939.

ROGER McDONALD
Components; Two Summers in Moravia; Bachelor Farmer; Flights; The Hollow Thesaurus: *Airship*, University of Queensland Press, 1975.

RHYLL McMASTER
Profiles of my Father: previously unpublished in book form.
Tanks; A Round Song: *The Brineshrimp*, University of Queensland Press, 1972.

LES A. MURRAY
An Absolutely Ordinary Rainbow; Once in a Lifetime, Snow: *The Weatherboard Cathedral*, Angus and Robertson, 1969.
The Names of the Humble; The Powerline Incarnation: *Selected Poems: The Vernacular Republic*, Angus and Robertson, 1976.
Portrait of the Autist as a New World Driver: *Lunch & Counter Lunch*, Angus and Robertson, 1974.

SHAW NEILSON
The Soldier is Home; Take Down the Fiddle, Karl!; The Sundowner; The Crane is My Neighbour; In the Street; The Orange Tree; You Cannot Go Down to the Spring: *The Poems of Shaw Neilson*, Angus and Robertson, 1965.
Flowers in the Ward: *Witnesses of Spring*, Angus and Robertson, 1970.

BERNARD O'DOWD
The Bush: *The Bush*, Thomas Lothian, 1912.

GEOFF PAGE
Country Nun: *Smalltown Memorials*, University of Queensland Press, 1975.

A. B. ('BANJO') PATERSON
The Road to Hogan's Gap; The Travelling Post Office; Waltzing Matilda; The Man from Snowy River: *The Collected Verse of A. B. Paterson*, Angus and Robertson, 1921.

RODERIC QUINN
The Fisher: *The Hidden Tide*, Bulletin Newspaper Co., 1899.

ELIZABETH RIDDELL
Suburban Song; The Soldier in the Park; The Children March: *Forbears*, Angus and Robertson, 1961.

ROLAND ROBINSON
The Wanderer: *Selected Poems*, Angus and Robertson, 1971.
Deep Well: *Deep Well*, Edwards and Shaw, 1962.

JUDITH RODRIGUEZ
Eskimo Occasion, Rebeca in a Mirror; At the Nature-Strip; *Water Life*, University of Queensland Press, 1976.

DAVID ROWBOTHAM
Mullabinda; Prey to Prey: *Selected Poems*, University of Queensland Press, 1975.

J. R. ROWLAND
A Traveller; London: *The Feast of Ancestors*, Angus and Robertson, 1965.

THOMAS W. SHAPCOTT
Schoenberg Op. 11; Webern; Flying Fox; The Bicycle Rider; Near the School for Handicapped Children; Sestina with Refrain; The Litanies of Julia Pastrana: *Selected Poems*, University of Queensland Press, 1978.
Autumn: *Shabbytown Calendar*, University of Queensland Press, 1975.

R. A. SIMPSON
Antarctica; Diver; Lake: *Diver*, University of Queensland Press, 1972.

PETER SKRZYNECKI
Feliks Skrzynecki; Cattle: *Immigrant Chronicle*, University of Queensland Press, 1975.

KENNETH SLESSOR
Country Towns; A Bushranger; North Country; South Country; William Street; Out of Time; Five Bells; Polarities; Beach Burial: *Selected Poems*, Angus and Robertson, 1975.

VIVIAN SMITH
Fishermen, Drowned Beyond the West Coast: *The Other Meaning*, Lyre-Bird Writers, 1956.
Reflections; Summer Band Concert; At an Exhibition of Historical Paintings, Hobart: *An Island South*, Angus and Robertson, 1967.

DOUGLAS STEWART
Glencoe: *Glencoe*, Angus and Robertson, 1947.
Marree; Ruins; The Silkworms; The Garden of Ships; Two Englishmen; At the Entrance: *Collected Poems 1936–67*, Angus and Robertson, 1967.

RANDOLPH STOW
The Singing Bones; The Sleepers; The Jungle; Ruins of the City of Hay; Dust: *A Counterfeit Silence, Selected Poems*, Angus and Robertson, 1969.

**ANDREW TAYLOR**

The Invention of Fire: *The Invention of Fire*, University of Queensland Press, 1976.

Developing a Wife: *The Cool Change*, University of Queensland Press, 1971.

**JOHN TRANTER**

The Death Circus: *Red Movie*, Angus and Robertson, 1972.

Crying in Early Infancy: *Crying in Early Infancy: 100 Sonnets*, Makar Press, 1977.

**DIMITRIS TSALOUMAS**

A Rhapsody of Old Men: previously unpublished in book form.

**URUMBULA SONG**

Urumbula Song: translated by T. G. H. Strehlow in *Hemisphere*, Vol. 6, No. 8, 1962.

**MARIA VALLI**

The Crows: *Australian Poems*, University of Queensland Press, 1972.

**CHRIS WALLACE-CRABBE**

Citizen; The Dirigible: *Selected Peoms*, Angus and Robertson, 1973.

The Rebel General: *The Rebel General*, Angus and Robertson, 1967.

**KATH WALKER**

We Are Going; Dawn Wail for the Dead: *We Are Going*, Jacaranda, 1964.

**FRANCIS WEBB**

This Runner; The Sea; The Gunner; Airliner; Pneumo-encephalograph; Harry; Old Timer; Ward Two and the Kookaburra; Homosexual; A Man; The Old Woman; Wild Honey: *Collected Poems*, Angus and Robertson, 1969.

**WENBERI**

Wenberi's Song: translated by A. W. Howitt in *The Journal of the Anthropological Institute of Great Britain and Ireland*, Vol. XVI, No. 3, 1887.

**MAX WILLIAMS**

The Empty House: *The Poor Man's Bean*, Prism, 1975.

**WONGURI-MANDJIGAI SONG**

The Wonguri-Mandjigai Song Cycle of the Moon-bone: translated by R. M. Berndt in *Oceania*, Vol. XIX, No. 1, 1948 (with small modifications and transliteration of proper nouns from the International Phonetic Alphabet to English by Professor Berndt, 1981).

**JUDITH WRIGHT**

Wings; Australia 1970: *Collected Poems*, Angus and Robertson, 1971.

Bullocky: *The Moving Image*, Meanjin Press, 1946.

JUDITH WRIGHT *contd*

Country Dance; Woman to Man; Eli, Eli: *Woman to Man*, Angus and Robertson, 1949.

Request to a Year: *The Two Fires*, Angus and Robertson, 1955.

Habitat IV; Habitat VI; Tableau: *Alive*, Angus and Robertson, 1973.

FAY ZWICKY ˙

Summer Pogrom: *Isaac Babel's Fiddle*, Maximus Books, undated.